English as a lingua franca

Marie-Luise Pitzl

English as a lingua franca in international business

Resolving miscommunication and reaching shared understanding

VDM Verlag Dr. Müller

Impressum/Imprint (nur für Deutschland/ only for Germany)
Bibliografische Information der Deutschen Nationalbibliothek: Die Deutsche Nationalbibliothek verzeichnet diese Publikation in der Deutschen Nationalbibliografie; detaillierte bibliografische Daten sind im Internet über http://dnb.d-nb.de abrufbar.

Alle in diesem Buch genannten Marken und Produktnamen unterliegen warenzeichen-, marken- oder patentrechtlichem Schutz bzw. sind Warenzeichen oder eingetragene Warenzeichen der jeweiligen Inhaber. Die Wiedergabe von Marken, Produktnamen, Gebrauchsnamen, Handelsnamen, Warenbezeichnungen u.s.w. in diesem Werk berechtigt auch ohne besondere Kennzeichnung nicht zu der Annahme, dass solche Namen im Sinne der Warenzeichen- und Markenschutzgesetzgebung als frei zu betrachten wären und daher von jedermann benutzt werden dürften.

Coverbild: www.purestockx.com

Verlag: VDM Verlag Dr. Müller Aktiengesellschaft & Co. KG
Dudweiler Landstr. 99, 66123 Saarbrücken, Deutschland
Telefon +49 681 9100-698, Telefax +49 681 9100-988, Email: info@vdm-verlag.de

Herstellung in Deutschland:
Schaltungsdienst Lange o.H.G., Berlin
Books on Demand GmbH, Norderstedt
Reha GmbH, Saarbrücken
Amazon Distribution GmbH, Leipzig
ISBN: 978-3-639-22507-5

Imprint (only for USA, GB)
Bibliographic information published by the Deutsche Nationalbibliothek: The Deutsche Nationalbibliothek lists this publication in the Deutsche Nationalbibliografie; detailed bibliographic data are available in the Internet at http://dnb.d-nb.de .

Any brand names and product names mentioned in this book are subject to trademark, brand or patent protection and are trademarks or registered trademarks of their respective holders. The use of brand names, product names, common names, trade names, product descriptions etc. even without a particular marking in this works is in no way to be construed to mean that such names may be regarded as unrestricted in respect of trademark and brand protection legislation and could thus be used by anyone.

Cover image: www.purestockx.com

Publisher:
VDM Verlag Dr. Müller Aktiengesellschaft & Co. KG
Dudweiler Landstr. 99, 66123 Saarbrücken, Germany
Phone +49 681 9100-698, Fax +49 681 9100-988, Email: info@vdm-publishing.com

Copyright © 2010 by the author and VDM Verlag Dr. Müller Aktiengesellschaft & Co. KG and licensors
All rights reserved. Saarbrücken 2010

Printed in the U.S.A.
Printed in the U.K. by (see last page)
ISBN: 978-3-639-22507-5

To my mom,
my dad,
and my friends

CONTENTS

Acknowledgements   4

1   INTRODUCTION   5

2   THE JUNGLE OF THEORY: A CRITICAL OVERVIEW OF DIFFERENT APPROACHES TO 'MISCOMMUNICATION'   8

2.1   Introduction   8
2.2   Pragmatics and conversation analysis: the problematic bias of communication breakdown, failure and repair   9
2.3   Intercultural communication and sociolinguistics: culture as the only culprit?   14
2.4   The dialogical approach: acknowledging 'miscommunication'   18
2.5   Summary and conclusion   22

3   FINDING A NON-NATIVE SPEAKERS' PATH: AN ELF PERSPECTIVE ON 'MISCOMMUNICATION'   23

3.1   Introduction   23
3.2   The ELF position   23
    3.2.1. Pronunciation problems and the 'Lingua Franca Core'   25
    3.2.2. ELF pragmatics and the absence of 'miscommunication'   26
    3.2.3 'Let it pass', 'communicative leniency' and the risk of interactional vulnerability   27
3.3   Core terms and definitions: understanding, miscommunication, misunderstanding and non-understanding   29
3.4   Diagnosing 'miscommunication': the potential covertness of 'miscommunication' and the role of the analyst   33
3.5   Negotiating 'miscommunication': indication and interactional management of 'local non-understanding'   35
    3.5.1 Procedures for indicating 'non-understanding'   36
    3.5.2 The 'negotiation of meaning'   42
3.6   Examining another type of 'miscommunication': the possibility of 'strategic miscommunication'   46
3.7   Analyzing 'global miscommunication': the interrelatedness of understanding and context   48
    3.7.1 Micro-context: 'frame', 'footing' and 'contextualization'   49

3.7.2 Macro-context: the role of shared knowledge, culture and institutional conditions — 52
3.8 **Attempts at explaining 'miscommunication': the multicausality of 'miscommunication'** — 55
3.9 **Summary and conclusion** — 57

4 THE DATA: BUSINESS MEETINGS AMONG ELF SPEAKERS — 59

4.1 **Introduction** — 59
4.2 **General information about the data** — 59
4.3 **Methodological aspects of the data collection** — 60
4.4 **Properties of business meetings** — 61
   4.4.1 Structure — 62
   4.4.2 Degree of formality — 65
   4.4.3 Goals and objectives — 66
   4.4.4 Participant relationships and roles — 68
   4.4.5 The power of the chair person — 69
4.5 **Summary and conclusion** — 72

5 ANALYSIS: TYPES OF 'MISCOMMUNICATION' IN ELF AND THEIR INTERACTIONAL MANAGEMENT — 73

5.1 **Introduction** — 73
5.2 **Local non-understanding and the negotiation of meaning** — 73
   5.2.1 Shortened sequences: trigger – indicator – response — 74
   5.2.2 Basic sequences: trigger – indicator – response – reaction — 78
   5.2.3 Enlarged sequences: 'waffling' and additional explanations — 82
   5.2.4 High involvement sequences: 'fragile' activities and the need for clarity — 86
   5.2.5 Complex sequences: multiple indicators and negotiation cycles — 92
5.3 **Local misunderstanding and the negotiation of meaning** — 109
5.4 **Self-initiated negotiation of meaning as a means of preventing miscommunication** — 112
5.5 **Non-understanding or strategic miscommunication?** — 115
5.6 **Global misunderstanding: being in the wrong 'frame'** — 122
5.7 **Summary and conclusion** — 128

6 CONCLUSION — 131

REFERENCES — 135

APPENDIX   141

Data A: Meeting A   141
Data B: Meeting B   163
VOICE Transcription and mark-up conventions (Version 3.0, June 2003)   178

Acknowledgements

I would like to thank my supervisor, Prof. Barbara Seidlhofer, for her continuous help and advice. In many discussions, she was never tired to provide valuable comments and, through her own commitment, she continuously increased my interest in the fascinating topic of English as a lingua franca.

Furthermore, I am highly indebted to the two companies for allowing me to record their meetings. My special thanks go my two contact persons, who made the necessary arrangements, organized a trip to Luxembourg and allowed me to be present and record the meetings. Without the courtesy of those companies, my research would not have been possible and I am grateful for their readiness to support my project.

Likewise, I want to express my deepest thanks to all the participants of the two meetings. It was their consent which opened to door to analyzing ELF business interactions to me.

And last but not least, I would like to thank my parents and my friends for being there for me and for never getting tired of providing emotional support.

1 INTRODUCTION

Let's start with what is obvious: People converse in English every day, all over the world, and they do so successfully. They meet, they negotiate, they do business together. They talk on the telephone and stay in touch via email. They read and write reports, files and contracts. They publish scientific papers and participate in international conferences. In the 21st century, we find ourselves in a world of globalization in which language and communication play a role more central in economic, political and cultural life than ever before (Graddol 1997: 3). And at the core of this development stands English in its function as a 'global language' (Crystal 1997).

When we ask ourselves who the speakers of this global English are, we find that it is no longer the 'Inner Circle' (Kachru 1992a: 356), i.e. the native speakers, who hold the majority. The 'Outer Circle', i.e. those who speak English as a second language, and the 'Expanding Circle', i.e. those who speak it as a foreign language, are taking over (ibid.: 356). Particularly the number of speakers of 'English as a foreign language' (EFL) is increasing rapidly. Even today, there may be more EFL speakers than the sum of those who speak it as a first and second language (Graddol 1997: 13). Estimates go up to one billion EFL speakers (Crystal 1997: 54) and the global demand for English is still increasing. As a consequence, the majority of English interactions take place between non-native speakers to whom the language functions as a 'lingua franca', i.e. "an additionally acquired language system that serves as a means of communication between speakers of different first languages" (Seidlhofer 2001: 146).

This global state of affairs has led to a shift in perspective in linguistic research. The 'ownership of English' and the native speakers' custody of the language have been called into question (Widdowson 1994). The need for largescale research and a broad empirical basis on 'English as a lingua franca' (ELF) has been stressed by many scholars (e.g. Firth 1996; Seidlhofer 2001). Initial studies relying on ELF data (e.g. Firth 1996; Meierkord 1996; Jenkins 2000; Kordon 2003) confirm the assumption that "[e]xperienced users of English as a foreign language may acquire communicative skills which are different from those of native speakers" (Graddol 1997: 13). Yet, in these first four years of the new millennium, research in this field is only beginning to emerge and there are still vast areas of ELF discourse which are waiting to be explored. It is the purpose of the present study to make a small contribution to this corpus of ELF research that is in the process of being built.

The focus chosen in this study is 'miscommunication' in English as a lingua franca and the data I am relying on to investigate this phenomenon is business data, business meetings to be precise. The central purpose of the study is to sketch some of the features that appear to be characteristic of 'miscommunication' in ELF interactions. The aim is to create a first and initial (but certainly not complete) picture of what 'miscommunication' looks like in an ELF context and how it is interactionally reacted to and handled by ELF speakers. In other words, the study can be brought down to two central research questions:

- Which types of 'miscommunication' can be found in ELF interactions?
- How do ELF speakers manage these different types of 'miscommunication' within an interaction?

In addition, some potential causes of 'miscommunication' in ELF situations are also discussed as a side aspect.

As a starting point, chapter 2 presents a short overview of some of the literature in the broad field of 'miscommunication'. Since a widely used term such as 'miscommunication' may be applied to very different communicative situations, it appears necessary at the onset to survey some of theoretical approaches that have been taken towards 'miscommunication' and to present some of the research that has been done in this area. The idea is to create a rough picture of 'what there is' with regard to research and literature on 'miscommunication' and to discuss this state of affairs critically from an ELF perspective.

Chapter 3 then lays the theoretical foundation for the analysis of 'miscommunication' in ELF interactions in this book. First, existent ELF findings[1] are summed up with regard to the implications they have for an analysis of 'miscommunication'. Afterwards the core terms and definitions of the present study and the role of the analyst are discussed. As a central pillar for analysis, the chapter presents a model for the local 'negotiation of meaning' and a spectrum of indicating procedures which non-native speakers have been shown to use in order to initiate such negotiation sequences. Furthermore, the question of intentionality and the possibility of strategic miscommunication are considered. With regard to global miscommunication, the relation of understanding and context is examined. In this respect, Goffman's notion of 'frame' and the importance of macro-contextual features such as shared knowledge, culture and institutional constraints is considered. The theoretical part

---

[1] Up until 2004, i.e. when this study was completed.

is then brought to an end with some remarks about the multicausal nature of 'miscommunication'.

Chapter 4 is concerned with a characterization of the data collected for the purpose of this study. After providing some general information about the two recorded business meetings, some methodological aspects of the data collection are considered. The remaining portion of chapter 4 is dedicated to a discussion of some properties of business meetings. Features such as structure, formality and objectives are appraised with regard to both meetings. In addition, participant roles and relationships as well as the power of the chair person are briefly observed.

The core of the study, namely the qualitative analysis of different types of 'miscommunication' in ELF interactions, is presented in chapter 5. A large portion of the chapter is devoted to the negotiation of meaning of local non-understandings, which are analyzed with regard to their structural characteristics, interactional management and some potential causes. A local misunderstanding and two self-intiated negotiations of meaning are also examined. Furthermore, some examples exhibiting the possibility of strategic miscommunication are analyzed. As a last type of 'miscommunication', an instance of global misunderstanding is examined in relation to the notion of 'frame'.

2 THE JUNGLE OF THEORY: A CRITICAL OVERVIEW OF DIFFERENT APPROACHES TO 'MISCOMMUNICATION'

2.1 Introduction

The past two decades have brought about an abundance of research and literature on 'miscommunication'. This increased interest in 'miscommunication' has been accompanied by "a plethora of terms" (Tzanne 1999: 33). Many of these terms are used with little to no consistency (Gass & Varonis 1991: 123) and "different researchers use different terms to describe the same phenomenon, or the same term to discuss different, but not totally unrelated phenomena" (Tzanne 1999: 33). Hence, sometimes one feels lost in a theoretical and terminological jungle in which comparing and juxtaposing findings is difficult. This chapter therefore functions as a brief overview of the predominant approaches to 'miscommunication'. Although all of these traditions have unquestioningly contributed much to our understanding of language use, they will be discussed critically with regard their conception of 'miscommunication' and related phenomena.

Section 2.2 examines the two most common and long standing approaches to 'miscommunication', namely pragmatics and conversation analysis. While pragmatics has put forward a broad spectrum of studies on 'communication breakdown' and various 'failures', conversation analysis has focused on disclosing the prevailing structural patterns of 'repairs'. Both approaches, however, seem to regard 'miscommunication' solely as a negative phenomenon and many researchers strive to find strategies for eliminating it. Section 2.3 focuses on sociolinguistics and intercultural encounters. It takes a look at the tradition of intercultural communication research where communicative problems have come to be explained mostly – and often exclusively – through the participants' cultural differences. Section 2.4 looks at works, e.g. in a dialogical theory tradition, which take a more positive attitude towards 'miscommunication'. These works note the proximity of communication and 'miscommunication' in spoken discourse and acknowledge 'miscommunication' as an inevitable communicative phenomenon. Some studies even focus on what 'misunderstanding', to give an example, may positively contribute to social relationships, socialization and cross-cultural communication.

2.2 Pragmatics and conversation analysis: the problematic bias of communication breakdown, failure and repair

During recent years there has been a tremendous increase in studies on 'miscommunication', many of which are situated in the field of pragmatics and share a common focus on 'communication breakdowns' (Tzanne 1999: 33). Yet, as is obvious by looking at the following list, the variety of terms that are used may give rise to confusion[2]:

- misperception
- mishearing
- misapprehension
- misinterpretation
- misfit
- misunderstanding (e.g. Dascal 1985b & 1999; Ochs 1991; Tzanne 1999; Weigand 1999)
- nonunderstanding (e.g. Bremer et al. 1996)
- incomplete / partial understanding (e.g. Gass & Varonis 1991)
- miscommunication (e.g. Coupland, Wiemann & Giles 1991)
- pragmatic failure (e.g. Thomas 1983)
- communication / communicative / conversation failure
- problematic talk (e.g. Coupland, Giles & Wiemann 1991)
- conflict talk
- communication breakdown (e.g. Meierkord 1996; Milroy 1984)
- repair (e.g. Bazzanella & Damiano 1999; Meeuwis 1994; Schegloff 2000; Wong 2000).

While this open list clearly indicates the richness and the diversity of research on 'miscommunication', it is obvious that a detailed discussion of all these terms would certainly go beyond the scope of this study. Suffice it to say that most of the terms are taken to denote "unintentional incorrect comprehension" (Tzanne 1999: 36).

What should be noted, however, is that many of these terms like 'communication breakdown', 'communication failure', 'pragmatic failure' and indeed also

---

[2] Terms assembled from Tzanne (1999: 37), Weigand (1999: 763), and Linell (1995: 176), parentheses added. An elaborate and concise overview of many of the terms can be found in Tzanne (1999: 35-43). The terms mainly used in this paper are 'miscommunication', 'misunderstanding' and 'non-understanding'. A definition of these will be provided in section 3.3.

'miscommunication' are strikingly negative and seem to have become derogatory, denoting unwanted and adverse conversational states which should be worked against – an attitude I was not really aware of when I first got interested in 'miscommunication'. Consequently one encounters positions where 'miscommunication' is defined as unresolved 'misunderstanding' which "cannot serve the purpose of coming to an understanding" (Weigand 1999: 770). It is distinguished from terms such as 'misunderstanding' and 'non-understanding' which may still lead to understanding (Weigand 1999: 771). Thus, as Dascal (1999: 754) remarks, Weigand takes the term 'miscommunication' to indicate "a breakdown in communication" (Dascal 1999: 754). In cases like these, the term 'miscommunication' is taken to indicate the ultimate 'default' situation in a conversation, a situation so to speak where everything goes wrong. Although not always openly stated, a similar attitude seems to linger in many studies dealing with the phenomenon.

As already indicated by the list of the diversified terminology above, many studies do not focus on 'miscommunication' as a whole, but e.g. on 'misunderstanding'. Weigand's (1999) theoretical paper falls into this category. In order to arrive at some constitutive features of what might be called the standard case of misunderstanding, Weigand (1999: 764-768) sketches and dismisses four methodological frameworks. First, she mentions the cross-cultural communication approach, which she holds to be irrelevant for her purpose, because she presumes the standard case of language use to foster co-membership of culture and community (Weigand 1999: 764). Considering current global trends and developments, such as the rapidly increasing number of EFL speakers[3] and the omnipresence of new communication technologies like email, such a claim no longer seems to be valid – if it ever was.

Secondly, Weigand (1999: 764) eliminates for her standard case "[d]eviant or side aspects" of 'misunderstanding'. For her, such "side aspects" (ibid.: 764) are planned and unresolved misunderstanding as well as cases in which a misunderstanding is prevented. Such an 'a priori' dismissal, however, bears the risk of impoverishing analysis. As all of these "side aspects" (ibid.: 764) appeared to be relevant for the data analyzed in this paper, some unexpected, but very intriguing relations, e.g. about non-understanding and strategic miscommunication, would not have been examined, had these aspects been excluded at the onset.

---

[3] For estimates of foreign language, second language and first language speakers of English between 1950 and 2050 see Graddol (1997: 60).

Thirdly, Weigand (1999: 765) takes her standard case to be incompatible with a "view which considers language use as inherently problematic" and which regards 'miscommunication' as a part of the act of communicating, a view promoted e.g. by Coupland, Wiemann & Giles (1991)[4]. The last framework Weigand outlines – the one she seems to associate herself with most of all – refers to 'misunderstanding' in a "harmonious model, where the interlocutors belong to the same community" (Weigand 1999: 766). But after all, this view seems to be based on an idealization of talk that is difficult to maintain even with native speakers (NSs) and certainly cannot be maintained with ELF data. This limited focus and the exclusion of significant aspects of the phenomenon already suggest that any attempt to define a standard case of 'misunderstanding' or also 'miscommunication' may well turn out to be a hunt for an academic chimera and, even if we were to define one, it would be unlikely to be of help if one is working with authentic data.

A similar position is also held by Dascal (1999: 757), who says that "[p]erhaps 'non-standard' cases are not marginal or sporadic – as assumed by Weigand – but rather quite central and frequent". While attempting to examine the different roles of linguistic devices in the management of misunderstanding in conversation, Dascal (1985b: 443) distinguishes four layers of significance of an utterance. However, he acknowledges that

> in most cases more than a single layer is involved. In fact, misunderstanding – as understanding – results from particular forms of *interaction* between the different layers (Dascal 1985b: 443, original emphasis).

This statement not only hints at the multi-causal nature of 'misunderstanding' and 'miscommunication'[5], but also underlines the improbability of the standard case to occur in real life.

One of the so-called non-standard environments of 'miscommunication', namely cross-cultural communication, has also been dealt with by some linguists within the field of pragmatics. The researcher to be mentioned here in the first place is Jenny Thomas, who coined the term 'pragmatic failure' (Thomas 1983: 91). Thomas (1983: 93) distinguishes between 'misunderstanding' at the level of propositional content and at the level of pragmatic force, and it is this second type of 'misunderstanding' which she labels

---

[4] As will be outlined in more detail in section 3.3, it is this view that is adopted in this study, since even Weigand (1999: 766) acknowledges that if one is interested in the "documentation of authentic conversations [...] well-formed structures and mis-structures cannot be clearly separated".
[5] The multicausality of 'miscommunication' will be discussed in section 3.8.

'pragmatic failure', defining it as "the inability to understand 'what is meant by what is said'" (Thomas 1983: 91).

Further Thomas specifies two types of 'pragmatic failure'. While 'sociopragmatic failure' refers to the social conditions placed on language use, 'pragmalinguistic failure' occurs when

> the pragmatic force mapped by S onto a given utterance is systematically different form the force most frequently assigned to it by native speakers of the target language, or when speech act strategies are inappropriately transferred from L1 to L2 (Thomas 1983: 99).

Two things are noticeable in this definition. For one, it reflects the native speaker authority that has customarily been taken for granted for a long time[6], even though Thomas (1983: 91) herself states the 'pragmatic failures' are not restricted to interactions between native speakers and non-native speakers (henceforth NSs and NNSs). Yet, in her definition it is the NS's assessment that decides whether something counts as a 'pragmalinguistic failure', even if no NS is present. Secondly, the reference to inappropriate transfer from L1 to L2 reflects an attitude that will be all the more pronounced in the next section, namely the tendency in intercultural communication research to locate the causes of communication problems exclusively in the participants' cultural and linguistic differences.

Some researchers in pragmatics, however, choose a different angle, that is, they focus on what actually happens in a conversation. Working with a corpus of spoken Italian, Bazzanella and Damiano (1999) examine how participants interactionally handle 'misunderstandings' and 'miscommunication'. While the following statement expresses a pattern that is indeed highly relevant for any researcher examining instances of 'miscommunication', namely the speakers' choice between indicating and avoiding indication[7], it does so in a peculiar and not unproblematic way:

> After a misunderstanding has been recognized [...], the participant who has realized it, irrespective of her/his **responsibility** in the misunderstanding, has to choose between two possibilities: s/he can point it out and make a **repair** [...], or she/he can decide to disregard it. In the latter case [...], either a topic shift or a **communication breakdown** can follow. (Bazzanella & Damiano 1999: 823, emphases added)

There are three aspects in this statement I would like to comment on. First of all, one speaker is held responsible for the 'misunderstanding', i.e. s/he is being 'blamed' for its 'creation'. Secondly, it features the concept of 'repair' implying that a participant

---

[6] Cf. the debate about the 'ownership of English' (Widdowson 1994: 377-389; 2003: 35-44).
[7] Cf. section 3.5.1 on the procedures for indicating 'non-understanding'.

addressing a 'misunderstanding' (or 'miscommunication') makes an active attempt to fix something that is damaged. Thirdly, the possibility that the conversation may continue quite smoothly if a 'repair initiation' (Schegloff 2000: 207) is not made is ruled out – either the topic has to be abandoned or a breakdown will follow.

Relating to the first aspect above, i.e. the speakers' responsibility for 'miscommunication', Tzanne (1999: 44) states that she prefers to "discuss miscommunication in terms of 'failure' rather than 'blame'" as she considers the latter to be "associated with evaluative judgments following communication breakdown" (ibid.: 44). Nevertheless, she maintains the term 'failure' which she takes to "describe the result of the communicative process" (ibid.: 44). Relating to the third point mentioned above, this raises the question whether every instance of 'miscommunication' necessarily points towards a 'failure' of the 'communicative process'. There is evidence to suggest that, especially in ELF conversations, this is not the case (e.g. Firth 1996; Kordon 2003), because even though information transfer may be impaired or delayed, the communicative process can nevertheless be successful on an interpersonal level (e.g. phatic communion, establishment or maintenance of rapport due to face-saving behavior).

With regard to the second point made above, a brief comment about the very commonly employed concept of 'repair' seems to be called for. Coined as a term by conversation analysts, 'repair' refers to

> practices for dealing with problems or troubles in speaking, hearing, and understanding the talk in conversation (and in other forms of talk-in-interaction, for that matter). [...] We proposed that these practices for dealing with trouble form an orderly *organization* of practices (Schegloff 2000: 207, original emphasis).

Among the practices that fall within the domain of 'repair' in conversation analysis (CA), Wong (2000: 247) mentions "[c]onfirmation checks, clarification requests, restatements, repetitions, understanding checks, and the like". Therefore, one gets the impression that, on the one hand, no clearly defined set of repair strategies exists, but on the other hand, a 'repair' is something that is always actively initiated, either by the speaker of the "trouble source" (Schegloff 2000: 208) as 'self-initiated repair' or by its recipient as 'other-initiated repair', an attitude which reflects a conventional CA position[8].

As CA primarily focuses on the structural and organizational components and the sequential development of conversations, conversation analysts assume "[e]pisodes of repair

---

[8] For a discussion of this traditional CA position and an alternative lingua franca position in CA see Firth (1996: 251-253).

activity" (Schegloff 2000: 207) to be composed of parts, most importantly a 'repair initiation' and a 'repair outcome'. The 'repair initiation' is seen to mark a "possible disjunction with the immediately preceding talk" (ibid.: 207). Consequently, any instance of 'miscommunication' from a CA perspective is seen to hold the progress of the conversation and "replace or defer whatever else was due next" (Schegloff 2000: 208). It is perceived to be a mere 'side sequence' and it is therefore marginalized. While such a view may reflect the structural development from an organizational perspective, it does not necessarily reflect participants' actual experience during the progression of a talk, especially not in ELF conversations, where NNSs are prone to expect the occasional need for clarification.

After this first short overview of literature, terms and attitudes, I would like to record three initial points about the view of 'miscommunication' adopted in this paper. Firstly, 'miscommunication' does not always have to lead to and surface as a 'repair activity'. Participants may realize the occurrence of 'miscommunication' or they "may remain unaware of it for a long time, and sometimes never know that it ever occurred" (Tzanne 1999: 2). Secondly, an instance of 'miscommunication' is not necessarily a 'failure' – 'miscommunication' can happen at various levels. Therefore a problem at one level may leave other levels unaffected or even have positive effects on them. Thirdly, 'miscommunication' does not necessarily have to be 'repaired'. It varies greatly in its degree of severity and, if it is not addressed or negotiated, it may, but certainly does not have to, lead to a 'breakdown'. As Tzanne (1999: 2) states,

> misunderstandings do not always develop in the same way, but [...] they can follow different courses of development, and have different outcomes, effects and consequences each time (Tzanne 1999: 2).

As this statement suggests, 'miscommunication' is a highly complex and not ineluctably negative phenomenon which can have highly diverse causes, appearances and consequences. It is the aim of this study to sketch some of the potential appearances it may exhibit in ELF conversations.

2.3 Intercultural communication and sociolinguistics: culture as the only culprit?

The attitude that 'miscommunication' is a negative phenomenon, however, is not restricted to pragmatics and CA, but is also very common in intercultural communication research, where with rare exceptions 'miscommunication' is "not invoked in the literature as a technical term but as representative of a genre of interaction outcomes that are undesirable" (Banks, Ge & Baker 1991: 104). In its key sense, 'miscommunication' is therefore perceived as having social consequences for the interactants (Banks, Ge & Baker 1991: 105). Among these social consequences are "misattribution of motives" and "unwarranted actions" (ibid.: 105), "mutual frustration, alienation and pejorative stereotyping" (Gumperz & Roberts 1991: 52). While it is certainly legitimate to point out that 'miscommunication' in an intercultural environment may have such severe social effects – particularly so with regard to encounters where cultural differences are reinforced by an (institutional) imbalance of power between the participants[9] – it is equally important to note that this is not always the case. Social consequences do not inevitably occur.

Intercultural encounters where speakers "in spite of repeated attempts, [...] utterly fail in their efforts to negotiate a common frame" (Gumperz 1982: 185) have resulted in a premise which came to be a central pillar in intercultural communication research, namely the abandonment of the distinction between cultural and social knowledge and linguistic signaling processes (Gumperz 1982: 186). Consequently, it came to be generally accepted that "[s]ocio-cultural conventions affect all levels of speech production and interpretation" (ibid.: 186). Although this statement constitutes a claim of universal validity, it should be noted that socio-cultural conventions are certainly not the only intricate mechanisms underlying, affecting and influencing linguistic behavior.

Based on the premise outlined above, Gumperz has coined the term 'contextualization cues', which refers to
> constellations of surface features of message form [...] by which speakers signal and listeners interpret what the activity is, how semantic content is to be understood and how each sentence relates to what precedes or follows (Gumperz 1982: 131).

'Miscommunication' which occurs when speakers fail to recognize or misinterpret such 'contextualization cues' is "regarded as a social faux pas" (Gumperz 1982: 132) and leads to misjudgments of the speaker's intent. Many communicative difficulties in intercultural encounters are consequently explained by the fact that participants rely on "systematically different contextualization conventions to carry out their interactive strategies" (Gumperz & Roberts 1991: 61).

---

[9] Cf. Gumperz and Roberts (1991)

This idea that speakers may 'coat' the same language with a contrasting repertoire of 'contextualization cues' has become well-established in intercultural communication research (Meeuwis 1994: 392). One remarkable contribution of this approach certainly is the assumption that neither party is 'right', but on the contrary that both sides contribute to 'miscommunication' (Banks, Ge & Baker 1991: 113). Yet, a note of caution also seems appropriate:

> While not denying the significant role contextualisation cues play in the construction of an interactional context, I envisage insuperable problems in assigning contextualisation cues an overpowering explanatory value when it comes to interpreting participants' cultural identities in an intercultural encounter. (Sarangi 1994: 412)

The same can likewise be said about an analysis of 'miscommunication': If a researcher assigns 'contextualization cues' such an "overpowering explanatory value" (ibid.: 412), the resulting analysis will almost necessarily be biased in that direction.

Even though this interactional-sociolinguistic research tradition undoubtedly "deserves credit for having produced fine-grained analyses of naturally occurring intercultural encounters" (Sarangi 1994: 411), the problems that arise from the working assumptions outlined above do not end at an overemphasis of 'contextualization cues'. A further and much more serious consequence of these working assumptions is a very reductionist perspective in findings about intercultural (mis)communication, namely a perspective in which cultural differences overshadow all other potential causes of understanding problems:

> In sum, then, the **relevant** sorts of misunderstandings addressed as miscommunication emerge from cultural differences, either exclusively or partially, in intercultural encounters. (Banks, Ge & Baker 1991: 107, emphasis added)

Of course, it is only logical for intercultural communication researchers to focus on communicative difficulties which arise when speakers with different cultures interact. The problem is that this focus often already seems to determine the reasons for any difficulties that occur.

Researchers like Scollon and Wong Scollon (1995: 125) want to "talk about large groups of people and what they have in common". In order to do this, they have to emphasize the commonalities, which however plays down possible differences among individuals (ibid.: 125). Yet, as they explicitly acknowledge themselves,

> [c]ultures do not talk to each other; individuals do. In that sense, all communication is interpersonal communication and can never be intercultural communication (Scollon & Wong Scollon 1995: 125).

The solution for this dilemma which researchers of intercultural communication often find is to restrict attention only to "those aspects of culture which research has shown to be of direct significance" (Scollon & Wong Scollon 1995: 126). Thus, they work with a limited and predefined view of 'culture', an "analytic construct" to use Sarangi's (1994: 409) term.

Such a proceeding leads to analyses of 'miscommunication' which overemphasize cultural differences at the expense of other factors, to the point where the researchers themselves "come to 'stereotype' intercultural communication as more 'intercultural' than 'communicative' in nature" (Meeuwis & Sarangi 1994: 311). This "analytic stereotyping" (Sarangi 1994: 409) of course bears the "risk of circularity" (ibid.: 413). If one is working with an a priori definition of an intercultural context which builds on differing 'cultural' attributes of the participants, then it is not only not surprising, but in fact very likely that any instance of 'miscommunication' is traced back to just these cultural differences (Sarangi 1994: 414).

A practice related and also similar to the 'analytic stereotyping' of intercultural context is the frequent mention of L1 transfer as an explanation of odd linguistic behavior and 'miscommunication'. While some idiosyncrasies or other characteristics may definitely be regarded as interferences from the speakers' mother tongues, one has to be cautious with limiting any causal explanation to an L1 transfer. As Meeuwis (1994: 395) notes with regard to one example in his data, to state that "mother-tongue transfer […] is the only cause of this misunderstanding" (ibid.: 395) would certainly oversimplify the complex factors involved in this – and any other – interaction. Therefore, one can only agree with Ellis when he says:

> [I]t is important not to overstate the role of the non-native speaker's L1 and culture. […] While acknowledging the importance of transfer, we also need to recognize that other factors are involved. (Ellis 1994: 187)

And in fact, there are some researchers who not only recognize and acknowledge the existence of other factors, but who also include their potential influence into analysis.

Among these researchers is Tzanne (1999: 32), who, instead of relying unquestioningly on participants' differences or similarities, suggests integrating the dynamic interpretive context of interaction. She notes that "exclusive preoccupation with participants' stable background features" (Tzanne 1999: 15) may obscure or even conceal completely the importance of other *social roles* interactants can play [...] or the role of *physical context* to the interpretation of talk-in-interaction (Tzanne 1999: 15, original emphasis).

As a consequence, it is obvious that a more open-minded approach to the investigation of intercultural encounters is called for, an approach which takes "situated activity types and participants' roles and power relations" (Tzanne 1999: 7) into account and considers them in relation to the continual and jointly constructed situational context of an interaction.

In conclusion, we can say that research on intercultural communication has certainly shown how 'contextualization cues' and other linguistic behaviors are influenced by a speaker's (native) culture and how 'miscommunication' resulting from cultural differences may have potentially severe social consequences for speakers. Yet, as ELF researchers we need to ask ourselves the question

> whether one's ethnic identity is *the only identity* this person can be found to assume in an encounter, and thus whether this identity is *always* relevant to the interpretation of this person's goals in *all* kinds of encounters in which s/he may take part (Tzanne 1999: 7, original emphasis).

While the answer to such a question should be plain, I hope the preceding discussion has succeeded in outlining how long this attitude has nevertheless been maintained in research. In conceiving of ELF speakers as speakers of their own right – and not primiarily in terms of their native language and culture – I am discarding such a notion in favor of a more open-minded and less ethno-centric approach.

2.4 The dialogical approach: acknowledging 'miscommunication'

The two preceding sections have shown how most of the pragmatic and intercultural research on 'miscommunication' has in fact adopted what Coupland, Wiemann and Giles (1991: 1) call the "Pollyanna perspective", treating any kind of communication problem as "aberrant behavior which should be eliminated" (ibid.: 1). Such a demand, however, of course does not only call for the elimination and avoidance of 'miscommunication', but it also presupposes that 'miscommunication' can be eliminated, a claim which, it seems, is worth questioning.

Focusing on daily conversations between equal participants, Blum-Kulka and Weizman (1988: 219) argue for the "inevitability of unresolved misunderstandings in ordinary talk". They attempt to show how participants tolerate a rather high degree of non-acknowledged, unresolved potential misunderstandings in interpersonal communication

(Blum-Kulka & Weizman 1988: 220). While the authors state that misunderstandings are not necessarily resolved by negotiation (ibid.: 220), they also stress the fact that the levels at which a 'misunderstanding' – or another type of 'miscommunication' – exists may remain covert[10] (Blum-Kulka & Weizman 1988: 219). In their conclusion, they stress that 'miscommunication' is inevitable because of participants' face interests, which induce speakers to keep up a certain level of ambiguity (Blum-Kulka & Weizman 1988: 235). Agreeing with Tannen (1986), the authors therefore propose that "communication is inherently ambiguous" (Blum-Kulka & Weizman 1988: 235).

As Wardhaugh (1998: 252) reports, a similar attitude towards the ambiguity of language is also reflected in ethnomethodological research:

> Apparently, conversation proceeds on the assumption that a certain vagueness is normal, that ordinary talk does not require precision, and that many expressions that are used in conversation are not to be taken literally. This vague, imprecise, and non-literal nature of ordinary talk is deemed to be entirely reasonable, and for someone to question it is to act unreasonably. (Wardhaugh 1998: 252)

Even though this statement primarily refers to ordinary conversations among NSs, it certainly contains far-reaching implications for any type of spoken interaction. It makes clear that once we come to work with spoken discourse, the distinction between correct and incorrect, ambiguous and unambiguous is no longer clear-cut, but becomes unclear and blurred.

From this angle, it is hardly possible to disavow the contention that "language use and communication are in fact pervasively and even intrinsically flawed, partial, and problematic" (Coupland, Wiemann & Giles 1991: 3). At the same time, it has to be acknowledged that discoursal 'problems' occur at multiple levels and dimensions and differ greatly in severity (ibid.: 3). Therefore, they can neither be collectively labeled irrelevant nor seriously threatening. It is getting more and more obvious that

> the connections between understanding and misunderstanding [are] both more intimate and more complex than I – and many others – had previously assumed (Dascal 1985b: 441-442).

The "paradoxical formula" that Dascal (1985b: 442) brings this observation down to is that "a significant part of understanding speech has to do with misunderstanding" (ibid.: 442).

The "monological focus" (Good 1999: 10) found in a good deal of research is eschewed particularly by researchers working in a "dialogical or dialogistic theory

---

[10] Cf. section 3.4

tradition" (ibid.: 10) like Coupland, Wiemann and Giles (1991) and Linell (1995). In this tradition, there is nothing like 'the correct and complete understanding' of an utterance (Linell 1995: 181). Understanding is conceived of as "partial and fragmentary" (Linell 1995: 184) and communication as a "matter of degree" (ibid.: 184). Consequently, 'miscommunication' is not seen as something essentially different from 'communication' (ibid.: 184). The relation between understanding and 'miscommunication' is intimate, so that apparent difficulties may sometimes pave the way to a higher degree of understanding[11]:

> Indeed, salient (and perhaps fruitful) misunderstandings occur, because parties try to understand each other, and hence such episodes may increase the depth of understanding in ways that, without them, would be difficult to come by. (Linell 1995: 184-185)

For Linell (1995: 185) this interrelatedness does not only open up the potential for arriving at an in-depth understanding via 'miscommunication', but it also relates to the fact that 'miscommunication' and 'misunderstanding' are "dialogically constituted and collectively generated" (ibid.: 185) in conversation.

Since the attitude reflected in most works investigating 'miscommunication' is fairly different from the one sketched above, it is easy to overlook the explanatory potential of 'miscommunication' and the ways in which it may positively contribute to interaction and social relationships (Coupland, Wiemann & Giles 1991: 3). Yet, there are some researchers, like Brown and Rogers (1991), who focus on interpersonal relationships. As, in their opinion, intimate relationships are a matter of negotiating competing tensions, rather than eliminating differences, they demand neither continuous harmony nor conflict (Brown & Rogers 1991: 147). From their perspective, 'miscommunication' is unavoidable and necessary for the management of interpersonal tension (ibid.: 147).

Within their "epistemology of pattern", Brown and Rogers (1991: 149) see social life as a process of interrelating, a process which is inherently problematic. In this process, any moment or behavior derives its significance from other moments and behaviors (ibid.: 149). As a consequence, the authors state that

> as such, no given behavior-moment-state can be deemed *inherently* more healthy, more functional, more desirable, or more miscommunicative than any other (Brown & Rogers 1991: 149, original emphasis).

---

[11] A similar approach is taken by Weizman (1999: 837), who, by means of analyzing a short story in Hebrew, "endeavours to show how apparent miscommunication is exploited by the speakers to build up towards an implicit mutual understanding between them" (ibid.: 837).

Furthermore, it is proposed that sequential patterns and contextualization are crucial to the interpretation of behavior[12] (Brown & Rogers 1991: 150). Within such a perspective, the concept of 'miscommunication' clearly loses its all negative face and is "radically redefined from a mis-hap to a happening" (Brown & Rogers 1991: 163).

Ochs's (1991) study on miscommunication and children certainly adopts a similiar perspective. Her focus is on 'misunderstanding' by which she means a "communicative activity in which one or another participant signals noncomprehension or potential noncomprehension" (Ochs 1991: 45). These misunderstandings are taken to be structured in local and universal ways (ibid.: 45). The universal structure of misunderstandings appears to traverse cultures and languages (ibid.: 45). Furthermore, Ochs (1991) finds that the verbal strategies for signaling and responding to unintelligibility are universal characteristics of misunderstandings[13]. Consequently, she notes that this shared universal knowledge facilitates communication among speakers with different mother tongues (ibid.: 56). This is the case because

> [s]peakers from all sorts of communities are able to coordinate their actions while engaged in the activity of misunderstanding because they share a partial understanding of how that activity is structured (Ochs 1991: 56).

While the general structure of such misunderstanding activities is universal and traverses languages and cultures, the preferences for particular forms of signaling or responding to unintelligibility are "tied to the local social order and local theories of communication and understanding" (ibid.: 56).

Ochs (1991: 58) relates misunderstandings to the process of socialization and sees them as "opportunity spaces for constituting and learning social order" (ibid.: 58), not only for children but also for people who immigrate into a foreign country. In this view, misunderstandings are more then language activities – they are social and cultural activities as well (ibid.: 59).

> From this point of view, misunderstandings are not loci in which social life breaks down. Rather, to the contrary, misunderstandings structure social life. Each misunderstanding is an opportunity space for instantiating local epistemology and for structuring social identities of interactants. Once we focus our ethnographic microscopes on misunderstandings, we can appreciate their extraordinary complexity

---

[12] Cf. Goffman's notion of 'frame' and Gumperz's notion of 'contextualization', which will be discussed in section 3.7.1.
[13] Cf. Vasseur, Broeder and Roberts's (1996: 73-90) multi-language model of procedures for indicating 'non-understanding'. A detailed discussion of this model will be given in section 3.5.1.

and impact on human culture through the process of language socialization. (Ochs 1991: 60)

It is bold statements and findings like these which underline the importance of empirical research on 'miscommunication' in different contexts, as they stress the widely varying positive functions this phenomenon can have. Consequently, the attitude expressed by other researchers that without negative social consequences like misattribution of motives and unwarranted actions research on 'miscommuncation' would be "of trivial interest" (Banks, Ge & Baker 1991: 105) seems unjustified. On the contrary, it is high time we follow Coupland, Wiemann and Giles's postulation to "rescue 'miscommuncation' from its theoretical and empirical exile, and explore its rich explanatory potential in very diverse contexts" (Coupland, Wiemann & Giles 1991: 2).

2.5 Summary and conclusion

While pragmatics has certainly endowed us with the ground work – and also core terms – in the field, researchers have often shown a tendency to treat 'miscommunication' as an unfavorable communicative phenomenon. Similarly, CA has given us valuable insights into the structural development of 'repairs', but due to its extremely organizational focus, it tends to take away some of the liveliness of interaction and to disregard participants' real life experience. Sociolinguistics has provided fine-grained analyses of naturally occurring conversations, mostly focusing on 'miscommunication' that is perceived as a social faux pas and has social consequences for the participants. As a result, the tradition of intercultural communication research, which tends to predetermine participants' cultural identities and analyze 'miscommunication' accordingly, has established itself. A considerably different view is represented by a branch of research informed by dialogistic theory. Working with the assumption that communication and 'miscommunication' are intricately linked, this tradition explores the positive effects 'miscommunication' can have and acknowledges its explanatory power. It is in this view that 'miscommunication' clearly ceases to be regarded as a purely negative phenomenon, but rather comes to be accepted as an intrinsic part of any interaction.

3 FINDING A NON-NATIVE SPEAKERS' PATH: AN ELF PERSPECTIVE ON 'MISCOMMUNICATION'

3.1 Introduction

After the short overview of different approaches to 'miscommunication' in chapter 2, chapter 3 presents the theoretical models, terms, definitions and assumptions which are used for the analysis of 'miscommunication' in ELF interactions in this paper. As a first step, section 3.2 outlines the general point of view of ELF research and some tendencies concerning 'miscommunication' which existent ELF findings suggest. Section 3.3 discusses core terms and definitions, focusing on 'miscommunication' as well as 'understanding', 'non-understanding', and 'misunderstanding'. Some problems the analyst has to face are addressed in section 3.4, including the circumstance that many instances of 'miscommunication' remain covert and never surface in discourse. The systematic structural analysis of instances of 'local non-understanding' is the focus of section 3.5. Two models are presented in this respect, namely a model for the 'negotiation of meaning' and a continuum of indicating procedures. Section 3.6 is dedicated to the possibility of strategic miscommunication. The interrelatedness of 'understanding' and 'context' is examined in section 3.7. The notions of 'contextualization', 'frame', and 'footing' are considered in relation to the dynamic development of 'micro-context', while shared knowledge, culture and institutional conditions are regarded as 'macro-contextual' features. Finally, section 3.8 touches upon the multicausal nature of 'miscommunication'.

3.2 The ELF position

English as a 'lingua franca' (ELF)[14] is a research focus which has emerged over the last decade and is still continuously gaining ground in linguistic research.[15] The term 'lingua franca' refers to "an additionally acquired language system that serves as a means of communication between speakers of different first languages" (Seidlhofer 2001: 146). A

---

[14] Other terms which are sometimes used more or less interchangeably with ELF are English as an international language (EIL) (e.g. Seidlhofer 2002a), English as a global language (e.g. Crystal 1997), English as a medium of intercultural communication (e.g. Meierkord 1996), and 'interlanguage talk' (ILT) (e.g. Jenkins 2002).

[15] The current section represents the state of the art of ELF research in 2004 and does not take into account recent publications and developments from late 2004 onwards.

'lingua franca' therefore is a 'contact language' (Firth 1996: 240), a language with "no native speakers" (Seidlhofer 2001: 146). In a world in which countries and cultures are moving closer together through global business, international organizations and new communication technologies, ELF interactions are extremely frequent and most likely are to gain even greater importance in the decades to come[16]. Due to the situation outlined, ELF interactions, i.e. interactions involving "members of two or more different linguacultures" (House 1999: 74), often take place in 'influential networks' like business[17], politics, science, technology and media (ibid.: 74).

The need for empirical research on ELF has been stressed by Seidlhofer (2001), who points out the need for "closing the conceptual gap" (ibid.: 133) that still exists between the state of real world affairs, empirical research and teaching curricula. What is called for with regard to this empirical work and what marks ELF research as something clearly different from e.g. intercultural communication research is the conceptualization of the ELF speaker

> as a *language user* whose real-world interactions are *deserving* of unprejudiced description, rather [...] than as a person conceived *a priori* to be the possessor of incomplete or deficient communicative competence, putatively striving for the 'target' competence or an idealized 'native speaker' (Firth 1996: 241, original emphasis).

A similar attitude is reflected by Haegeman (2002: 138), who is wary of researchers basing their conclusions on "a fixed set of characteristics such as age, sex, NNS" which they assume the speakers to bring into every conversation. Haegeman (2002: 138) argues that these characteristics are not relevant per se, but only can be made relevant by the speakers through interaction. Therefore, the researcher has no reason to set up e.g. a NS vs. NNS distinction from outside (Haegeman 2002: 159-160). But in order to arrive at the "unprejudiced description" that Firth (1996: 241) calls for, we need to abandon a priori distinctions and categorizations and likewise "unrealistic notions of achieving 'perfect' communication through 'native-like' proficiency in English" (Seidlhofer 2002a: 22). It is obvious that such an assumption also has to inform an analysis of 'miscommunication' in ELF interactions.

---

[16] For a detailed discussion of the current status of English in the world and potential future scenarios see Graddol (1997).

[17] The importance of English as an internal company language is stressed e.g. by Vollstedt (2002). Mainly relying on data collected in a series of case studies in international companies with German and French headquarters, she examines as Meierkord & Knapp (2000: 15) acutely state "the scope and extent to which English has established itself in the area of business communications and analyzes the factors which influence the language shift from the parent company's language to English".

3.2.1. Pronunciation problems and the 'Lingua Franca Core'

Concerning the issue of what is intelligible in ELF talk, very valuable groundwork in the area of phonology has been provided by Jennifer Jenkins. She has established a 'Lingua Franca Core' comprised of pronunciation features found essential to understanding among NNSs (Jenkins 2000: 134-162; 2002: 96-98). What is remarkable with regard to these features is that e.g. sounds like 'th' were found non-essential and were excluded from the core (Jenkins 2002: 98). A similar view is expressed by Seidlhofer (2001: 149) with regard to lexico-grammar, when she states that

> features which are regarded as 'the most typically English', such as 3rd person –s, tags, phrasal verbs and idioms, [...] turn out to be non-essential for mutual understanding (Seidlhofer 2001: 149).

Successful ELF communication therefore seems to come about despite features which would be termed 'incorrect' or 'unidiomatic' by NS standards (Seidlhofer 2001: 148). Initial findings like these already indicate that one seems to be clearly mistaken if one were to attempt to define 'miscommunication' (or communicative success) in ELF in terms of correctness, although it may be tempting to do so for some researchers. If anything, one can only come to grips with 'miscommunication' in ELF in relation to appropriateness[18]. Yet such a demand immediately raises a crucial question which is yet to be fully answered: what is appropriate in ELF interactions?

At the level of phonology, Jenkins's 'Lingua Franca Core' already provides a fairly satisfactory answer to this question. Furthermore, it also relies on a premise which can be regarded as central in ELF research: appropriateness is determined by intelligibility. In this respect, Jenkins (2002: 87-89) also looks at the link between intelligibility and 'miscommunication' and determines some categories of phonological error which most often prove problematic for speakers in her data. The categories Jenkins names are

> consonant sounds, tonic (or nuclear) stress, vowel length, and non-permissible (according to the rules of English syllable structure) simplification of consonant clusters (Jenkins 2002: 88).

With regard to these categories, Jenkins (2002: 87) notes that "although pronunciation was by no means the sole cause of ILT [interlanguage talk] communication breakdown, it was by far the most frequent and the most difficult to resolve". As Seidlhofer (2001: 142)

---

[18] A similar demand is made by Widdowson (1998: 705-716; 2003: 93-106) concerning the need for appropriating 'authentic' or 'real' English to the (learning) environment of a foreign language classroom.

remarks, however, phonology is a fairly "closed system" and this, it seems to me, may be a possible explanation for the disruptive potential that Jenkins observes with regard to phonological problems: Since we are looking at a 'closed system' in phonology, it may be rather difficult for participants to compensate for problems that occur within this system (i.e. unintelligible pronunciation) by relying on features which are outside the system (e.g. context or gestures).

3.2.2. ELF pragmatics and the absence of 'miscommunication'

In contrast to phonology, pragmatics is "a more open-ended affair" (Seidlhofer 2001: 142), which, however, makes it much more difficult to arrive at 'conclusive' findings. With regard to 'miscommunication' and pragmatics, House (1999: 73) sets out to an analysis with the hypothesis that "misunderstandings in ELF talk are caused by differences in interactants' pragmatic-cultural norms". Although she acknowledges that misunderstandings regularly occur between members of the same language community and are "the rule rather than the exception in our own familiar linguaculture" (House 1999: 76), she nevertheless assumes misunderstandings to be much more critical when members with different cultural backgrounds interact. Her data, however, which consists of 30 minutes of taped quasi natural ELF group discussions (ibid.: 79) do not confirm her initial hypothesis, because no open misunderstandings are noticeable (ibid.: 80). What she finds are only minor misunderstandings "inherent in the nature of interaction with minor local routine disruptions" (ibid.: 79). Yet, the data also exhibit remarkable stretches of 'parallel talk' in which "participants 'play their own game' without really listening to the interlocutors" (ibid.: 80). As Seidlhofer (2001: 143) notes, however, this last feature could be due to the particular type and purpose of the interaction analyzed, and thus it is far from certain that this constitutes an essential characteristic of ELF talk.

Meierkord's (1996) extensive, pragmatically oriented analysis of dinner table conversations in a British dormitory also supports the assumption that ELF interactions take place rather smoothly. In her data with an overall length of 13.5 hours (Meierkord 1996: 67), Meierkord only finds nine instances of 'miscommunication'. Five instances relate to individual speakers' problems concerning vocabulary and are negotiated immediately (ibid.: 195). With regard to these negotiations, Meierkord (1996: 205) makes two remarkable observations: firstly, less competent speakers seem to exhibit a higher degree of cooperation than speakers with greater proficiency; and secondly, even if clarifications still remain ambiguous, they are accepted if they are judged to be inconsequential for the further progression of the interaction.

Furthermore, Meierkord (1996: 205) notices four instances where attempts for clarification are not made and a 'communication breakdown' occurs. She notes, however, that these examples are, as a rule, not caused by the participants' cultural differences:

> Die vorgestellten Beispiele verdeutlichen, daß die im vorliegenden Korpus auftretenden *communication breakdowns* in der Regel nicht als durch die unterschiedliche kulturelle Zugehörigkeit der SprecherInnen bedingt interpretiert werden können. (Meierkord 1996: 216, original emphasis)

In Meierkord's interpretation, most "communication breakdowns" in her data originate in differing personal attitudes towards the topic or different amounts of background knowledge (ibid.: 216). Consequently, it is not surprising that the participants react to the occurrence of a 'communication breakdown' by a shift in topic (ibid.: 216). Yet, nine instances of communicative problems in more than 13 hours certainly are rather few. Therefore, smooth interaction represents the rule in Meierkord's ELF corpus (ibid.: 193).

3.2.3 'Let it pass', 'communicative leniency' and the risk of interactional vulnerability

Attempting a reorientation of CA towards the interpretation of ELF data, Firth (1996: 241) analyzes a corpus of business telephone conversations involving Danish export managers and their international clients. In this analysis, Firth (1996: 243) defines the 'let it pass' concept as an "interpretive procedure" the hearer adopts when faced with problems in understanding the speaker's utterance:

> The hearer thus lets the unknown or unclear action, word or utterance 'pass' on the (common-sense) assumption that it will either become clear or redundant as the talk progresses. (Firth 1996: 243)

Although the principle is not unique to ELF interactions, Firth (1996: 243) calls it a "commonly-deployed resource in lingua franca interactions". Even though this concept certainly displays participants' "shared intentionality" (Weizman 1999: 843) and "charitable attitude" (Dascal 1999: 757), it is also closely linked to 'miscommunication'.

First of all, a 'let it pass' procedure may occur when the analyst is able to identify an apparent 'misunderstanding', but "since neither party orient to or *display* awareness of the 'misunderstanding' [...], it is rendered *interactionally irrelevant*" (Firth 1996: 243, original emphasis). Yet, the question that immediately poses itself to the analyst is how s/he can determine whether the 'misunderstanding' was missed by the participant(s) or whether it was simply allowed to pass (ibid.: 244). In the first case, participants are unaware of the occurrence of any communicative problem, in the latter, they are – or at least one participant is – aware of it, but they decide to 'ignore' it[19]. What is more, Firth (1996: 244) states that by adopting a 'let it pass' strategy participants "may act *as if* they understand one another – even when they in fact do not" (original emphasis). Normally such a behavior might be labeled deceptive, but in ELF interactions it seems to be perfectly acceptable. It would seem that lack-of-uptake, minimal responses and paraverbal behavior such as laughter – i.e. typical 'let it pass' features – can also be interpreted as indirectly and implicitly pointing towards 'miscommunication'[20], at least for the analyst.

As a characteristic of ELF conversations, the 'let is pass' principle exemplifies the "constructive, collaborative feel" (Seidlhofer 2001: 148) these interactions usually display. It indicates the participants' "remarkable ability and willingness to tolerate anomalous usage and marked linguistic behaviour" (Firth 1996: 246), an attitude that Meeuwis (1994: 398) has subsumed under the term 'communicative leniency'. Findings so far suggest that ELF speakers

> display a particular style largely characterized by cooperation leading to successful communication rather than misunderstanding (Meierkord 2002: 120).

The participants adopt the position that their talk is "understandable and 'normal' – even in the face of misunderstandings and abnormalities" (Firth 1996: 256).

Yet, as is often the case, there are two sides to this coin, as there is an "interactional *vulnerability*" (Firth 1996: 244, original emphasis) inherent to such a high degree of cooperation and especially to the 'let it pass' procedure. In other words, the remarkable degree of cooperation and the willingness to leave a communicative problem pending, so to speak, may mask instances of 'miscommunication'. In some contexts, talk is inherently more 'robust', while in others it is much less so (Firth 1996: 248). Accordingly, there are certain activities, like e.g. spelling a name, which are inherently more 'fragile' than others

---

[19] It is precisely this awareness that, in my terminology, distinguishes a 'misunderstanding' (unawareness) from a 'non-understanding'(awareness) (see section 3.3).
[20] Cf. Vasseur, Broeder and Roberts's (1996: 76-82) implicit procedures for signalling 'non-understanding' ('symptoms'), which will be discussed in section 3.5.1.

(ibid.: 248). In these 'fragile' situations, "the need arises for the participants to accomplish and to make explicit their substantive understanding on a turn-by-turn basis" (ibid.: 250).

If, in such a 'fragile' situation, all participants adopt a 'let it pass' behavior, a "general superficial consensus may indeed mask deeper sources of trouble" (House 1999: 75). The talk, thus, is interactionally vulnerable through the 'let it pass' strategy. Indeterminacy can be left unattended, which can prolong ambiguity "theoretically ad infinitum" (Blum-Kulka & Weizman 1988: 236). Taken to an extreme, participants may leave the interaction with "contradictory envisionments of what has been going on" (Blum-Kulka & Weizman 1988: 236). Therefore, it seems that in 'fragile' situations minor 'local' disruptions – if not addressed and negotiated – may lead to more 'global' discrepancies. Therefore, it is highly interesting to investigate how 'miscommunication' is managed in the face of such a high degree of cooperation among ELF participants and which types of 'miscommunication' occur – and surface – in such an environment.

3.3 Core terms and definitions: understanding, miscommunication, misunderstanding and non-understanding

With regard to the terminology used in this study, there are three core terms, which need to be defined and described: 'miscommunication', 'non-understanding', and 'misunderstanding'. But before entering a discussion of these terms, however, it is necessary to address another concept, namely that of 'understanding'. First of all and most importantly, it needs to be noted that 'understanding' in this study is defined by taking primarily an interactional sociolinguistic and dialogistic perspective and that it is therefore seen as "interactive and jointly constructed" (Roberts 1996: 17). It is not seen as a passive ability, but as "a dynamic, public and cooperative activity in which both sides [i.e. speaker and listener] are actively engaged" (ibid.: 17). Consequently, 'understanding' is primarily analyzed in terms of participants' "shared and mutual understanding" (Linell 1995: 179). As 'understanding' in this perspective is clearly a goal for both listener and speaker (Linell 1995.: 180) – and not only for the listener – it is obvious that participants "collaborate on constructing shared understanding" (ibid.: 180). Yet, the process of 'understanding' is difficult to deal with for the analyst, because although "the process of understanding is not a private one, it is largely an invisible one" (Roberts 1996: 18).

It is quite obvious that 'understanding' – as shared understanding – in this perspective is usually, as Linell (1995: 184) notes, "partial and fragmentary" and that in this sense, "miscommunication cohabits with communication in dialogue" (ibid.: 184). Consequently, 'miscommunication' in this book is clearly not regarded as 'aberrant behavior' which should be eliminated, as in fact it cannot be eliminated and is always and inevitably an intrinsic part of spoken interaction, be it among NSs or NNSs of any language. The concept of 'miscommunication' in this study will therefore closely – with only one restriction[21] – follow Linell's definition which specifies 'miscommunication' as talk

> generating or mobilizing and sometimes leaving discrepancies between parties in the interpretation of what is said or done in the dialogue (Linell 1995: 176-177).

'Miscommunication' in this paper is thus used as an umbrella term, addressing all instances of "understanding problems" (Bremer 1996) – a term which will be used synonymously with 'miscommunication'. These 'understanding problems' can have highly diverse causes and appearances and "widely varying degrees of severity" (Coupland, Wiemann & Giles 1991: 3) and accordingly are not per se 'dangerous' or 'threatening' to the conversation. Mirroring the notion of 'understanding' outlined above, one could also say that the term 'miscommunication' in this book refers to instances in an interaction at which 'understanding' is not shared among participants.

Before I turn to the two other terms in need of definition, 'misunderstanding' and 'non-understanding' that is, some preliminary remarks about what has been said so far seem appropriate. First, it should be noted that 'understanding' and 'miscommunication' above are conceived of primarily in emic terms, i.e. as experienced by the participants of an interaction, and not as judged by the analyst. Yet, this emic conception is not absolute either, as it is restricted by the fact that even participants themselves may be unaware of 'miscommunication'. Furthermore, since the analyst is an observer, who as such is per definition outside the speech event, s/he can only discuss instances of 'miscommunication' which become apparent and observable, i.e. which 'surface' in the conversation. As a third point, one should be aware that even with those instances that surface it may be highly

---

[21] Linell's original definition refers to "talk **non-deliberately** generating or mobilizing and sometimes leaving discrepancies between parties in the interpretation or understanding of what is said or done in the dialogue" (Linell 1995: 176-177, emphasis added). While within a conceptual framework, deliberate 'miscommunication' can be clearly separated from non-deliberate 'miscommunication', the analysis has shown that such a distinction can be highly problematic for the analyst with regard to naturally occurring data. Therefore, I will refrain from a priori excluding deliberate miscommunication and have therefore left out the word 'non-deliberately' from the definition.

difficult for the analyst to assess from outside what is going on in the participants' minds and how they experience a particular situation[22].

Similar to Gass and Varonis's (1991: 124) diagram, in which they distinguish two subcategories of 'miscommunication' – 'misunderstanding' and 'incomplete understanding' – the two basic types of 'miscommunication' distinguished in this study, a distinction following Bremer (1996: 40), are 'misunderstanding' and 'non-understanding' (see Figure 1). The prime distinguishing factor between those two phenomena is the participants' degree of awareness: immediate awareness (of at least one participant) of an 'understanding problem' points towards a 'non-understanding', while an instance of 'miscommunication' of which neither participant is aware at the time of its occurrence represents a 'misunderstanding'.

```
                    miscommunication
                   ↙                ↘
          non-understanding      misunderstanding
             (awareness)           (unawareness)
```

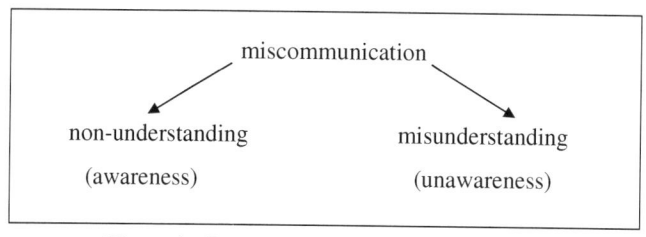

Figure 1: Core terms of miscommunication

The term 'misunderstanding' has been used by many researchers. Milroy (1984: 15) roughly defines it as a "simple disparity between the speaker's and the hearer's semantic analysis of a given utterance". Bremer (1996: 40) calls it a "mismatch" in which "the listener achieves an interpretation which makes sense to her or him – but it wasn't the one the speaker meant". The issue of both the speaker's and the listener's unawareness is even more pronounced in Tzanne's description which sees 'misunderstandings' as instances "where the hearer has misinterpreted, but remains under the false impression that s/he has understood correctly, the communicative intention of the speaker" (Tzanne 1999: 33).

Even though these three definitions all provide valid descriptions of what makes an instance of 'miscommunication' a 'misunderstanding', they are slightly problematic, as they could all be read as more or less implicitly conveying the notion that the 'responsibility' for

---

[22] These two aspects, namely the fact that many instances of 'miscommunication' remain covert for the analyst and the fact that it can be highly difficult for the analyst to assess participants' experience at a particular moment, will be addressed in more detail in section 3.4.

'misunderstanding' lies with the listener, as s/he appears to be the one who fails to grasp the speaker's intended meaning and/or intention. Yet, in particular with regard to the interactive and jointly constructed nature of 'shared understanding', this is not the case. As Linell astutely observes

> [t]he speaker is assigned the status of interpretive authority when it comes to the meaning of his/her own utterances. But this holds most unambiguously for reference, not necessarily for descriptive (or other) aspects of meaning. In other words, the speaker knows what the intended referents are, but s/he may be mistaken in her/his choice of words for describing them. Thus, when A says something and B does not share or come to share A's understanding of the matter, we are not always justified in saying simply that B misunderstands. (Linell 1995: 180-181)

Consequently, regarding 'misunderstanding' but also 'non-understanding', the perspective taken in this paper is that no single participant can be held responsible for the "creation" of an instance of 'miscommunication' or regarded as its "maker" (Tzanne 1999: 38).

The most suitable and most neutral definition of 'misunderstanding' that I encountered is the following:

> a misunderstanding occurs when a communication attempt is unsuccessful because what the speaker intends to express differs from what the hearer believes to have been expressed (Humphreys-Jones 1986: 1 quoted in Tzanne 1999: 39).

It comprises the 'mismatch' of meaning and/or intention as well as the unawareness of all participants "without assigning *blame* to either participant" (Tzanne 1999: 39, original emphasis) and it is this non-judgmental attitude which is adopted in the present study. Furthermore, due to participants' unawareness, it is obvious that a 'misunderstanding' can only be recognized retrospectively, once it has surfaced, e.g. through an incoherent response. In some cases, it may not surface at all and therefore participants may never realize that the 'misunderstanding' ever occurred.

The same attitude, namely one which does not blame participants for 'miscommunication', is also adopted with regard to 'non-understanding'. Bremer (1996: 40) states that a 'non-understanding' occurs "when the listener realises that s/he cannot make sense of (part of) an utterance". In other words, one participant – usually the listener – realizes before making her or his next contribution that s/he and her or his co-participant(s) do not share understanding. In most cases this realization, however, does not correspond to a total lack of understanding, as 'non-understanding' – much like 'understanding' – is a "graded phenomenon" (Bremer 1996: 40), which may range from a total lack of understanding to more or less complete understanding (Allwood & Abelar 1984: 29). Since in the case of a 'non-understanding' at least one participant is always aware of the existence of an 'understanding problem', s/he will have the choice between indicating the 'non-understanding' and avoiding indication[23], i.e. adopting a 'let it pass' behavior.

3.4 Diagnosing 'miscommunication': the potential covertness of 'miscommunication' and the role of the analyst

Participants may be unaware of 'miscommunication' and, even if they are aware of it, they may decide not to indicate an 'understanding problem' explicitly. As a consequence, instances of 'miscommunication' are "not easy to identify or categorize" (Linell 1995: 186). Thus, it may be that case that although an exchange

> carries a high potential for inherent misunderstandings, this potential remains, as it were, 'under the surface' in the sense that there is no verbal evidence for its existence. In other words, in no part of the dialogue does either party endeavor to show that her intentions were misinterpreted by her partner, or to find out whether she herself has interpreted correctly her partner's intentions. Misunderstanding, if existent at all, is *not negotiated* (Blum-Kulka & Weizman 1988: 229, original emphasis).

Such a behavior, however, bears two main problems for the analyst: first, it may be impossible to decide for the analyst whether an instance of 'miscommunication' exists; secondly, if an instance of 'miscommunication' can be pinpointed, it may be difficult to decide whether participants – or at least one participant – are aware of it ('non-understanding'), but prefer to make no explicit reference to it, or whether neither participant is aware of an 'understanding problem' ('misunderstanding').

As a consequence, many instances of 'miscommunication' will remain covert for the analyst and/or for the participants. In this respect, Linell (1995: 187) distinguishes three types of what he calls "miscommunication events" (MEs): latent, covert, and overt. 'Overt' MEs pose no problem for the analyst as they have "clear reflections and manifest properties" (ibid.: 187) in the interactional data. Most instances of 'miscommunication' presented in this paper can be assigned to this category. What Linell labels 'covert' MEs can be discovered via "traces or indirect reflections" (ibid.: 187) that can be (re)interpreted into the data. While 'overt' MEs are most likely realized by participants, 'covert' MEs are likely to be perceived as "uncomfortable moments" (Erickson & Shultz 1982 referred to in Linell 1995: 187) in an interaction. Finally, Linell's category of 'latent' MEs is characterized by

---

[23] For a further discussion of these two options and the particular procedures that can be employed to indicate 'non-understanding' see section 3.5.1.

the fact that these instances of 'miscommunication' leave "no traces or symptoms in the interactional data" (Linell 1995: 187). Even though there is "a factual or perceived discrepancy in understanding" (ibid.: 187) between participants, this discrepancy is interactionally invisible and therefore not observable for the analyst.

Although "the absence of superficial problems of meaning exchange is no indication of the absence of miscommunication at deeper levels" (Coupland, Wiemann & Giles 1991: 7), the analyst nevertheless has to find ways for offering assessments that go beyond his or her own "subjective platform" (McGregor 1985: 3). Such assessments are most easily offered by resorting to listeners' responses and taking the sequential interactional development of talk into consideration. Yet, also when relying on participants' observable behavior,

> the analyst is faced with the difficulty of stating with even a fair degree of certainty what a speaker 'meant' by some utterance or specifying precisely what the communicative effect of the utterance was for the listener (McGregor 1985: 3).

This is particularly so since attentional and interpretative skills as well as individual listening behavior would seem to vary from participant to participant (McGregor 1985: 5-6).

This point becomes even more problematic once we acknowledge the fact that we are working with ELF data and

> enter into the analytic equation the possibility that (some of) the participants have neither fully developed nor stable nor shared competence and, more importantly, that they themselves demonstrate cognizance of such a state of affairs (Firth 1996: 252).

As a consequence to these potential properties, "assigning interactional significance" (ibid.: 252) to various linguistic behaviors such as gaps, restarts and pauses becomes increasingly difficult for the analyst. Due to the variability of linguistic competences and L1 backgrounds in different ELF constellations, the analyst is confronted with a greater array of variables which may influence participants' behavior and this poses an additional problem. Consequently, it is not surprising that it may not only be difficult to 'diagnose' instances of 'miscommunication' in a stretch of data, but also to decide with regard to those instances that 'surface' which type of 'miscommunication' one is looking at.

In this respect, the distinction between 'misunderstanding' and 'non-understanding' as two different types of 'miscommunication' appears to be quite clear-cut at first. When it comes to the actual analysis of linguistic data, however, it becomes obvious that assigning instances of miscommunication to these two categories is not always as straightforward as it may seem:

> It is very difficult for the analyst to assess from outside just how aware someone is of the uncertainty of his/her hypothesis. And it would exactly be this kind of awareness that decides whether a failed interpretation was a – well-concealed – lack of understanding or a real misunderstanding (Bremer 1996: 41).

For example, an answer that in the course of interaction turns out to have been a hypothesis may, on the one hand, have been intended as a hypothesis by the speaker, which would presuppose his/her awareness and therefore be an instance of 'non-understanding'. On the other hand, the speaker may not have been conscious at all of the fact that s/he was forming a (wrong) hypothesis on the basis of an incoherent interpretation, in which case the analyst is looking at a 'misunderstanding'. Even though they may be indistinguishable in their surface appearance, the conceptual distinction between these two types, nevertheless, will be maintained for the analytical framework and also in the analysis whenever this is possible.

3.5 Negotiating 'miscommunication': indication and interactional management of 'local non-understanding'

It is obvious that sequences in which participants deal with 'understanding problems', i.e. in which 'miscommunication' surfaces and is negotiated, vary in length and salience (Linell 1995: 190). It is logical to assume that the length of negotiation mostly corresponds to the gravity and depth of the 'understanding problem', so that shorter sequences may be more easily traced back to a causal core utterance by the participants and the analyst, while longer negotiations may lack such a focal cause. As my analysis will show, 'non-understandings' are mostly negotiated and resolved in rather 'local' sequences. 'Misunderstandings' on the contrary either surface by chance or are indicated retrospectively with time lag, which makes it more difficult for participants and analyst to trace back any of their particular causes. Therefore, misunderstandings usually take up longer stretches of discourse to resolve.

Therefore, I will apply Linell's (1995: 190) distinction between 'local' and 'global' MEs to the analysis of my data and distinguish mainly between 'local non-understanding' and 'global misunderstanding'[24]. If 'non-understandings' are labeled 'local', they "originate, develop and [are] closed over a more or less limited sequence" (ibid.: 190). What will be considered in the following two sections is how these 'local non-understandings' surface in

---
[24] In my data, I also found one instance of a negotiated 'local misunderstanding' (see section 5.3).

discourse, i.e. what procedures participants have at their disposal in order to indicate a 'non-understanding', and how non-understandings are interactionally managed, i.e. how meaning is sequentially negotiated among participants.

3.5.1 Procedures for indicating 'non-understanding'

When a 'non-understanding' occurs, i.e. when at least one interactant notices a lack of shared understanding, this interactant has essentially two immediate choices: s/he can indicate the 'non-understanding' and thereby initiate a 'negotiation of meaning'[25] or s/he can avoid indication (Vasseur, Broeder & Roberts 1996: 69; Varonis & Gass 1985: 74). In the literature (e.g. on 'repair' in CA), one often encounters a view according to which a participant who avoids (direct) indication is alleged insincerity, as s/he is seen to conceal something and thereby to intentionally deceive his or her co-participants. I want to note at the onset that this view is not shared in this study. The attitude adopted here is clearly not a judgmental one (like 'indication is good' vs. 'avoiding indication is bad'), particularly so since, as will become apparent, 'indication' in this paper is not understood as 'direct indication', while in most other studies it is.

A participant's decision between the two options of indicating and avoiding indication, it seems, is primarily influenced by two major factors, which are highly variable from encounter to encounter, but also within any one encounter, namely activity-type and face considerations. It is evident that there is a connection between the type of activity and the need for indication and clarification of 'miscommunication'. Speech event types "which aim at exchanging concrete and precise information hardly allow for a lack of clarity" (Vasseur, Broeder & Roberts 1996: 71), while an informal chat among friends will not have to meet such requirements. Furthermore, a conversation may contain activities like spelling which are inherently more 'fragile' than others (Firth 1996: 248). Particularly, but not exclusively, with regard to interactions that feature a strong interpersonal component, the second factor, face considerations, may override the need for clarification. Although an indication (or repeated indications) of 'non-understanding' may be much more face-threatening for NNSs in the presence of NSs, who concomitantly tend to assume the position of authority in NNS-NS interactions, face considerations are certainly also relevant in ELF and NS-NS interactions. Participants' relative power and competence in relation to

---

[25] For the model for the 'negotiation of meaning' see section 3.5.2.

their co-participants are certainly variables at play here (Vasseur, Broeder & Roberts 1996: 90). Consequently, there are always "rules of etiquette and politeness" (Linell 1995: 183) which tend to mitigate or inhibit the direct indication of non-understanding.

Despite potentially restraining factors, conversations will always contain contributions and sequences which are not entirely directed towards the topic, but which contribute to the "meta-level management of interaction and understanding" (Linell 1995: 183) like "feedback seeking and giving, metacommunicative comments, repairs, reformulations, and extended negotiations of meaning" (ibid.: 183). In order to locate those points in a conversation at which these 'negotiations of meaning' take place, it seems necessary to begin analysis with a well defined system of procedures which NNSs have been shown to deploy. Categorizations of indicating procedures like the ones presented by Varonis & Gass (1985: 76-77) and Wong (2000: 248) entail a major drawback, because they are mostly limited to direct and explicit indicating procedures. Therefore, these schemes are necessarily incomplete, since they do not cover the whole range of procedures available to participants.

A comprehensive and systematic model of procedures for indicating 'non-understanding' for NNSs is presented by Vasseur, Broeder and Roberts (1996: 73-90)[26]. Most importantly, they set up a "continuum of procedures" (ibid.: 76) which covers the whole spectrum of more or less commitment (directness, explicitness) and focusing (specificity). Corresponding to those procedures Varonis and Gass (1985) and Wong (2000) have identified, one end of the continuum is taken up by 'signals' which are "direct and consciously produced" (Vasseur, Broeder & Roberts 1996: 75) by speakers in order to indicate a 'non-understanding' and initiate a negotiation sequence. Yet – and this is its biggest asset – the model is not restricted to these direct and explicit 'signals', since they are opposed to the indirect and inexplicit 'symptoms' at the other end of the continuum.

---

[26] The data that Vasseur, Broeder and Roberts (1996) and Bremer et al. (1996) use involves so-called majority and minority speakers, i.e. NSs and NNSs, and is not ELF data. As the focus is on the minority speakers throughout most of the analysis in their work, however, the procedures for indicating non-understanding are from a minority, i.e. NNS, perspective and, it seems, equally relevant for ELF data. What also has to be noted is that most of the minority speakers in their data are adult immigrants most of whom did not have proper foreign language training in school and have a rather low level of competence.

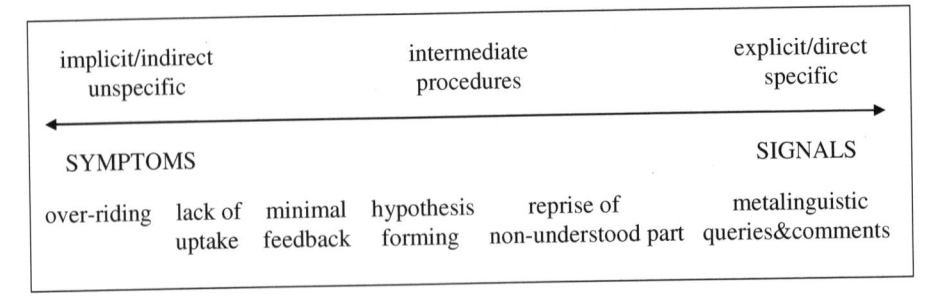

```
     implicit/indirect            intermediate             explicit/direct
        unspecific                 procedures                 specific
    ◄─────────────────────────────────────────────────────────────────►
        SYMPTOMS                                              SIGNALS

    over-riding   lack of    minimal     hypothesis    reprise of            metalinguistic
                  uptake    feedback      forming    non-understood part   queries&comments
```

Figure 2[27]: Model for the main procedures for indicating non-understanding

What is essential to these 'symptoms' is that they are defined as "behaviours which are not necessarily meant to signal non-understanding but which are interpreted as revealing non-understanding" (ibid.: 75). Another, although by far not as extensive, list of procedures including 'symptoms' and 'signals' can be found in Linell (1995: 188).

Vasseur, Broeder and Roberts (1996: 86) list three main direct and explicit procedures for indicating 'non-understanding' and initiating and/or requesting clarification, namely 'reprise of the beginning or part of a non-understood utterance', 'minimal queries', and 'metalinguistic questions and comments'. 'Reprise', which in other variants can also be used as an intermediate procedure, refers to a "much more expanded and dynamic notion than repetition [and] covers a whole range of procedures which consists of taking up the other's words" (ibid.: 83). The 'reprise of the beginning or a part of a non-understood utterance' is rather specific and functions as "an active means of confronting non-understanding" (ibid.: 86).

The second explicit procedure, namely 'minimal queries' such as *what?, sorry?* or as in my data *again?*, is usually unspecific (Vasseur, Broeder and Roberts 1996: 88). Dascal (1985b: 447) also refers to such queries as "misunderstanding preventing devices". Because they are unspecific, minimal queries usually point to a sort of general 'understanding problem' (e.g. of a whole utterance). Furthermore, they certainly depend on their "positioning adjacent to the trouble-source turn" (Schegloff 2000: 223) in order for them to be understood as requests for clarification. The third explicit procedure, 'metalinguistic questions and comments', may either be general or very specific in indicating the precise source of the trouble (Vasseur, Broeder & Roberts 1996: 86). While a 'metalinguistic comment' such as *I don't understand* is rather general, 'metalinguistic questions' such as

---
[27] Figure 2 taken from Vasseur, Broeder and Roberts (1996: 77)

what is x? are quite precise in indicating the (linguistic) object that the 'non-understanding' primarily relates to (ibid.: 88).

In the middle of the continuum, "between the avoidance of signaling and explicit metalinguistic comments" (Vasseur, Broeder & Roberts 1996: 82), there are intermediate procedures which are mainly based on 'hypothesis-forming'. 'Hypothesis-forming' is defined as "the basic interpretive process of all understanding" (ibid.: 82). It can surface in various forms and usually puts the co-participants 'on the track' of a 'non-understanding' (or also a 'misunderstanding', as un/awareness may be indiscernible). Vasseur, Broeder and Roberts (1996: 82) list three types in which hypothesis-forming as an intermediate procedure can be expressed by participants: 'tentative responses', 'reprise as comprehension check', and 'reformulation as comprehension check.

```
                    intermediate procedures
                      hypothesis-forming
           ↙                 ↓                  ↘
       tentative          reprise as          reformulation as
       responses     comprehension check    comprehension check
```

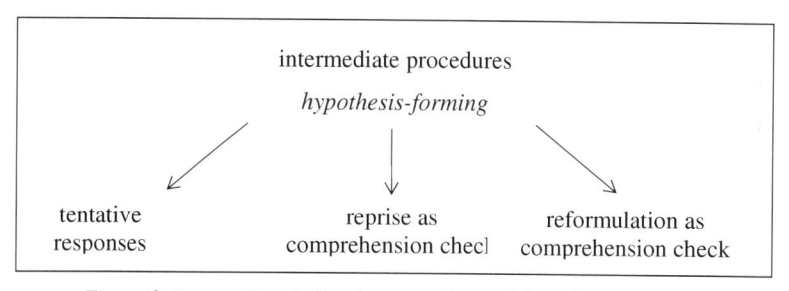

Figure 3: Intermediate indicating procedures of 'hypothesis-forming'

The intermediate strategy which is least interactionally visible is a tentative response, since it involves neither conscious signaling of a 'non-understanding' nor a passive wait and see behavior (ibid.: 82-83). In making a tentative response, a participant risks a response on the basis of what s/he guesses to have been conveyed without taking up any of the formal features of the preceding utterance (ibid.: 82-83). If the response in this way is cohesive and appropriate, the other participants "cannot suspect that there has been any problem" (ibid.: 83). Correspondingly,

> [o]nly incohesive utterances are interpreted as symptoms of non- or misunderstanding. In this way, a tentative response may implicitly convey misunderstanding, that is to say an illusion of understanding. (Vasseur, Broeder & Roberts 1996: 83)

Clearly much more interactionally visible than tentative responses are the two other intermediate procedures: 'reprise as comprehension check' and 'reformulation as comprehension check', since the "reprise of an isolated form with interrogative prosody is a clear comprehension check" (ibid.: 83). Such a behavior shows interactional involvement as well as "willingness to participate and gives some clue as to what has been understood" (ibid.: 84). An even more sophisticated procedure than reprise is reformulation, which constitutes a "re-elaboration of the other's discourse (or part of it)" (ibid.: 84). In reformulating what another participant has said, a speaker tries to ensure that understanding is shared among interactants.

On the implicit, indirect end of the continuum, Vasseur, Broeder and Roberts (1996: 77) list some symptomatic procedures which not necessarily indicate 'non-understanding' but may lead other participants – and also the analyst – to suspect that there is one. These procedures, closely corresponding to the behaviors identified by Firth (1996) as 'let it pass' principle, certainly require "more interpretative work" (Vasseur, Broeder & Roberts 1996: 77) from co-participants. Yet, it has been observed in ELF interactions that a participant in fact may "orient[] to the possibility that G [the interlocutor] has not adequately understood" (Firth 1996: 251), even if there is no explicit indication, but only a very implicit symptom. In this particular case, Firth (1996: 252) notes that "[t]he 0.7 second 'gap', however, is again treated as being indicative of G's failure to understand" and is subsequently followed by a direct indication and a negotiation sequence.

Finally, the three core 'symptoms' of 'non-understanding' which Vasseur, Broeder and Roberts (1996: 77-78) list are 'over-riding', 'lack of uptake', and 'minimal feedback'. 'Over-riding', which arguably is in danger of being misinterpreted as uncooperative or impolite behavior (especially by NSs it would seem), is defined as

> a particular interactional phenomenon in which [participants] apparently ignore the others' utterance and carry on with the topic they have already introduced or stay with the schema which they have brought to the encounter (Vasseur, Broeder & Roberts 1996: 77).

In adopting such a strategy, the participant may thus be perceived as flouting the maxim of relevance (ibid.: 77). Yet, over-riding in a conversation may, of course, not only point towards 'non-understanding', but may be due to topic concerns which 'over-ride' another subject that is being discussed (ibid.: 78).

'Lack of uptake' can take various appearances (or non-appearances) in an interaction such as

> [s]ilence, non-verbal behaviour, such as shoulder-shrugging, head-shaking, paralinguistic behaviour like laughter, coughing, mumbling or any 'filler': *er, hm, you see* (Vasseur, Broeder & Roberts 1996: 78, original emphasis).

Out of these various forms lack of uptake can have, the function of laughter seems to deserve special attention. Even from the traditional position of CA, Schegloff (2000: 219-220) has noted that "[t]here appears to be a deep relationship between laughter and repair". In this tradition, laughter is considered unfavorable and potentially problematic, since it is perceived to delay the repair. Furthermore, Schegloff notes that it is "retroactively rendered illegitimate because it registers a claimed grasp of the preceding talk" (Schegloff 2000: 222). In such a traditional and NS-oriented view, laughter is by no means analyzed as a potential 'symptom' of 'non-understanding'.

Turning to ELF data, the opinion expressed by analysts is a quite different one. In NNS-NNS interactions, participants can be found to laugh about 'themselves', i.e. to display "an orientation to the 'non-fatal', even humorous, nature of [their own] anomalous usage, and inviting H [the other participant] to do likewise" (Firth 1996: 254). In a similar way, Meierkord (1996: 199) notes that laughter in the course of the negotiation of meaning may serve as a face-saving device:

> Zur Entschärfung der dieser Situation inhärenten Gefahr des Gesichtsverlustes einer der SprecherInnen, die nicht umhinkommen, ihre sprachlichen Defizite zu dokumentieren, dient auch der Einsatz des Lachens (Meierkord 1996: 199).

What should be noted is the fact that in ELF conversations, even though participants may have various degrees of competence, any participant's face is much more likely to be threatened by 'non-understanding' resulting from linguistic deficits, while e.g. in NNS-NS interactions it will almost inescapably be the NNS's face which is threatened. Therefore, in ELF situations all participants are equally likely to employ laughter simultaneously as a 'symptom' of 'non-understanding' and as a face-saving device.

Repeated 'minimal feedback' such as *yes, hm, yeah* and *mhm* in response to one or more utterances has the potential of being very ambiguous (Vasseur, Broeder & Roberts 1996: 78). This ambiguity may be particularly pronounced in what Vion (1986 referred to in Vasseur, Broeder & Roberts 1996: 78) has termed 'linear phases', namely longer stretches in a conversation during which one participant only replies by uttering minimal responses. This participant adopts a 'wait and see' strategy (Voionmaa 1984 referred to in Vasseur, Broeder & Roberts 1996: 78) comparable to the 'let it pass' principle. Such 'linear phases' can be a means of "keeping the interaction going" (Vasseur, Broeder & Roberts 1996: 78-79) and in this respect may also serve as implicit indicating procedures and as a face-saving devices at the same time.

It is obvious that participants usually will not resort to one single procedure, but will regularly combine various procedures and adapt them. As far as negotiating and resolving 'local non-understanding' is concerned, Vasseur, Broeder and Roberts consider explicit procedures to be more effective:

> In contrast to the option of not indicating problems and relying on implicit procedures (lack of uptake or simple feedback) in order to maintain apparent understanding, the use of metalinguistic indicators always results in better understanding, because it clearly, precisely and cooperatively triggers working sequences. (Vasseur, Broeder & Roberts 1996: 88)

However, they also note that it is not a "wide repertoire of direct procedures" (ibid.: 89) that ensures the most fruitful management of understanding. Rather, they point out that "the most flexible, adaptive and effective use" (ibid.: 89) of all indicating procedures in an "emerging context" (ibid.: 89) is significant for shared understanding. Such a flexible use of direct, intermediate and implicit procedures allows participants to "find a balance between continuing the interaction and frequently halting it for clarification" (ibid.: 89). Successful interactional management of 'miscommunication' means maintaining relative smoothness, cooperation and normality in a conversation, while at the same time ensuring a sufficient amount of shared understanding. A close examination of the way participants manage 'miscommunication' is certainly one way of finding out how 'successful' an interaction – and maybe particularly an ELF interaction – is.

3.5.2 The 'negotiation of meaning'

Since any instance of 'miscommunication' only becomes visible by chance ('misunderstanding') or if it is followed by one (or more) indicating procedure(s) ('non-understanding'), this grid of various indicating procedures seems to be a valuable starting point for locating sequences in which 'non-understanding' becomes the subject of discussion, i.e. is negotiated among participants. While, as Seidlhofer (2002a: 19) notes, the reciprocal engagement in negotiating meaning is certainly a typical feature of all spoken interaction, it has been found that such negotiations are particularly frequent in NNS-NNS interactions (Meeuwis 1994: 395; Varonis & Gass 1985: 71). In this respect, Varonis and Gass (1985) have coined the term "negotiation of meaning" and they propose a model which is extremely functional, since its basic structure rests on only "four functional primes" (Varonis & Gass 1985: 73). Therefore it can be flexibly adapted to the analysis of any negotiated 'local non-understanding'.

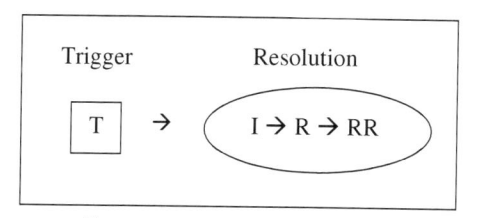

Figure 4[28]: Model for the negotiation of meaning

Varonis and Gass's (1985: 74) model is divided into two main parts termed 'trigger' and 'resolution'. The 'trigger' (T) is defined as "that utterance or part of an utterance on the part of the speaker which results in some indication of non-understanding on the part of the hearer" (ibid.: 74). Consequently, the 'trigger' only can be located via the first part of the 'resolution', the 'indicator' (I). Yet, the negotiation clearly does not end at this point. The 'indicator' will be followed by a 'response' (R) and by a 'reaction to the response' (RR) (ibid.: 74).

Comparing NS-NS, NS-NNS and NNS-NNS interactions, Varonis and Gass (1985: 83) find that in their data NNS-NNS discourse involves more of such 'non-understanding routines' than the other two types of discourse. The ideological assumptions connected with this finding, however, devalue these negotiation sequences as well as the NNSs themselves and therefore cannot be subscribed to from an ELF perspective:

> [T]he more involved non-native speakers are in a dyad, the more time interlocutors will spend moving down, or in other words, in the negotiation of meaning, rather than moving forward, in other words, in the progression of the discourse (Varonis & Gass 1985: 83).

Although the authors distinguish these negotiation sequences from 'side-sequences' in the sense of conversation analysis (Varonis & Gass 1985: 73), they still hold the opinion that 'negotiation of meaning' in every instance halts the progress of a conversation, which they in turn seem to conceive of as having mainly a transactional function. It appears that in this very one-sided view the possibility of these negotiation sequences contributing something positive to an ongoing interaction, e.g. on an interpersonal level, is ruled out, whereas within an ELF perspective it is very well imaginable that successful 'negotiation of

---

[28] Figure 4 is taken from Varonis and Gass (1985: 74).

meaning' may contribute something positive to an interaction e.g. to the emergence of rapport (cf. e.g. Kordon 2003).

Nevertheless, this model of negotiation of meaning allows the systematic analysis of some instances of 'miscommunication'. As it focuses on the sequential development of the negotiation of 'local non-understanding', it may, combined with the analysis of the indicating procedures employed, get us somewhat closer to the items, inferences and ambiguities that these 'local understanding problems' are actually caused by. Furthermore, the model's basic structure can be enlarged at any point through the inclusion of comprehension checks between the four primes (Varonis & Gass 1985: 75).

On the whole, it should be noted that such negotiation sequences, while they would still belong to the 'local' category of 'miscommunication', may also take up more extensive stretches of discourse, as they can become a negotiation loop in which e.g. a 'response' or a 'reaction to a response' may be simultaneously an 'indicator' as well and thereby initiate another negotiation sequence. This loop character is expressed in the following model of 'NNS miscommunication' (Gass & Varonis 1991: 129) which I have expanded by adding into its structure the central terms used in this study (Figure 5 below). This model of 'NNS miscommunication' encompasses all possible routes that 'miscommunication' may (locally) take within an ELF interaction.

Path 1a represents what Gass and Varonis (1991: 125) and I have termed 'misunderstanding'. The "conversation proceeds with no overt evidence of interruptions for clarification" (Gass & Varonis 1991: 128) and results in a "semantic mismatch" (ibid.: 128), while the participants are unaware of this state of affairs. Path 1b involves the "recognition of a problem" (ibid.: 128) or, in other words, awareness of a lack of shared understanding by at least one participant, i.e. in my terms a 'non-understanding'. In case of a 'non-understanding', the model presents three possible scenarios: (1) following path 2a, a participant can decide to terminate the thread of conversation, e.g. by shifting the topic; (2) opting for path 2b, the participant indicates the 'non-understanding' and thereby initiates a 'negotiating of meaning'; (3) choosing path 4/1b, the participant "ignore[s] the difficulty and proceed[s] with the conversation" (ibid.: 128), in other words, s/he 'avoids indication' and 'lets' the disruption 'pass'.

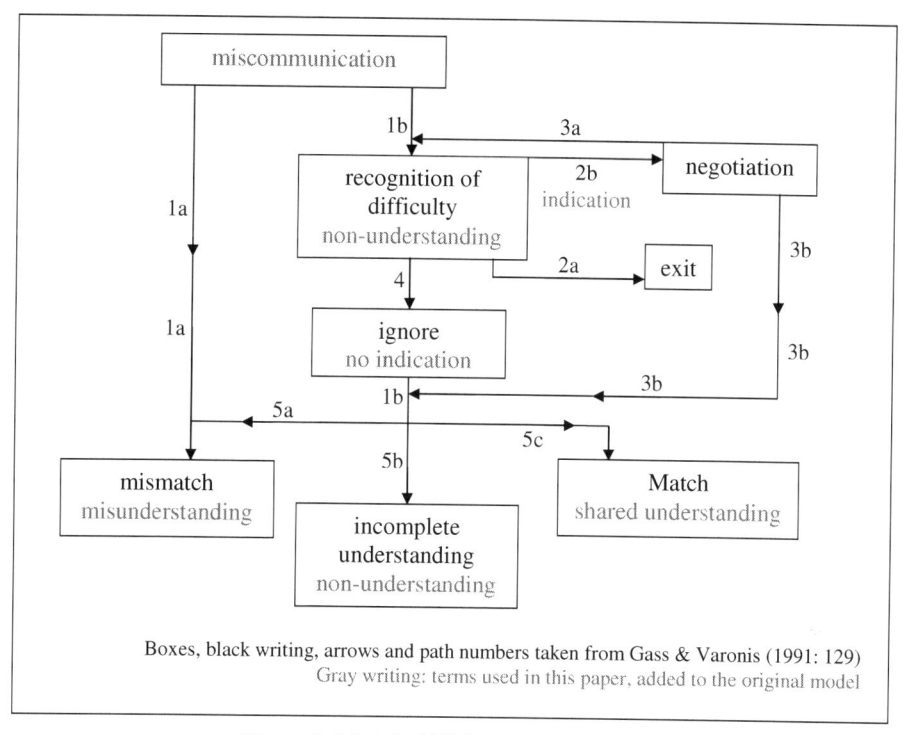

Figure 5: Model of NNS miscommunication

Once a 'negotiation of meaning' has taken place (path 2b has been followed), two other options present themselves to the participants: they may "recognize that there is still a problem" (Gass & Varonis 1991.: 128) or they may "return to the main thread of the conversation" (ibid.: 128). The first option, path 3a, represents the "recursive function" (ibid.: 128) of the indication of 'non-understanding'. In this case, there is "another recognition of difficulty" (ibid.: 128) and the participant is facing again the possibilities of 'ignoring' (4/1b), 'terminating' (2a) and 'indicating' (2b). It is here that the basic 'negotiation sequence' may, through another indicator, turn into a 'negotiation loop' (2b → 3a → 2b etc.). With the second option, path 3b, the 'negotiation of meaning' ends and the conversation proceeds on a more topical and not so much metacommunicative focus again, while I think, however, that for the participants involved in a conversation the distinction between these two foci is not always clear-cut.

Once the participants have "determined which of these paths to follow" (Gass & Varonis 1991.: 128) – although in my opinion it is also open to question to which extent such choices are consciously made or just unconsciously happen – there are essentially "three possible outcomes" (ibid.: 128). The 'negotiation of meaning' may be successful in resolving the 'non-understanding', in which case there is a "match in message transmission/reception" (ibid.: 128). In other words, shared understanding is achieved (path 5c). Secondly, the 'non-understanding' may be not or not fully resolved and therefore there is still incomplete understanding – or 'non-understanding' in my terms (path 5b). As a third outcome, participants may believe that the 'non-understanding' has been resolved and shared understanding has been achieved, while there is actually a mismatch, i.e. a 'misunderstanding' arises (path 5a). In order to decide which of the possible outcomes actually occurs, Gass and Varonis (1991: 128) propose to imagine "an objective interpreter of the true state of the world that can determine the congruity between the intended message and the received message".

Gass and Varonis's (1991: 129) model nicely brings together the various types of 'miscommunication' that may occur in NNS-NNS conversations. It outlines the various paths and routes that participants may unconsciously follow or actively decide to take and it sketches the possible outcomes that these different courses of development can have. Yet, there are is another type, or rather subtype, of 'miscommunication' which may occur under certain conditions – conditions highly relevant for the data analyzed in this paper – and which for this reason deserves special attention and thus will be separately discussed in the following section: strategic miscommunication.

3.6 Examining another type of 'miscommunication': the possibility of 'strategic miscommunication'

Strategic or intentional miscommunication is something many researchers (e.g. Weigand 1999: 764) dismiss a priori, since it is considered to be the exception rather than the rule and therefore judged irrelevant. Such an attitude is also expressed by Banks, Ge and Baker who state that

> it is not a case of miscommunication if the failure of one participant to understand the interaction at hand results from the other's intentional efforts to baffle, confuse, or manipulate. In other words, miscommunication is not a matter of intentionally caused misunderstanding: When discovered, this sort of misunderstanding is usually called deception. (Banks, Ge & Baker 1991: 106)

There are two points I would like to make with regard to such an attitude. First of all, 'strategic miscommunication', being labeled "deception" by some researchers, as just quoted, is conceived of as a participant's effort to "baffle, confuse, or manipulate" (ibid.: 106) and such a behavior is without exception seen to flout the maxim of quality or the maxim of relevance (e.g. if the answer to a posed question is intentionally not provided). Yet, it would seem, it is possible to imagine situations where such a slightly manipulative and 'strategic' behavior is not only not perceived as a violation of the cooperative principle, but will be seen as inherent to the particular communicative event. If the occasion of a business meeting is a sales visit of company B's representative at company A, it is not surprising that this representative will in fact 'act as sales representative' and will try to make company B appear in a favorable light. Of course, this will involve 'strategic communication' and accordingly also 'strategic miscommunication' at times. Yet, this behavior is not perceived as abnormal or uncooperative by the other participants, but is in fact even expected. The particular communicative situation, the participants' communicative goals and their resulting behavior, i.e. the 'rules of the game', are actually part of the participants' shared knowledge and therefore mark them as members of the same (business) community. As a consequence, 'strategic miscommunication' – i.e. recognizable instances of 'miscommunication' which are caused by participants' strategic behavior – is to be expected in my data and it would be unreasonable to exclude it a priori.

The second point with regard to Banks, Ge and Baker's attitude I would like to make is that the researchers themselves – by saying "[w]hen discovered" (ibid.: 106) – point towards an analytical problem: 'strategic' intentions provoking 'miscommunication' are not always visible, neither for the analyst nor for the other participants. As a consequence, 'strategic miscommunication' cannot always be clearly distinguished from 'non-strategic miscommunication'. Accordingly, a 'non-understanding' may be 'intentional', in order to "create certain implicatures and thus convey messages indirectly to [the other] interlocutors" (Tzanne 1999: 35) and may be "closely related to interlocutors' face considerations" (ibid.: 35).

Yet, whether "deliberately used by speakers in order to gain an advantage over their interlocutors" (House 1999: 78) or mainly employed as a face-saving device, 'strategic miscommunication' is clearly relevant for the data analyzed in this study. As Dascal astutely notes,

[i]t is often difficult to distinguish between a failure to grasp the 'point' (and the associated 'conversational demand') of an utterance, and a deliberate avoidance to relate one's reply to that 'point' (Dascal 1985b: 448).

Consequently, 'strategic miscommunication' will be primarily discussed in relation to 'local non-understanding', since in some cases the intentions which lead to what surfaces as a 'non-understanding' in the conversation appear to be 'strategic'. Nevertheless, as an analyst one can never be completely sure about participants' intentions at any one point in a conversation and therefore 'strategic miscommunication' and 'local non-understanding' turn out to be indistinguishable at times.

3.7 Analyzing 'global miscommunication': the interrelatedness of understanding and context

Understanding always relies both on context and on the decoding of an utterance. In intercultural encounters, to which ELF interactions clearly belong, however, contextual considerations are of particular importance, as participants do not share the same linguistic and cultural resources (Roberts 1996: 24). If one wants to deal with "interaction in a holistic way – a way that takes account of social relationships, feelings and perceptions" (ibid.: 24), a dynamic approach to context is called for. Such an approach can be found in Goffman's sociological concept of 'frame' (Goffman 1975), his related notion of 'footing' (Goffman 1981a) and in Gumperz's sociolinguistic notion of 'contextualization' (Gumperz 1982). This view of context mainly focuses on the dynamic construction and development of context within a situation and can therefore be called "micro-centered" (Meeuwis 1994: 403): "'Context', in this view, equals 'micro context'" (ibid.: 405).

Then again, every situation also has a 'pretext' (Meeuwis 1994: 403), which influences it, and this is what I will refer to as 'macro-context'[29]. The concept of 'macro-context' mainly relates to "conversation-external features" (Meeuwis 1994: 405) which play an active part in the "situational locus of (intercultural) interaction" (ibid.: 405). It refers to the consideration of power relations, dominance and social equality (ibid.: 403) as well as to institutional constraints and, with regard to ELF, also the impact of culture. 'Micro-context' and 'macro-context' both influence interaction and can be seen as "two extreme ends of the continuum of context" (Dua 1990: 130).

---

[29] Some 'macro-contextual' features of business meetings and their particular quality within my data will be discussed in section 4.4.

3.7.1 Micro-context: 'frame', 'footing' and 'contextualization'

The term 'frame' was originally coined by Bateson (1972: 186) as a 'psychological concept' that "is (or delimits) a class or set of messages (or meaningful actions)". Such a frame may be consciously recognized and even given a lexical representation (e.g. 'job', 'interview', or 'meeting'), but it is also possible that there is no explicit verbal reference to it and that the subject has no consciousness of it (ibid.: 186-187). Besides its 'inclusive' and 'exclusive' nature – by including certain messages or meaningful actions, it simultaneously excludes others – and its reliance on "premises" (ibid.: 187), a frame is also 'metacommunicative':

> Any message, which either explicitly or implicitly defines a frame, *ipso facto* gives the receiver instructions or aids in his attempt to understand the messages included within the frame (Bateson 1972: 188, original emphasis).

However, Bateson (1972: 188) states that the reverse is also true, namely that every message which is metacommunicative is or defines a frame.

Goffman (1975) enlarges Bateson's concept and defines it as the "principles of organization which govern events – at least social ones – and our subjective involvement in them" (Goffman 1975: 10-11). These (interpretative) frames are activated in any encounter and they "serve to transform generalized, abstract or context independent cultural knowledge, to generate situated practices" (Gumperz & Roberts 1991: 53). They are the conceptions participants have of their current social activities (Drew & Heritage 1992a: 8) and consequently they determine participants' social and also linguistic behavior within this social activity:

> Given their understanding of what it is that is going on, individuals fit their actions to this understanding and ordinarily find that the ongoing world supports this fitting. (Goffman 1975: 247).

What becomes obvious is that participants need to share frames in order to create the conditions which are necessary for shared interpretation (Roberts 1996: 24). Otherwise disruptions are bound to occur.

Frames, however, are not static, but constantly negotiated and changed (Tannen 1986: 99; Tzanne 1999: 10). They have a "reflexive and fluctuating character" (Drew & Heritage 1992a: 8) and are "interactively achieved" (Ribeiro & Hoyle 2000: 4). The framing that happens at any moment is "part of what establishes the frame for what goes on next" (Tannen 1986: 99). This continuous 'reframing' consequently changes the ongoing interaction (Ribeiro & Hoyle 2000: 3) and it also changes how the participants position themselves within this interaction. Moving from one frame to another, participants are involved in "moment-by-moment reassessments and realignments" (Drew & Heritage 1992a: 8), and it is this continuous (re-)positioning of participants that Goffman (1981a) addresses by the notion of 'footing'.

'Footing' is a particular kind of frame which identifies the relationships between participants (Tannen 1986: 90). It refers to "the alignment we take up to ourselves and the others present as expressed in the way we manage the production or reception of an utterance" (Goffman 1981a: 128). A participant's alignment or 'projection' is held across a stretch of behavior, which can be of considerable length or rather short (ibid.: 128). In the course of speaking, participants "constantly change their footing, these changes being a persistent feature of natural talk" (ibid.: 128). These changes may range from "the most subtle shifts in tone" to "gross changes in stance" (ibid.: 128). However, most of the time participants "do not simply change footing, but rather *embed* one footing within another" (Ribeiro & Hoyle 2000: 7, original emphasis)[30]. In such a process of "lamination" (Goffman 1981a: 154), a participant may not terminate a prior alignment, but rather "hold it in abeyance" (Goffman 1981a: 155) with the understanding that it may be reactivated at any point[31]. In this sense, one alignment can be fully enclosed within another (ibid.: 155). 'Footing' and changes in 'footing' are effected through language and linguistic behavior[32], but at the same time they also influence it. So the relation can be seen as interdependent.

'Framing' and 'footing', however, do not always take place smoothly, but may be impaired by 'misframing' and 'frame breaking'. A participant's beliefs as to how an event is to be framed may be "uninduced and erroneous" (Goffman 1975: 308) and may lead to "action on the basis of wrong premises" (ibid.: 308). Thus, a participant behaving this way 'misframes' the social activity – or its current state – and exhibits "wrongly oriented behavior" (ibid.: 308). As any longer activity can be perceived as being organized into a main track and various side tracks, 'misframings' may occur in the management of each of

---

[30] E.g. a teacher in a classroom will never abandon his or her primary footing as 'teacher'. Yet, depending on the particular situation, the 'teacher' may also act as 'adviser', 'helper', 'examiner', 'judge' etc. S/he thus never gives up the 'teacher' position, while s/he also embeds other footings within this stance.
[31] Cf. Chafe's (1987: 26-33) scale of activation states in which he distinguishes between 'active concepts', 'semi-active concepts', and 'inactive concepts'.
[32] Goffman (1981a: 128) mentions that code-switching or sound markers such as pitch, volume, rhythm, stress, and tone quality are involved, but it seems that the linguistic strategies for changing 'footing' – and 'frame' – are certainly not limited to these, partially very subtle, linguistic cues, but also include non-verbal and paralinguistic behaviors as well as lexical choice (cf. Gumperz's characterization of 'contextualization cues' (Gumperz 1992: 231)).

these several tracks (ibid.: 319). From the perspective of a participant who is interacting with someone who 'misframes' the event, the other's 'wrongly oriented behavior' signals "a break [...] in the applicability of the frame" (ibid.: 347). Thus, the notions of 'misframing' and 'breaking frame' can be regarded as two sides of the same coin, or in Goffman's words: "[i]t is plain that when an individual misframes events, his subsequent action will break the frame" (ibid.: 348).

'Frame' and 'footing' point towards the fact that "situations and participants' roles and goals are open to constant definition and redefinition" (Tzanne 1999: 11) and thereby capture the essentially dynamic nature of interaction. In a frame perspective, it is then obvious that context is not seen as separate from interaction (Ribero & Hoyle 2000: 4) and it is this type of context which I call 'micro-context'. At the beginning of every encounter, participants negotiate "a frame of interpretation" (Gumperz 1982: 167), which means they agree "on what activity is being enacted and how it is to be conducted" (ibid.: 167). The strategy they use in order to accomplish this aim is called 'contextualization' and refers to

> speakers' and listeners' use of verbal and nonverbal signs to relate what is said at any one time and in any one place to knowledge acquired through past experience (Gumperz 1992: 230).

Therefore, it is through talking that the conditions which make an intended interpretation possible are established (Gumperz 1982: 159).

The process, by means of which the participants then arrive at a certain interpretation, has been termed 'conversational inference' by Gumperz. 'Conversational inference' is defined as

> the situated or context-bound process of interpretation, by means of which participants in an exchange assess others' intentions, and on which they base their responses (Gumperz 1982: 153).

Through 'contextualization cues' and other strategies speakers constantly indicate how their own utterances are to be interpreted and simultaneously illustrate how they have interpreted others' utterances (Gumperz 1982: 154). They are therefore constantly involved in a continuous feedback circle, crucial for their interpretations and also for the degree of understanding that is achieved. 'Micro-context' thus becomes increasingly dynamic and is consequently closely linked to the achievement of understanding.

With regard to an analysis of 'miscommunication', it therefore can be assumed that there are some instances of 'miscommunication' – most probably 'misunderstandings' it seems, as participants are unlikely to be aware of these instances at the time they occur –

which can be traced back to disruptions in 'framing', 'footing' and 'contextualization'. One participant 'misframes' and consequently arrives at a – from the point of view of the other participant – 'wrong conversational inference' and in her/his subsequent (linguistic) reaction breaks the frame, which may cause a 'moment of awkwardness'. This type of 'miscommunication' thus does not happen on a 'local' linguistic level, but rather on a 'global' discourse level.

3.7.2 Macro-context: the role of shared knowledge, culture and institutional conditions

Even though 'micro-context', namely the context which is continuously (re)constructed by the participants during an interaction and inherently dynamic in nature, may indeed influence understanding severely and lead to instances of 'global misunderstanding', it is not the only type of context worth considering with regard to an analysis of 'miscommunication' in ELF business meetings. "Pretext" (Meeuwis 1994: 403), or 'macro-context' as I prefer to call it, refers to features and characteristics that are already determined prior to the beginning of an interaction. This 'macro-context' consists of various aspects like participants' relations and the amount of (general and specific topic related) shared knowledge, the interactants' (similar or diverse) cultural backgrounds and also pre-existing institutional or situational constraints, and is certainly relevant for any interaction. Nevertheless, it would be inappropriate to take the nature and impact of these various aspects for granted. Rather it should be examined by the analyst – as far as this is possible – which features of the 'macro-context' are actually made relevant by the participants and how relevant they are.

With regard to 'miscommunication', it has been shown that the connection between shared knowledge and the occurrence of understanding problems can be very intimate (e.g. Meierkord 1996: 210-217). There are even analyses of 'miscommunication' in which researchers focus in particular on those instances in which communication problems are due to wrong assumptions about what can be regarded as 'given' information by all participants. For example, Weizman (1999: 838) reserves the term 'miscommunication' for "cases wherein a speaker uses the given-new distinction in a way that does not match the interlocutor's assumptions about givenness". 'Givenness', in this respect, is understood "in sense of 'shared knowledge'" (idib.: 838). However, Weizman's analysis features two participants who have intimate knowledge of each other, namely a married couple. When participants are not that well acquainted with each other – as is typical for ELF interactions and especially the case in my data, which consist of business interactions – it does not seem feasible to apply such a definition of 'miscommunication'.

Therefore, generally speaking, instances of 'miscommunication' which appear to be primarily caused by different amounts of knowledge are not included in my analysis, since I would contend that tackling such differences in knowledge and thereby increasing the amount of detailed and topic-related shared knowledge are essential functions of business meetings. Consequently, adopting the participants' perspective, it would not seem logical to label such 'negotiations of knowledge' 'miscommunication'. It is, however, possible that such negotiation sequences lead to other language-related instances of 'miscommunication' or merge with them, so that the distinction made here is clear as a conceptual one, but might still become blurred in the process of analysis at times.

Nevertheless, the impression that 'shared knowledge' as a 'macro-contextual' factor does not relate to the analysis of 'miscommunication' in this study at all would certainly be incorrect. Rather, on the contrary, the participants in my data belong to the same "secondary international community" (Widdowson 1997: 145), because they work in the same domain of business. Consequently, 'shared knowledge' does play quite an important role. In their domains of business, the participants in both meetings share a great deal of specific, work related knowledge. It is the membership in these "expert communities" (ibid.: 143) and the resulting amount of shared knowledge that are relevant in the (business) meetings.

The "maximal domain within which knowledge is shared among participants" (Auer 1995: 10) is 'culture', a domain which is a particularly important 'macro-contextual' factor with regard to ELF. The view on the role of culture in ELF interactions varies among researchers and is, of course, also always informed by the particular data the researcher has collected. In the current case, I agree with Meierkord (2002: 126) that doing business may be the prime reason for using a lingua franca in the first place. Thus, the English used for business, trade, science or technology is primarily 'English for specific purposes' (ESP), which emphasizes "communication and information rather than community and identity" (Widdowson 1997: 143). Constellations and co-participants' cultural backgrounds vary from ELF interaction to ELF interaction. Even though participants "are aware of the fact that their interlocutors do also use a language that is not their mother tongue" (Meierkord

2002: 128) and adapt their own speech – in a foreign language – in ways they consider appropriate, they will commonly be "uncertain about the [cultural and linguistic] norms obtaining in their interlocutors' mother tongues" (Meierkord 2002: 127). In a way, ELF speakers can therefore be seen to 'co-construct English' in the process of conversation (Seidlhofer 2002b: 273).

House (1999: 84) calls "this non-influence of ELF speakers' linguaculture coupled with the non-availability of ELF as a means of identification" the 'culture irrelevance hypothesis'. Native language and culture are "eclipsed" (ibid.: 84), since the focus of interaction is on individual concerns rather than on group identity and because English is primarily used as a means of communication (ibid.: 84). Nevertheless, House also mentions that

> interactants are individual ELF speakers belonging to something vague, fluid and immaterial as the 'community of ELF speakers', which is always constituted anew in the on-going talk (House 1999: 84).

Since behavior depends largely on what culture a speakers wants to construct in a particular interaction, they may discard their national culture in favor of constructing another one (Meierkord 2002: 129), e.g. the culture of the respective domain of business. Like Widdowson (1997: 144) notes, they learn and use English in order to "become member of expert communities and to communicate with other members [...] whatever primary culture they come from".

The culture constructed in such an interactive process, more precisely the 'culture constructed in cultural contact', has been termed 'interculture' (Koole & Ten Thije 1994: 69). This notion is based on the assumption that "culture does not only determine linguistic action" (Meierkord 2002: 119) but is also the product of it. With regard to ELF this process can be described in the following way:

> Since lingua franca communication entails the lack of one prevailing norm due to the multitude of codes which are available for application, and since interaction requires – at least at the subconscious level – negotiation of norms and signs, it might seem reasonable to argue that this process implies the construction of a new inter-culture. (Meierkord 2002: 120)

Culture is therefore clearly conceived of as something which is constantly being "made and remade" (Sarangi 1995: 9) and is "an active rather than passive process" (ibid.: 9).

As a consequence, it is possible to argue that there is something like an 'ELF culture', only it is not predetermined, but constructed in each interaction. The participants of

ELF interactions should therefore in the first place be conceived of as co-members of this 'ELF culture' and not primarily as members of different native cultures. As has been outlined above, ELF speakers – regardless of their first language and cultural background – share a considerable amount of common characteristics. So in very many ways, they are all 'in the same boat' and so it is in fact not very surprising that they exhibit a strong tendency towards remarkably cooperative behavior and 'communicative leniency'. Adopting such a perspective, the analyst has no predetermined 'analytic construct' of culture available and the 'analytic stereotyping' which often occurs in intercultural communication research can be avoided. In a way, such an approach entails the transference of the 'macro-contextual' factor 'culture' from the 'macro-contextual' to the 'micro-contextual' level, since its nature can only be determined by looking at an actual interaction.

As a last 'macro-contextual' factor, situational and institutional constraints on an interaction will be mentioned. Linell (1995: 181) states that all understanding is *"situated and activity-specific*, which means that it is subject to premises, purposes and rationalities tied to social activities and situations" (original emphasis). As a consequence, situations vary, for example, in their depth of intended understanding (Linell 1995: 182) – an informal 'chit-chat' will be quite different from an academic seminar or also a business meeting. With regard to business meetings, whose structure may be more or less prescribed and formal, there are consequently always institutional constraints on the situation which may influence the interaction more or less.

3.8 Attempts at explaining 'miscommunication': the multicausality of 'miscommunication'

As Linell (1995: 183) describes the process of understanding as multilayered and multifaceted, it is obvious that "[s]omething can go wrong at different levels of the understanding process" (ibid.: 183). If one accepts the assumption that 'miscommunication' involves "discrepancies in interpretation between interlocutors" (ibid.: 188), it seems necessary, before one even starts investigating into the causes of 'miscommunication', to identify a number of possible 'objects' which such discrepancies may concern:

(identity of) words spoken vs. apprehended (cf. mishearings);
references and referential perspectives;
meaning specifications (aspects of semantic potentials activated);
cognitive, emotive or conative attitudes towards things talked about;

levels of intentionality (e.g. seriousness vs. joking);
frames, perspectives adopted in interpretation (Linell 1995: 188).

Yet, by solely looking at these various levels at which a 'mismatch' in interpretation may occur, it appears unlikely that instances of 'miscommunication' will normally be monocausal, i.e. caused by only one single, clearly identifiable element.

Indeed, findings suggest that rather the opposite is the case, namely that 'simple' causes are the exception (Bremer 1996: 38). Allwood and Abelar (1984: 37) state that all the examples of 'misunderstandings' in their data "arise as a consequence of jointly operating factors". Therefore, they promote a "multicausal relationship" (ibid.: 37). Dascal (1999: 755) notes that this interaction of various causes is in itself a phenomenon which is rather difficult to grasp, since the causes may be "either reinforcing or cancelling each other" (ibid.: 755). In order to underline his contention, Dascal provides the following example:

A mispronunciation may engender a miscomprehension, but it can also be automatically corrected by a hearer when the mispronounced expression doesn't fit the communicative intention s/he attributes (correctly or incorrectly) to the speaker; and a (correct or incorrect) attribution of intention or interpretation of a contextual feature may produce a mishearing or misreading. (Dascal 1999: 755)

What makes this state of affairs even more difficult, however, is the fact that "the analyst cannot know for certain which utterance or utterances may have been of particular salience in leading to the communicative sequences" (McGregor 1985: 2) and likewise also the 'non-understandings' and 'misunderstandings' that occur.

The web of tightly linked and constantly interacting potential causes, however, does not end here. Any instance of 'miscommunication' is the result of a complex interaction between linguistic (and non-linguistic) 'discoursal contributions' and 'contextual factors', like shared knowledge, communicative purposes or frames (Linell 1995: 188-189). Consequently, it is certainly correct to say that "[a]ny degree of (non) understanding results from a complex fusion of particular, local inferences and general or global knowledge" (Roberts 1996: 14). The relation that exists between the required amount of linguistic information and the amount of shared knowledge can be described as inversely proportional:

The more limited the knowledge from contextual sources such as immediate situation or world knowledge, the greater the dependency on linguistic information is, and thus the greater the degree of difficulty for the participant with a different cultural and language background. (Bremer 1996: 56)

The more general or specific topic-related knowledge participants share, the less they are forced to rely on precise linguistic expression and comprehension in order to achieve shared understanding. Accordingly, a linguistic item or structure that constitutes a difficulty in one context or situation may be completely unproblematic in another.

Yet, even within one interaction and at any one particular point of it, more than one context may be "in play" (Auer 1995: 13). Since there are more contexts available, participants will "switch to and fro between these multiple contexts" (ibid.: 13). As a consequence, the analyst is always confronted with "many levels of contextual frames which [may or may not] affect the interpretation of speaker 'intent'" (McGregor 1985: 3). Participants will be "constantly engaged in making sure that they orient to the same (yet changing) context(s)" (Auer 1995: 13), as it is only in this context that their behavior becomes meaningful. Considering all the various linguistic and contextual levels which interact within every interpretation, it would be naïve to assume that the causes of 'miscommunication' are easily identifiable. Rather, one has to accept the "multiple causality" (Linell 1995: 189) of 'miscommunication' and examine each individual instance as thoroughly as possible without predetermined or rash conclusions.

3.9 Summary and conclusion

In chapter 3, I have attempted to provide the theoretical terms, concepts, models and considerations that will be employed for the analysis of 'miscommunication' in this study. The core terms that are used besides 'miscommunication' are 'non-understanding' and 'misunderstanding. 'Non-understanding' is associated with 'local' instances of 'miscommunication' for the most part. With regard to such 'local non-understandings', a continuum of indicating procedures has been presented. Direct or indirect indications then tend to initiate a 'negotiation of meaning', which may be very focused and short or lead to longer 'negotiation cycles'. In examining how such 'negotiation sequences' sequentially develop, we may gain valuable insights into how ELF speaker interactionally manage 'local' instances of 'miscommunication'.

In addition to such 'local negotiations of meaning', there are, however, other types of 'miscommunication' which need to be considered. Since the analyst, as an outsider, can never be completely sure about a speaker's intentions at a particular point of time, the possibility of 'strategic miscommunication' cannot be ruled out and deserves a place in the framework of analysis. Furthermore, 'misunderstandings' on a 'global' discourse level may occur. These 'misunderstandings' are not realized by participants for a considerable span of time and only through some instance or other surface in the conversation. A close analysis of the 'micro-contextual' development of conversational 'frames' may provide clues as to how such 'global misunderstandings' come about.

4 THE DATA: BUSINESS MEETINGS AMONG ELF SPEAKERS

4.1 Introduction

The following chapter will present the characteristics of the data that were collected for the purposes of this study. After providing some general information about the two data sets in section 4.2, some methodological aspects of the data collection, like the degree of authenticity and the role of the observer, will be discussed in section 4.3. The core section of this chapter, section 4.4, will examine some typical features of business meetings in general and relate them to the two meetings recorded for the current analysis. Since aspects like structure, formality, objectives, participant roles and the power of the chair are assumed to be of relevance on a macro-contextual level, their respective quality in the two meetings will be briefly analyzed.

4.2 General information about the data

The data which are analyzed in this paper consists of two data sets, both of which are recordings of business meetings among ELF speakers. Meeting A was recorded at the branch office of an international forwarding agency in Luxembourg in January 2004. The overall length of the meeting is more than three hours and it consists of various subsections involving different participants. Since an analysis of the whole meeting would go beyond the scope of the present study, only the first hour – consisting of two subsections with three participants each[33] – has been transcribed and analyzed. All participants (S1, S2, S3, S4) are NNSs of English. While S1, S3 and S4 are from Germany and have German as L1, S2's mother tongue is Dutch. All, except S2, work for the forwarding agency at which the meeting took place and which is subsequently referred to as (COMPANY1) and its branch office as (COMPANY1a) in extracts A.1 and A.2. S2 is a sales executive of an airline, called (COMPANY5) in A.1 and A.2, and the meeting took place on the occasion of his sales visit. As a consequence, the overall subject of the meeting is air cargo with regard to destinations in the Middle East and Far East.

Meeting B was recorded at a food company in Austria in February 2004. The meeting also runs for more than three hours, the first two hours of which have been

---

[33] See extracts A.1 (involving S1, S2, and S3) and A.2 (involving S1, S2, and S4) in the appendix.

transcribed and analyzed[34]. The meeting involves five participants (P1, P2, P3, P4, and P5) all of whom are present throughout the whole interaction, except for some very short stretches during which P5 leaves the room in order to fetch some samples or bring coffee. P3, P4 and P5, who are Austrian and have German as L1, are employees of the food company, referred to as (COMPANY2) in extracts B.1 to B.16. As the company's name is synonymous with its main product, (COMPANY2) is also used as a product label very often. P1 and P2 are representatives of a big Asian business group which distributes (COMPANY2), i.e. its products, in South Korea. Similarly to meeting A, meeting B also takes place on the occasion of the business partners' visit. The main subject of the two hours transcribed and analyzed is the past year's sales of the product in Korea. Since P1 and P2's first language is Korean, it should be noted that the two meetings differ greatly in 'language distance': While meeting A only involves European participants with the first languages German and Dutch, meeting B involves Europeans, namely Austrians with German as L1, and Asians, namely Koreans.

4.3 Methodological aspects of the data collection

My intention to collect data in the realm of international business was mainly due to the fact that I was looking for conversations in which there was something at stake for participants, i.e. in which speakers needed to accomplish certain goals and to exchange precise information. Furthermore, international business constitutes an area in which ELF is of particular importance for people on an every day basis. As a consequence, I wanted to record my data 'inside', so to speak, where things actually happen. To ultimately get 'inside', however, is not easy, since it is obvious that many business meetings are rather delicate as far as content is concerned and, of course, one needs permission even to be present at a meeting if one is not an employee. I was lucky to have one internal contact person in each of the two companies at which I recorded my data. After having been informed about my research interest, these two persons arranged for me to be present and to record a meeting, while, however, neither of the two took part in the recorded meeting themselves.

Due to the particular procedure that has been outlined above, all participants of the meetings were informed and consented to my presence and the recording prior to the

---

[34] See extracts B.1 to B.16 in the appendix.

occasion of the meeting. Before all participants arrived, I was, in both companies, given the opportunity to set up the recording equipment. The recording devices were clearly visible and participants had already been informed, therefore the procedure employed was overt recording. In addition, I was present during the meetings as an observer whose role can be described as 'passive participant':

> Passiv teilnehmend bedeutet, daß sich der Beobachter ganz auf seine Rolle als forschender Beobachter beschränken kann und wenig bis nicht an den zu untersuchenden Interaktionen bzw. sozialen Konstellationen teilnimmt. (Atteslander 1995: 112)

Since I was not a part of the ongoing interaction, as I was clearly not a meeting participant but an outsider, it was nevertheless possible for me, besides recording the meeting, to observe the interaction and take field notes.

Despite the visible presence of the recording devices and myself as an observer, participants seemed to focus almost exclusively on the ongoings of the meeting and only very scarcely on their status as objects of observation. Although it is true that the very act of recording is likely to distort the object of observation (Milroy 1987: 59), i.e. in this case the interaction in the meeting, the effect of what Labov (1978: 209) has termed the 'observer's paradox' seems to have been minimal. While "observation itself may generate artificial behaviour" (Stubbs 1983: 227), my personal impression was that, with regard to both data sets, this was not the case. This impression was also confirmed in a short conversation with S2, the chair of meeting A, who told me that in his opinion the meeting had taken place in very much the same way as it would have, had I not been present.

Since both business meetings were held in a regular business context and not especially set up for the purpose of this study, the data which are analyzed within this paper can be characterized as naturally occurring. Yet as any naturally occurring conversation – and also a meeting – cannot be fully understood and adequately interpreted without inspecting the context of its occurrence, the next section will be devoted to a brief outline of the macro-contextual features relevant with regard to business meetings.

4.4 Properties of business meetings

Business meetings are particular speech events which differ greatly from informal, unplanned or private interactions. They are inevitably subject to situational constraints and 'macro-contextual' characteristics like structure, formality, objectives and participant relations seem to play an important role. Yet, the particular quality of these 'macro-contextual' features cannot simply be taken for granted with regard to every business meeting. Therefore, it is the duty of the analyst to consider in how far these situational constraints and 'macro-contextual' features are made relevant by the participants within the meeting.

4.4.1 Structure

While it is certainly true that not all business meetings are planned in advance and set up in conference rooms, but that many of them occur also in informal, non-planned settings at corridors or at office coffee machines (Pan, Wong Scollon & Scollon 2002: 106-107), the two meetings analyzed in this study belong to the 'conference room'-type. Due to their pre-planned character, meetings of this type are easier to identify, but as has already been noted earlier usually more difficult to document for reasons of confidentiality (ibid.: 108). They normally exhibit a (more or less) clear structure which can be identified by the analyst. While there is "a danger of falling into structural descriptions of meetings" (ibid.: 108), it seems nevertheless to be a valuable starting point to consider some of the structural characteristics they expose.

Generally speaking, any meeting consists of various types of activities which are subject to an 'episodic ordering' (Cuff & Sharrock 1985: 154) through which the structuring of the proceedings is achieved. According to Holmes and Stubbe (2003: 65), most meetings are organized in a three-phase structure, in which an opening or introductory section, a central development section and a closing section can be distinguished. In addition, prior to the opening phase, there may be 'prebeginning activities', which "are done in anticipation of, even in preparation for, the start of the meeting" (Cuff & Sharrock 1985: 155). As opening sections typically will involve agenda setting, identification of problems or tasks (Holmes & Stubbe 2003: 65) as well as small talk, it may be difficult to distinguish them from 'prebeginning activities'. The central development section, in which the core topics of the meeting are discussed, is usually characterized by a high degree of engagement by participants, shorter turns, overlaps and numerous feedback (ibid.: 67). In the closing section, the proceedings are brought to an end and decisions that have been made are summed up.

Both meeting A and meeting B exhibit the basic tripartite structure that has been outlined above. As the chosen one and two hour stretches are in both cases taken from the beginning, the closing phase is considered in neither of the two data sets. Meeting B includes an introductory phase of considerable length in which, prior to the setting of the agenda, all participants introduce themselves or are introduced by other speakers from their company.

Example 1 (B.1)[35]

```
1    P4:    mhm (1) SO (do you) first of all PLEASE let me introduce
2           MYSELF?
3    P1:    okay?
4    P4:    ahm (.) i'm in the company fo:r (.) the- the seventh YEAR now,
5           (.)
6    P1:    okay
```

As will be discussed in more detail in section 4.4.5, P4 is the chair of meeting B and therefore it is only logical that he should be the one to start the introductory round. At the very beginning of the opening section – which could probably also be characterized as a 'prebeginning section' – he introduces himself and continues to give P1 and P2, the visitors, some more information about his responsibilities in (COMPANY2).

As a next step, P4 introduces his young colleague *max*[36] (P3) by explaining the other's position in the company in relation to him:

Example 2 (B.1)

```
26   P4:    and (.) beginning of this ye:ar ah (1) ah we hired also max,
27   P1:    <2> mhm </2>
28   PX-2:  <2> mhm </2>
29   P4:    who will
30   PX-m:  mm (.)
31   P4:    basically it will be (.) TOGETHER that we: that we ah (2) are
32          here for you for your
```

---

[35] All data examples are given in the appendix. The line numbers and the labels in parentheses (A.1, A.2, B.1., etc.) correspond to those used in the appendix. The transcription conventions conform to those for VOICE (Version 3.0, June 2003), which are included in the appendix. The most recent version of the VOICE Transcription Conventions, including spelling conventions, is available on the VOICE Project website: http://www.univie.ac.at/voice. The spelling conventions conform to those of the MICASE Corpus (in early 2004). The most recent version of the MICASE Transcription Conventions is available at http://micase.elicorpora.info/micase-statistics-and-transcription-conventions/micase-transcription-and-mark-up-convent. Additional information about names, company names and pseudonyms used in the transcripts are provided in the appendix prior to extracts A.1 and B.1.

[36] All names occurring in the transcripts are psyeudonyms.

Finally, P4 ends the introductory round of his team by introducing *nina* (P5) and pointing out her status as an informant who has knowledge of the relations and past business history of (COMPANY2) and the Korean company:

Example 3 (B.1)

42	P4:	ah:m (1) the only thing is that ahm (.) since we have never MET
43		and <3> (NAME1) </3> is not here,
44	P1:	<3> mhm </3>
45	P1:	mhm
46	P4:	there was a past history and the knowledge
47	P1:	m<5>hm</5>
48	P2:	<5>m</5>hm
49	P4:	ahm is basically
50	P2:	<6> nina </6>
51	P1:	<6> you get </6> through:
52	P4:	in <7> NINA'S <7/>
53	P1:	<7> nina </7>
54	P2:	<SOFT> <7> @@ </7> @@ </SOFT>
55	P4:	in nina's hands

Besides structurally marking the opening – or pre-opening – phase of the meeting B, the above examples also hint at the importance of power relations among meeting participants as P4 speaks on behalf of his colleagues P3 and P5, an aspect which will also be considered in section 4.4.5.

This first introduction of the participants of the host company is followed by a period of small talk, after which P4 makes an active attempt to shape the structure of the meeting by posing an openly business-related question to P1:

Example 4 (B.3)

| 1 | P4: | ahm and (.) since WHEN are you distributing (COMPANY2)? |
| 2 | | (.) in korea? |

This question constitutes an activity which marks the definite beginning of the meeting and initiates a second opening or introductory phase. After providing an answer to the question, P1 in lines 22, 26 and 30 in turn introduces himself, his colleague *mister wu* and his company:

Example 5 (B.3)

22	P1:	I give you some (.)
23	P3:	<to P5> <SOFT> <L1=GERMAN> *(ist die milch eh genug?)*
24		</L1=GERMAN> <TRANS=is there enough milk?>
25	P5:	<SOFT> mhm </SOFT>

26	P1:	background
27	P5:	<to P3> <SOFT> <L1=GERMAN> *(x)* <6> *(xxx)* </6> *(xxxxx)*
28		</L1=GERMAN> </SOFT>
29	P4:	<to P1> <6> mhm </6>
30	P1:	of myself and mister wu as well as our company

Since the participants of the two companies have never met before, the introductory round of the opening phase is quite formal and elaborate in meeting B.

While meeting B involves the same five participants throughout its whole duration, meeting A consists of several subsections, the first two of which were selected for analysis in this study. As a consequence, with regard to meeting A, the three-phase structure cannot only be identified for the meeting as a whole, but also "within subsections embedded within the overall structure" (Holmes & Stubbe 2003: 65). Therefore, setting or readjusting the agenda – a typical opening phase activity – cannot only be observed at the very beginning of the meeting, but also the onset of its second subsection:

Example 6 (A.2)

1	S1:	hh okay let's let's first go to the general issues, (.) yeah? and
2		then i give a <1> call upstairs ah: </1>

Similar to meeting B, the first opening phase and the sub-opening phases are also characterized by small talk and personal introductory remarks which, however, end up being briefer and less formal than the ones in meeting B, since the participants of meeting A have met before.

4.4.2 Degree of formality

It is obvious that meetings may vary considerably in the degree of formality they exhibit. As has already been mentioned, both meetings analyzed here took place in conference rooms, were scheduled in advance and happened on the occasion of business visits. Therefore, it is evident that a certain degree of formality will result from such situational characteristics. Nevertheless, also meetings in a formal, prearranged setting such as a conference room may be more or less formal. One factor which is most likely to have an influence on the degree of formality is the size of the meeting. As Cuff and Sharrock (1985: 151) remark, "a meeting might be viewed in terms of size or composition, and it might be expected that other organizational features might depend on them". Holmes and Stubbe (2003: 60) note that smaller meetings, which they characterize as involving between two and four participants, tend to be located on the less formal end of the scale.

This observation has been confirmed by considering the formality of the two meetings analyzed. Meeting A, consisting of two subsections involving three participants each, appeared to be less formal than meeting B, in which five participants took part. In addition, the participants of meeting A were acquainted with each other prior to the meeting – a fact which can be assumed to decrease formality. At meeting A, participants scattered around the corner of a large conference table and there were no predetermined seating arrangements. As a consequence, neither the chair person nor any internal or external hierarchy was represented in the seating arrangements, which clearly had the effect of decreasing formality. Furthermore, there seemed to be no business dress code at (COMPANY1a), where meeting A took place. The only participant wearing a suit was S2, the airline's sales representative and therefore the visitor.

While meeting B can certainly not be called a particularly large meeting (five participants), it nevertheless appeared to be more structured and formal than meeting A. The conference room had been prepared with food and drinks in advance, writing pads and pens had been placed at the desk and the seating arrangements were fixed by the hosts prior to the arrival of the guests. Hosts and guests were facing each other, occupying the opposite sides of the conference desk. P4, who chaired the meeting, was flanked by P3 on the right and P5 on the left. Facing him on the other side of the desk was P1, while P2 was sitting opposite of P3. The impression of a relatively high degree of formality was further strengthened by the fact that all participants were wearing suits. Accordingly, as already exemplified by examples 1 to 5, meeting B proceeded in a clearly structured and formal way.

4.4.3 Goals and objectives

Since particularly in international organizations and enterprises "business and sales negotiations are done to a large extent through meetings" (Pan, Wong Scollon & Scollon 2002: 109), it is obvious that every meeting will have specific goals and objectives. Although they may not always be explicitly stated, a common understanding of the purpose of a meeting, and agreement about the role of different individuals attending, are important factors in accounting for how effectively a meeting runs (Holmes & Stubbe 2003: 61-62).

As is already indicated in this statement, the goals and objectives are primarily, but not solely, related to thematic and content concerns. Yet the function of a meeting also "always goes beyond a mere business deal" (Pan, Wong Scollon & Scollon 2002: 109).

Regarding overt 'business' goals, Holmes and Stubbe (2003: 63) distinguish three distinct meeting types: planning or prospective/forward-oriented meetings, reporting or retrospective/backward-oriented meetings, and task-oriented or problem-solving/present-oriented meetings. While it is common for meetings to involve elements of all three functions (ibid.: 63), the prime focus nevertheless has to be, or preferably should be, clear to all participants. In meeting A, the overall purpose seemed to be self-evident for all participants and was never explicitly stated. It was obvious to all interactants that S2 was coming for a sales visit at which the business relations between the forwarding agency (COMPANY1a) and the airline (COMPANY5) were to be discussed. Therefore, the meeting could be described as mainly prospective and forward-oriented involving some retrospective and task-oriented stretches. These objectives as well as the resulting participant roles were known to everyone and seem to have provided some shared 'frame' within which the beginning of the interaction could be safely managed.

Meeting B's purposes also seemed to be quite clear to all participants but were nevertheless explicitly stated by P4. This obvious instance of agenda setting in example 7 mostly likely resulted from the fact that P4, who had recently taken up the main responsibility for the business relations with Korea, had never met the Korean visitors, P1 and P2:

Example 7 (B.1)

64	P4:	that's why (1) maybe we will have also time to FIRST of all (.)
65		speak about your company,
66	P1:	mhm
67	P4:	in order for me to get a (.)
68	P1:	mhm
69	P4:	get a picture to know y- i mean (.) we have to come to korea
70		anyway:
71	P1:	mhm
72	P4:	to to to (1) to get deeper (.) in- involved in the market but i
73		appreciate your: your VISIT as a kind of first ah:m
74	P1:	<SOFT> (sure) </SOFT> (.)

75	P4:	ah:m let's call it (2) RE-START </2> since </2> last year was
76		not the: the: (.)
77	P1:	<2> <SOFT> mhm </SOFT> </2>
78	P4:	the best ye:ar, eh as i saw in the files maybe we can also talk
79		about that,
80	P1:	<SOFT> (sure) </SOFT> (.)
81	P4:	ahm (1) <L1=GERMAN> ja </L1=GERMAN>
82		<TRANSL=yes> and then we will present you also the news for
83		this year,
84	P1:	<SOFT> mhm </SOFT>
85	P2:	<SOFT> mhm </SOFT>

In this example, P4 mentions three core items on the agenda and one overall purpose of the meeting. In lines 73 and 75, he says that he appreciates the Koreans' visit as a re-start, which means that the prime objective of meeting B could be described as 'building and strengthening business relations and personal ties between the two companies'. This overall goal, it seems, is to be achieved via three main activities on the agenda: acquiring knowledge about the Korean company (lines 64-65), analyzing last year's business figures (lines 75-76, 78-79) and presenting the recent products of the Austrian company (lines 82-83). The agenda therefore involves one primarily present-oriented item (situation of the Korean company), one retrospective item (last year's sales) and one forward-oriented item (product news).

4.4.4 Participant relationships and roles

Some brief remarks about the influence of participant relationships and roles on the development of the meeting and its success have already been made. With regard to meeting B, P1 and P2, the representatives of the Korean company, were visiting (COMPANY2) in order to promote and increase their business ties. P3, P4 and P5, the Austrian hosts, received them as their guests. Since P4 had only recently taken on the responsibility for Korea, he was, as their new contact, in charge of the agenda, but he had not met P1 and P2 before, and neither had P3. The only one whom the guests seemed to have been acquainted with prior to the meeting was P5, the person familiar with the past history of the companies' business relations and the only female participant.

Examining meeting A, the participant relationships and roles appeared to be even more relevant than the ones in meeting B. This meeting also took place on the occasion of a business visit, a sales visit to be precise. All participants were acquainted with each other prior to the meeting, even though obviously familiarity among S1, S3 and S4 was much higher than their respective familiarity with S2, the visitor. The importance of S2's position as a visitor and guest, however, was much diminished by his role as a sales representative. In this function, S2 constantly promoted his airline, which had considerable influence on the interaction and led to some instances of strategic miscommunication[37]. Yet, S2's 'sales' behavior was not only tolerated but obviously also expected by the other participants. Due to this particular constellation, all participants seemed to be rather aware and conscious of their own as well as the others' roles during the meeting:

Example 8 (A.1)

```
675   S1:    what do you think if you could arrange it w- how long would it
676          take? (2) to put on tuesdays. (1) cuz LATER for the
677          HONGKONG discussion we will talk about the MONDAY
678          flight hh (.) hh so it would be important to have the monday
679          flight
680   S2:    mhm (.) okay,
681   S1:    <LOUD> @ @ @ @ @ so be CAREFUL what you're SAYING
682          now <4> @ @ @ @ </4> </LOUD>
683   S2:    <4> yah yah okay </4> okay @ (.)
684   S1:    @
685   S2:    always be careful what i'm saying <5> (but eh) </5>
686   S1:    <5> @ @ </5> @ @ (1)
```

Even though S1's remark in lines 681 and 682, which advises S2 to *be careful* abou what he says, is accompanied by laughter and is therefore to be taken as humorous, it nevertheless draws attention to S2's role as sales representative who tries to please (COMPANY1a)'s employees in order to promote business. This special role, as S2 himself states in line 685, strongly influenced S2's verbal behavior during the whole meeting and consequently this is also reflected in the data.

4.4.5 The power of the chair person

One particular participant role which is relevant with regard to any meeting is the position of the chair person. A chair may use "strategies which emphasis[e] his or her authority, such as very formally marking the opening and closing of the meeting" (Holmes & Stubbe 2003: 64-65) or s/he may downplay their authority and encourage the egalitarian nature of the

---

[37] See section 5.5

meeting (ibid.: 65). In meeting A, the opening sequence, which tends to give insight into the role of the chair, took place in the following way:

Example 9 (A.1)

1	S2:	shall we start?
2	S1:	yes, we start eh eh directly with marc <1> e:h </1> eh
3	SX-3:	<1> <SOFT> yeah </SOFT> </1>
4	S2:	okay
5	S1:	as he's eh: expect another visitor, he also will not join for lunch,
6		(.)
7	S2:	<2> okay </2>

Several aspects concerning the role of the chair become obvious in this short stretch of conversation. For one, the chair (S1) does not formally declare the meeting open, because it is not him who raises the subject of starting to talk business. This clearly deemphasizes his authority and is in line with the observation that meeting A is rather informal for a 'conference room'-meeting. As a second aspect, however, it should be noted that S2, in turn, does not declare the meeting open in line 1, but only raises the question, which is then confirmed by S1. Therefore, it is visible that it is indeed S1, who chairs the meeting and as a consequence possesses the authority to start it. What is noticeable furthermore is the fact that S1 speaks on behalf of his colleague S3, a strategy which is very similar to the introduction of P3 and P5 by P4 in examples 2 and 3.

Characteristic of the relative informality of the meeting and exemplary for the deemphasized authority of the chair is the fact that there is no explicit instance of agenda setting in meeting A. Yet, there are instances where it becomes clear that S1, the chair, nevertheless has an agenda in mind which he plans to maintain:

Example 10 (A.1)

133	S2:	now now in your internal picture, because you
134		mentioned ah:m (.) in you:r email to me that some
135		DIFFERENCE betwee:n some REGIONS? (.) maybe it's better
136		to explain me FIRST what what what happened <1> in this </1>
137		<2> scenario </2>
138	S1:	<1> hhh </1> <2> ahm </2> we will do this in in in the second
139		eh round when we talk with mia just eh for this point eh:
140		important is we are heading towards a a splitting of department,
141		(.)
142	S2:	<1> mhm </1>

When S2 poses a question which is likely to steer the meeting into a direction that S1 currently sees as unfit, S1 politely avoids discussing the subject at this point by indicating that it will be discussed later on in the second subsection with *mia* (S4).

As Holmes and Stubbe (2003: 66) note, it is common in meetings that "agenda setting [...] [is] strongly influenced by those in position of power or authority". This observation can also be made with regard to meeting B, where agenda setting is explicitly done by P4, as shown in example 7 above. By setting the agenda and by speaking on behalf of his fellow employees in the introductory round (see examples 2 and 3), P4 obtains an authority that is openly acknowledged by the visitor P1, when he makes a suggestion about the further proceeding of the meeting:

Example 11 (B.5)

1	P1:	and we brought some ah: (3) presentation material, (.) <1> for
2		</1> you,
3	P4:	<1> <SOFT> mhm </SOFT> </1>
4		<P1 hands material to P4 who hands one to P3 and keeps the
5		second one> (2)
6	P5:	(it's okay)
7	PX-2:	@ @ @
8	P4:	we'll we <2> look together </2>
9	P5:	<2> we always </2> share
10	P2:	<SOFT> @ @ @ </SOFT> (2)
11	P1:	and if you ALLOWED me about (.) let's say (2) an HOUR we
12		can go through, because
13	P4:	m<3>hm </3>
14	P1:	<3> it </3> gives you ah as as the CONTENT shows you
15	P4:	yeah (.)

It is obvious that P1 does not take it for granted that he will be able to do his presentation, since he seems to make reference to the possibility that P4, the chair, has made other plans for the concrete proceeding of the meeting and he, P1, would comply with those. As a result, he hands out the material and in line 11 stresses that if P4 *ALLOWED* him an hour, he would go through the presentation.

After this initial signal of compliance, P1 continues to outline what the presentation would include and which points would be discussed. When P1 has finished this enumeration, however, he does not immediately start the presentation, but pauses and explicitly asks P4's permission to do the presentation:

Example 12 (B.5)

```
36    P1:    is it okay that i (.) GO with this <6> presentation? <SOFT> okay
37           okay </SOFT> </6>
38    P4:    <6> PLEASE (.) PLEASE <L1=GERMAN> ja,
39           </L1=GERMAN> <TRANSL=yes> </6> (5)
```

It seems that the power relations among participants are quite clearly defined in meeting B and that the authority of the chair is very much acknowledged by colleagues as well as guests.

4.5 Summary and conclusion

In this chapter, I have presented some of the macro-contextual characteristics of the data analyzed in this paper. Two business meetings conducted in English as a lingua franca have been openly recorded at two internationally active companies. The recorded data were supplemented by field notes stemming from passive participant observation and were subsequently transcribed. Both meetings appeared to be clearly structured and rather formal due to the conference room-situation, whereas meeting B, however, turned out to be more formal than meeting A. The general goals and objectives of the meeting were known to all participants in both cases, although they were explicitly stated only in meeting B. The chair persons took responsibility for setting and/or maintaining the agenda as well as starting the meeting and introducing their colleagues.

5 ANALYSIS: TYPES OF 'MISCOMMUNICATION' IN ELF AND THEIR INTERACTIONAL MANAGEMENT

5.1 Introduction

Chapter 5 presents the various types of miscommunication that could be found in the three hours of business data analyzed. The majority of the observed instances of miscommunication can be characterized as 'local non-understandings' which are resolved via more or less complex negotiation of meaning. These are presented in section 5.2. The negotiation sequences range from short three line-exchanges (section 5.2.1) to complex and elaborate negotiation cycles, featuring various indicating procedures and non-understandings (section 5.2.5). Section 5.3 shows, however, that the negotiation of meaning may also occur in relation to a 'local misunderstanding'. Furthermore, negotiation sequences can be actively initiated by participants in order to prevent miscommunication, as section 5.4 exemplifies. The question of intentionality in miscommunication is discussed in section 5.5. This section outlines the problematicality of distinguishing between regular, i.e. unintentional, and strategic miscommunication. In conclusion, section 5.6 is concerned with 'global' miscommunication and sketches how a 'global' misunderstanding may be brought about if conversational parties do not share 'frames' over a considerable stretch of discourse.

5.2 Local non-understanding and the negotiation of meaning

Applying Varonis and Gass's (1985: 74) basic model for the negotiation of meaning, several instances of such negotiations of local non-understandings could be found in the data. Since an instance of 'non-understanding' by no means indicates 'no understanding at all', but rather is defined as a 'graded phenomenon' (Bremer 1996: 40) which covers the whole continuum from a complete lack of understanding to more or less complete understanding (Allwood & Abelar 1984: 29), it is obvious that negotiations vary greatly in their degree of complexity. While some are extremely straightforward, short and effective, others will consist of "multiple layers of trigger-resolution sequences" (Varonis & Gass 1985: 78). Partly, the degree of complexity the structures exhibit results from the types of indicating procedures that participants use and from the particular linguistic causes that have led to the non-understanding in the first place.

5.2.1 Shortened sequences: trigger – indicator – response

In this section, two extremely local and short instances of negotiation of meaning will be presented and analyzed with regard to their structure, the indicating procedures employed and the potential causes. The first example of an extremely local negotiation of meaning involves only three of the four 'functional primes' proposed by Varionis and Gass (1985: 73), since it does not feature a 'reaction to the response' (RR):

Example 13 (B.10)

11	P1:	we produced about three hundred <[vðær]> (1)	T
12	P4:	of those? (2)	I
13	P2:	<SOFT> yeah </SOFT>	R

Structurally speaking, example 13 consists of a 'trigger' utterance in line 11, which is followed by an indicating procedure in line 12 and a response in line 13. We are therefore looking at the most basic skeleton structure, in which meaning can be negotiated. Relying on Vasseur, Broeder and Robert's (1996) model, the utterance *of those?* constitutes an intermediate indicating procedure. P4 checks whether he has understood P1 one correctly by reformulating the last two words of P1's statement: *of that* (provided in phonetic transcription in line 11) becomes *of those* in line 12 and is accompanied by rising intonation, in order to signal the need for feedback. Once P4's reformulation is confirmed in line 13 – noticeably it is P2, and not P1, who picks up and reacts to the indicator – the non-understanding appears to be resolved and the conversation proceeds.

Although it is always difficult and almost never entirely possible to locate the causes of an understanding problem, an attempt will nevertheless be made to narrow down the possibilities concerning this example. If we consider the characteristics of the indicator, it seems fairly obvious that the trigger can be limited to the last portion of line 11, namely to the words *of that*, which are provided in phonetic transcription in example 13. There appear to be two levels at which these two words could have become problematic for P4, namely grammar and pronunciation. While a syntactic ambiguity is suggested by P4's employment of the deictic pronoun *those*, which stands in contrast to P1's pronoun *that*, this interpretation nevertheless is questionable if one considers the preceding talk and the contextual situation as a whole:

Example 14 (B.10)

```
1   P1:   and we eh: developed (1) (to) (.) to (a) fit eh size rack. eh
2         which=eh (.) i eh: showed the
3   P4:   mhm
4   P1:   pictures on page twenty-eight (1) and also we called it wire rack,
5         (2) so that was a bi- eh: that was our eh A and P eh (1)
6   P2:   <SOFT> seventeen </SOFT>
7   P1:   page seventeen?
8   P2:   <SOFT> mhm </SOFT>
9   P1:   oh yeah pa- sorry page seventeen
10  P5:   mhm (.)
11  P1:   we produced about three hundred <[vðær]> (1)          T
12  P4:   of those? (2)                                          I
13  P2:   <SOFT> yeah </SOFT>                                    R
```

When P1 talks about the rack in lines 1 and 4, he uses a singular form both times. It is therefore not surprising that he later, in line 11, also uses the singular *that*. One could argue that – looking solely the participant's verbal behaviour – the referent, namely *wire rack* in line 4, is rather removed from the pronoun in line 11 and that this could have caused ambiguity. Yet, as indicated in lines 4 to 10, there are pictures of the rack in the presentation material that all participants – also P4 – have in front of them. So when everyone turns to *page seventeen* to look at the picture, there is a non-linguistic referent for P1's *that*. As a consequence, it seems unlikely that – with the picture in front of him – P4 found P1's use of *that* ambiguous because of its syntactic quality.

In fact, it is seems much more plausible – and this is why phonetic representation has been chosen in the transcript – that P1's *of that* triggered a non-understanding on the part of P4 because of the way it was pronounced. While the rather quickly pronounced /vðær/ is certainly not incorrect by L1 standards, it may nevertheless be rather difficult to make out, especially for NNSs. In order to get a sense of how intelligible or unintelligible the pronunciation /vðær/ is for NNSs, it will be compared to the features of Jenkins's Lingua Franca Core, henceforth LFC (2000: 134-162; 2002: 96-98).

There are two main aspects of P1's pronunciation that need to be considered, namely the elision of the initial /ə/ and the use of the final voiced flap /ɾ/. Even though Jenkins gives no explicit rules as far as elision of vowels is concerned, she notes that weak forms themselves "may actually hinder intelligibility in EIL" (Jenkins 2000: 147). Therefore, it is easy to imagine that P1's dropping of the initial /ə/, which reduces the weak form /əv/ to /v/, impairs intelligibility, even though it would be an acceptable pronunciation in an L1 situation. The final /ɾ/ P1 pronounces would be an error in terms of the LFC, as the "LFC follows RP in its use of the consonant /t/" (Jenkins 2000: 140). This is the case because the General American (GA) usage of the flap /ɾ/ is "phonetically closer to /d/ than to /t/" (ibid.: 140) and therefore "has the potential to cause confusion" (ibid.: 140). According to Jenkins's findings, the pronunciation /vðæɾ/ therefore indeed exhibits features which might hinder ELF intelligibility. Yet, the dropping of the /ə/ and the substitution of the final voiced flap /ɾ/ doe not lead to complete unintelligibility and do not provoke a major disruption of the communicative flow. Although it is probably the pronunciation which causes the non-understanding, P4 is not utterly bewildered, but is in fact able to come up with the appropriate reformulation *of those?* almost immediately, which clears up the understanding problem.

The second example, similar to the preceding one, is also related to pronunciation and is resolved quickly. Again, the negotiation of meaning only involves the three basic components trigger, indicator and response:

Example 15 (B.14)

```
1   P4:    <L1=GERMAN> na ja </L1=GERMAN> <TRANSL=well> if
2          (.) if i m- may ehm (.) make a comment there,
3   P2:    mhm (1)
4   P4:    the (.) <['ɪmpʊls]> channel (.) ehm                        T
5   P1:    <['ɪmpʌls]> chann<1> el? </1>                              I
6   P4:    <1> the </1> <['ɪmpʊls]> channel or the C-V-S eh channel   R
7          (.) is very much ah (.) LICENSE driven. (.) meaning (1) it it's (.)
8          in the <['ɪmpʊls]> channel (1) the LICENSE is very important. (.)
```

Although the trigger turn in line 4 is short anyway, P1's indicating procedure in line 5 leaves no doubt about the fact that it is precisely the term *impulse channel* which triggers the non-understanding. The indicating procedure which is employed for this purpose is reprise, a feature which "covers a whole range of procedures which consists of taking up the other's words" (Vasseur, Broeder & Roberts 1996: 83). In this instance, the reprise involves the repetition of the term *impulse channel* with interrogative intonation. However, what is noticeable is that within this reprise P1 alters P4's non-standard pronunciation /ˈɪmpuls/ and uses the standard English pronunciation /ˈɪmpʌls/ instead, which suggests that the non-understanding might be phonetic in origin.

In establishing the LFC, Jenkins (2000: 159) suggests that, while vowel length is essential for intelligibility and consequently has to be maintained, "L2 regional qualities [are] permissible if consistent" (ibid.: 159) as long as the vowel /ɜː/ is preserved. As a result, vowel quality, "for example the difference between /bʌs/ and /bʊs/" (Jenkins 2002: 98), is included in her list of non-core features, as long as the particular quality is used consistently. In that respect, P4's first uttering of the word *impulse* with a changed vowel quality might have caused a slight irritation, i.e. a non-understanding on a very small scale, on the side of P1. In this case, P1's reprise clearly functions as a 'comprehension check'[38] and constitutes and intermediate procedure. Since P4 immediately repeats the crucial element with a slightly adapted, but again rather similar /ʊ/-pronunciation, P1 accepts this change in vowel quality and the phonetically caused non-understanding is resolved.

However, there is also an alternative interpretation which relates to the semantic meaning of the term *impulse channel* in this context. It is possible to imagine that P1's reprise in line 5 is in fact not meant as a comprehension check, of which a confirming repetition – or any other affirmative response such as 'yeah' – would be a successful resolution, but that the reprise is meant to request clarification of the term's meaning and constitutes an explicit indicating procedure. In this case, the non-understanding arises because of P1's being uncertain what P4 exactly means when he uses the term *impulse channel*. What is remarkable is that, from the point of view of the analyst, this interpretation holds as well as the one relating to pronunciation because of the way P4 responds in line 6. His response not only features a repetition of the term *impulse channel*, but also an explanation of it, namely *or the C-V-S eh channel*. As the term *C-V-S* (an acronym for 'convenience store') has been used very frequently in the portion of the meeting preceding

---

[38] In the sense of Vasseur, Broeder and Roberts (1996: 83)

this extract, the use of this alternative term would certainly have cleared up any semantic non-understanding that might have existed.

What is already observable, even in such a short stretch of conversation, is that proficient ELF speakers seem to engage actively and also very effectively in the negotiation of meaning. It seems that the two possible interpretations that have been outlined quite elaborately above also presented themselves to P4 and that he decided – obviously within the split seconds that one has available for making such decisions in the real time processing of an interaction – to account for both possibilities in his response. Since P4 opts for this combined strategy, rather than for either repetition or explanation only, the non-understanding is cleared up immediately and P4 is able to continue the thought started in line 4. It would seem that such a proceeding points to a rather skilled interactional management of non-understanding.

5.2.2 Basic sequences: trigger – indicator – response – reaction

While the preceding two examples only exhibit the first three components of Varonis and Gass's (1985) negotiation of meaning model, example 16 includes the whole four prime structure:

Example 16 (B.10)

4	P1:	pictures on page twenty-eight (1) and also we called it wire rack,	
5		(2) so that was a bi- eh: that was our eh A and P eh (1)	
6	P2:	<SOFT> seventeen </SOFT>	T
7	P1:	page seventeen?	I
8	P2:	<SOFT> mhm </SOFT>	R
9	P1:	oh yeah pa- sorry page seventeen	RR

As is evident from example 14, in which the surrounding sequence is shown, P1 is primarily talking to P4 in lines 4 and 5, when P2 adds the word *seventeen* in line 6. This correction is met by an indicating procedure (line 8), which is followed by P2's affirmative *mhm*. As a consequence, P1 reacts to P2's response by correcting his own statement of line 4 and by apologizing for the mistake he has made (line 9). The intermediate indicating procedure that P1 employs is, again, like in example 13, a 'reformulation as comprehension check' (Vasseur, Broeder & Roberts 1996: 84). As is characteristic of this procedure, P1 "submit[s] hypothetical meaning to [P2's] agreement" (ibid.: 84), when he repeats P2's word *seventeen* and adds the word *page* and in this way reformulates P2's utterance. It is the use of this particular indicating procedure which might put one on the right track in looking for a potential cause of this non-understanding, namely the distances that exisits between P2's *seventeen* in line 6 and its referent in line 4.

Since P2's utterance, containing only one word, is rather elliptical, the clear identification of the referent is essential for it to be understood. The referent *page twenty-eight*, however, is separated from the trigger by two other sentences and three short pauses (lines 4 and 5). As a consequence, there is a clear temporal and thematic gap between P1's *page twenty-eight* and P2's *seventeen*, which might prompt the non-understanding and P1's subsequent indicating procedure. Therefore, P2's *seventeen* could be called an 'elliptical utterance' (Bremer 1996: 53). Yet, the non-understanding, again, is presumably of a rather small degree, because P1 is able to correctly supply the missing information, i.e. *page*, in his indicator and thereby an affirmative response like *mhm* is enough to resolve the non-understanding[39]. One might, therefore, note at this point that ELF participants may exhibit a tendency to play a considerable part in joint negotiation work by submitting – if possible – hypothetical meaning to their interlocutors rather than requesting the others to provide an elaborate clarification.

But of course there are also instances where it will not be possible for an interlocutor to formulate a hypothesis and to submit it to the acceptance or rejection of the other participants. It seems that this may be the case either because the speaker does not achieve a deep enough understanding which would allow him or her to make a guess at what is meant, or because the trigger is of considerable length and causes a sort of 'general' non-understanding of a whole utterance. An instance of the latter can be observed in example 17:

Example 17 (A.1)

```
416   S2:                               this  is  more  or  less
417           the well (.) the level of rates which is at the moment (1) <7>
418           even (if) </7>
419   S3:    <7> are you </7> serving some some more destinations ah: in
420           the middle east?                                    T=Qu.
421   S2:    again?                                                  I
```

---

[39] It seems that one would not be doing full justice to example 16, if one did not at least mention the fact that both P2's trigger utterance and response were spoken in a rather soft tone and that this might have impaired P1's accousting perception. Yet, it needs to be borne in mind that P1 and P2 were sitting next to each other and that P2's place was remotest from the recording device, so that his utterances might have been in a low voice on the recording, but clearly intelligible for P1. Therefore, even though the softness is indicated in the transcript, I consider it unlikely to have caused the non-understanding.

```
422   S3:    do you have some more destinations in the middle east? or it's
423          purely dubai?                                                  R
424   S2:    YES. i PROMISE(D) you actually i've- sorry          RR=Ans.
```

Comparable to the preceding example, this extract also involves the basic four component structure of negotiation as the trigger utterance in lines 419 and 420 is followed by an indicator (line 421), a response (lines 422-423) and a reaction to the response (line 424). What is particularly noticeable about this example and can also be observed in other negotiation sequences is the fact that the trigger utterance is actually composed of a question, i.e. that the non-understanding happens – or comes to the surface – because one interlocutor poses a question to another. As soon as the question is answered (line 424), the non-understanding can be regarded as resolved.

In order for the question to be answered, however, a short stretch of negotiation is needed. The indicating procedure S2 uses is very direct and explicit and would be called a minimal query in Vasseur, Broeder and Roberts's scheme. As is characteristic of such minimal queries, S2's *again?* openly requests clarification and is easily identifiable as an indicator for the other participants, while it is at the same time unspecific about the precise cause of the non-understanding. As a consequence, such a procedure tends to point to some sort of general understanding problem (Vasseur, Broeder & Roberts 1996: 88) which would be related to the trigger utterance as whole.

It is this general interpretation that S3 primarily follows, when he responds to S2's indicator by repeating his initial question of lines 419 and 420 with a slight reformulation at the beginning. While the semantic core of S3's question, *some more destinations in the middle east*, remains intact, S3 changes the verb construction from a present continuous *are you serving* to a more simple *do you have*. By responding this way, S3 mainly seems to act on the assumption that S2 has simply not heard the question properly and therefore he repeats and simplifies it a little. Yet, when he then adds the short supplementary question *or it's purely dubai?*, S3 accounts for another possible interpretation, namely that his initial question might have been too imprecise in parts. By supplementing this small piece of information, S3 complements the comparative expression *some more* he has used in both the trigger utterance and the response.

By analyzing trigger as well as indicating procedure and response, which in this example successfully leads to an answer of the trigger-question, two main potential causes of this understanding problem can be distinguished. On the one hand, the non-understanding could be due to a perception problem caused by the overlap which occurs at the beginning of line 419. In line 418, S2 makes a pause and consequently a 'transition relevance place' occurs at which both S2 and S3 then start speaking simultaneously. As a result, there is not only a 'noise', which inhibits S2's perception, but also diminished attention, because it is S2 who is speaking. Since it is the beginning of the question whose perception is impaired in this way, this is likely to affect the rest of the utterance and to trigger a sort of general non-understanding of the whole utterance. A second interpretation fostered by S3's additional *purely dubai?*-question is that the expression *some more destinations*, in fact meaning 'destinations other than Dubai', proved problematic. This interpretation is less likely, however, since the rest of meeting A suggests that the required inference, i.e. some more destinations other than Dubai, would have been easy for S2 because of shared knowledge. Furthermore, it is highly probable that S2 would have opted for a different, more specific indicating procedure if this particular inference had been the cause of the non-understanding.

Although the next example still primarily exhibits the basic structure of trigger, indicator, response and reaction to response, it is slightly longer than the two non-understandings presented above, because it involves reactions by more than one speaker:

Example 18 (B.2)

4	P4:	<7> boah </7> (.) so you don't have any JET LAG or so?	T=Qu.
5	P2:	<SOFT> @ @ </SOFT>	
6	P1:	uh?	I
7	P4:	jet lag?	R
8	P1:	because we arrived eh PARIS (.)	RR1a
9	P2:	i am eh: <8> in europe for </8>	RR2b
10	P1:	<8> yah yah </8> eh: WEDNESDAY. (.)	...RR1a
11	P4:	oKAY, WOW	

Like in example 17, the trigger utterance in example 18 also is a question which is met with short laughter by P2 and an indicating procedure by P1, to whom the question most likely is addressed. After P4's subsequent response, it is P1 who reacts in the first place (RR1a), but is then joined in by P2, who also attempts to produce a reaction (RR2b). P2's reaction, however, remains incomplete due to the continuation of P1's reaction (...RR1a)[40]. What

---

[40] Responses (R) and reactions to responses (RR) which belong to the same trigger/indicating procedure will be numbered consecutively, i.e. R1, RR1, R2, RR2, etc. If more than one speaker responds or reacts to the response(s), this will be marked by a small letter which is added after the number, i.e. R1a, RR1a, R2b, RR2b, etc. If one 'logical unit', i.e. one response or one reaction, is split up due to overlaps, interruption or

already becomes obvious in this still rather basic structure is that the negotiation of meaning may take up longer stretches of discourse in an interaction.

Unlike example 17, P1's explicit, yet unspecific minimal query *uh?* is not followed by a complete repetition of the trigger question in case of example 18. In providing a response to P1's indicating procedure, P4 opts for reducing the trigger question to its semantic core, which he had already stressed in line 4, and repeats the term *jet lag?* with an interrogatory intonation. Although he is never given a direct and explicit answer – which would have been *no* – P1 renders an explanation about why he and P2 do not have jet lag in lines 8 and 10, which implies of course that they do not have let lag. Therefore, P4's perceives his question as having been answered and expresses this in line 11. Consequently, the non-understanding with regard to the trigger question is evidently resolved.

As far as the potential causes of this understanding problem are concerned, they are rather difficult to pinpoint in this instance, as there is hardly any evidence in the data on the basis of which assumptions can be made. Even though, there is an overlap an the beginning of line 4, there is a short pause before P4 starts phrasing his question, which means that there is no interference of simultaneous speech, which would have been a potential cause. Neither the particular form of the indicating procedure nor the shape of P4's response provide any hints as to what portion of the trigger posed problematic and why. In fact, the very simple nature of the response suggests that the non-understanding only was of a very small scale in the first place, i.e. an almost complete understanding, and that in context of the given situation the meaning of the question could be conveyed by very basic means, i.e. a noun phrase paired with a rising intonation.

5.2.3 Enlarged sequences: 'waffling' and additional explanations

As can already be inferred from example 18, the basic four prime structure of the negotiation of meaning may lead up to longer sequences which follow the actual clarification. In example 19, the basic structure actually resolves the non-understanding, but it entails a short exchange in which the reasons behind what has been the subject of negotiation are explained:

---

feedback of others and is continued at another point, it will retain the number it was first given but will be marked as a continuation with three initial dots, i.e. ...R1a, ...RR2b, etc.

Example 19 (B.16)

1	P1:	again ah we (.) expect that we would (.) GET (.) your	
2		contribution of ten per cent of our (1) (actual) we purchase	
3		which will: which we (.) we will ah provide you shortly (.) for	
4		our purchase plan (2)	
5	P1:	<to P2> <L1=KOREAN> *(3s)* </L1=KOREAN> (1)	
6	P2:	<to P1> <L1=KOREAN> *(4s)* </L1=KOREAN> (.)	
7	P1:	ah it will be (2) early (.) early march. okay? (.)	*T*
8	P4:	what?	*I*
9	P1:	the the FIGURE for the purchase (.) figure (bec-) <1> because	*R1a*
10		</1> (1)	
11	P4:	<1> <L1=GERMAN> *ach so* </L1=GERMAN> <TRANSL=oh i	
12		see> </1>	*RR1*
13	P2:	ah:	
14	P1:	we- we'll be back (.) we'll be back eh: (1) (the) twenty-eighth (2)	*R2a*
15	P2:	<SOFT> (end of) <2> (xx) </2> </SOFT>	*R3b*
16	P1:	<SOFT> <2> ah not </2> twenty-eighth </SOFT> (.) <3>	
17		twenty-SEVENTH </3>	*R4a*
18	P2:	<3> (twenty-seventh) </3> mhm (.)	*R5b*
19	P1:	i'll be <4> back </4> in in the office (.)	*R6a*
20	P4:	<4> <SOFT> mhm </SOFT> </4>	*RR2*
21	P4:	mhm	*RR3*
22	P1:	so i need (.) couple of more days to eh to (review) in detail (.)	
23		then we'll give you ah: our PURCHASE plan (.) for year two	
24		thousand four	*R7a*
25	P4:	right <5> because </5>	*RR4*
26	P1:	<5> (yeah:) </5> WITHOUT that (.) <6> (xx) </6>	*R8a*
27	P4:	<6> you cannot </6> really calculate <7> what </7>	
28		promotions you <8> can (have) </8>	*RR5*
29	PX-2:	<7> (xxx) </7>	
30	P1:	<8> of course you </8> SHOULD (.) you should have that	
31		number to to: (.) plan your your your part. (.)	*R9a*
32	P4:	right	*RR6*

Although the trigger utterance in line 7 is not a question, but a definite statement, it is nevertheless supplemented with an agreement seeking, interrogatory *okay?*, which certainly requires some kind of reaction or affirmation on the part of P4. But since a local non-understanding occurs, P4 is forced to use an indicating procedure (line 8) before being able to signal any approvement or disapprovment of P1's statement. P4's indicator is met with an adequate response (line 9), a response which is successful in resolving the non-understanding as one can see in P4's reaction in line 11. Yet, this particular reaction – even though it only consists of a minimal interjection – is provided not in English, but in P4's first language German. As a consequence, even though its function as a signal of understanding is probably clear to P1, who is a native speaker of Korean, its semantic meaning will probably have remained obscure to him.

The indicating procedure that is used by P4 is again an explicit minimal query. While it is possible to interpret his *what?* as an unspecific question referring to the trigger utterance as a whole, the way P4 says *what?* leads one to suspect that the query is in fact not unspecific this time, but points towards a particular portion of the trigger, namely the pronoun *it*. It is this latter point of view that P1 adopts in shaping his response. And because the response is effective in resolving the understanding problem, it appears that this interpretation is correct. In this way, the non-understanding seems to be caused by an 'elliptical utterance' (Bremer 1996: 53) whose subject (namely *it*) is ambiguous because it lacks a referent in close proximity. On the one hand, the referent is separated from the trigger by a short exchange between P1 and P2 in their L1 Korean (lines 5-6), which is likely to make the other partcipants' attention flag. On the other hand, P1's anaphoric *it* does not have a simple noun phrase as its referent, but condenses most of the information given in lines 3 and 4[41]. Accordingly, P1's usage of *it* challenges shared understanding in two ways and thereby causes the non-understanding.

While the non-understanding is quickly resolved by P1's specification of the referent and P4's exclamation, P1 still has not been given any approving (or disapproving) reply to P1's *okay?* in line 7 and the negotiation is extended by what House (1999: 81) calls 'waffling', i.e. the use of too many words as compensatory strategy. After the basic negotiation structure, which clarifies the fact that the purchase plan will be sent in early March, P1, occasionally supported by P2, obviously feels the need to explain why the purchase plan will be sent at this particular time, although P4 has in no way requested such an explanation. In fact, one gets the impression that P4 very much consents to the period of time mentioned by P1. But it seems that, since he does not openly signal this agreement immediately after having achieved understanding in line 11, P1 feels the urge to give reasons for their sending the purchase plan in early March. As a consequence, P1 and P4 agree on the schedule that requires this date (lines 14 to 25) and then jointly discuss the reasons why both companies need the purchase figures to plan their business (lines 25 to 32). While this sequence should not be devalued or judged superfluous as it most certainly

---

[41] See Bremer (1996: 54) for a similar example.

functions as a means of strengthening participants' business relations, it nevertheless develops out of the basic negotiation structure despite its being not imperative at this point.

Another enlarged – even though considerably shorter and more focused – negotiation structure is visible in example 20:

Example 20 (B.13)

1	P5:	<1> (xxx) </1>	
2	P1:	<1> it's like a INsurance </1> you know?	*T*
3	P4:	pardon me <clears his throat>	*I*
4	P1:	it's like an INsurance you buy (.)	*R1*
5	P4:	<@> right </@>	*RR1*
6	P1:	the CHANCE you (.)	*R2*
7	P4:	RIGHT	*RR2*
8	P1:	get in the <2> acci </2>dent is really really low	*...R2*
9	P4:	<2> right </2>	*RR3*

In this instance, the trigger utterance, which includes the comprehension check *you know?* at the end, is again followed by an explicit indicating procedure. While, as we can see from P4's reaction (line 5), P1's response (line 4) seems to clear up the non-understanding sufficiently, P1 nevertheless provides a second response (R2 and ...R2), which further clarifies the meaning of his utterance in line 2. Likewise, P4 also produces two additional reactions (RR2 and RR3) to the second response and thereby signals involvement, agreement and understanding.

Although P4, like the speakers in most of the examples discussed so far, uses a rather direct indicating procedure, the indicator this time is not a minimal query but the metalinguistic[42] comment *pardon me*. Like most minimal queries, this expression is also unspecific, pointing towards a more or less general non-understanding of the trigger utterance. It is, in the first place, interpreted in this way by P1, who repeats the trigger phrase *it's like an INsurance* adding the words *you buy* afterwards. If one analyzes the repeated portion of the trigger utterance, it is possible to locate two peculiarities which might have caused the non-understanding.

First of all, it needs to be noted that the words *it's like a INsurance* in line 2 are spoken during an overlap. Due to this 'noise' in the channel, P4 may not have heard them properly. A second peculiarity which may have caused the non-understanding is stress

---

[42] The term 'metalinguistic' is used in the sense of Vasseur, Broeder & Roberts (1996: 88-89) in this paper. In this sense, 'metalinguistic' questions and comments could be loosely described as explicitly '**relating to** what has been said' (i.e. to language) and **not** necessarily '**about** language'. 'Minimal queries' such as *again?* or *what?* can also be counted as a subcategory of such metalinguistic procedures.

placement in the word *INsurance*, as P1 places tonic stress on the first syllable of the word, whereas it should normally be placed on the second one. Although Jenkins (2002: 98) states that "the placement of word stress [...] varies considerably across different L1 varieties of English" and therefore defines word stress as 'non-core', it is nevertheless conceivable that the unusual stress distribution, together with the noise resulting from the simultaneous speech, may have led to the non-understanding. Even though P4 does not alter the stress distribution in *INsurance* when he repeats the trigger in line 4, P1's response prompts P4 to react with an affirmative *right*.

Nevertheless, P1 decides to provide another explanation in addition to R1, which leads to the extension of the structure in lines 6 to 9. This second response (R2) seems to stem from the fact that P1 had been drawing an analogy in lines 2 and 4. Previously to the stretch of conversation presented in example 20, the participants had been considering whether they should take a certain risk. P1's utterance *it's like a INsurance* was produced as a comment on this particular situation. In providing the second response, P1 seems to account for the possibility that P4's indicator might have pointed to a certain confusion as to why P1 was making this comment and what he wanted to express with it. Therefore, P1 opts – to be on the safe side, so to say – not only to resolve the non-understanding, but also to explain his analogy with R2 and ...R2. As his explanation is met with agreement by P4, any remaining possibility of non-understanding appears to have been resolved.

5.2.4 High involvement sequences: 'fragile' activities and the need for clarity

The enlarged structures discussed above show that the participants in the data analyzed show a great interest in exchanging precise information, which is of course likely to be a macro-contextual characteristic of any business meeting. This need for clarity is particularly prominent in those negotiations of meaning in which participants display high involvement strategies, i.e. in which participants, e.g. through the indicating procedures they use, exhibit considerable effort in resolving the non-understanding. They actively contribute to the clarification, rather than wait for the others to do the work.

Example 21 contains such a 'high involvement structure' which is linked to an immediately preceding non-understanding that has already been analyzed in example 17.

Example 21 (A.1)

422	S3:	do you have some more destinations in the middle east? or it's	
423		purely dubai?	*R=Qu.*
424	S2:	YES. i PROMISE(D) you actually i've- sorry	*RR=Ans.*
425	S3:	still not <1> get it @ @ @ @ </1>	
426	S2:	<1> i've (.) i for</1>got <2> @ (.) @ </2>	
427	S3:	<2> <SOFT> @ @ @ </SOFT> </2>	
428	S2:	i FORGOT eh you are recording this <3> (now) </3>	
429	S1:	<LOUD> <3> @ </3> @ <4> @ @ @ @ > </4> </LOUD>	
430	S3:	<4> @ @ @ @ </4>	
431	S2:	<4> @ @ </4> i forgot last year actually to mention it, yes. we-	
432		we have a lot of ah: destinations within (.) the middle east (1)	
433		<5> eh: </5>	*...Ans.*
434	S3:	<5> send me </5> (.) send me JUST a LIST (.)	
435	S2:	yes.	
436	S3:	with destinations you can offer, what kind of services, (1) <6>	
437		you </6> have, (1) <7> a:nd </7>	
438	S2:	<6> yes </6>	
439	S2:	<7> it's all </7> to to let you know now immediately it's all of	
440		course it's a TRUCKING (.) connection eh:	*T*
441	S1:	<SOFT> <FAST> from du<1>bai</1> </FAST> </SOFT>	*I*
442	S2:	<1> FROM </1> (.) our dubai station. (2)	*R*
443	S1:	<SOFT> okay. </SOFT>	*RR*

Recalling the initial non-understanding of example 17, the trigger utterance and accordingly also the response (lines 422 and 423) is a question which S2 starts to answer in line 424, but then interrupts himself with an insertion related to the fact that the meeting is being recorded. After this short digression, S2 finally provides an extensive answer in lines 431 and 432. The trigger utterance of example 21 (lines 439-440) is then an addition to this extensive answer. It is succeeded by an indicator and immediately resolved by a basic negotiation structure (R and RR).

While this negotiation is not remarkable with regard to its structural characteristics, it is noticeable with regard to the indicating procedure that is employed. By providing the supplementary comment *from dubai*, S1 makes use of an indicator "which is mainly based on hypothesis-forming" (Vasseur, Broeder & Roberts 1996: 82). Thereby S1 neither indicates the understanding problem directly, nor adopts a "passive wait and see attitude" (ibid.: 83) or 'let it pass' behavior (Firth 1996: 243-245), but opts for an intermediate strategy by "submitting hypothetical meaning to [his] partner's agreement" (Vasseur, Broeder & Roberts 1996: 84).

Along the lines of Vasseur, Broeder and Roberts's model of indicating procedures, the strategy can best be described as an intermediate procedure which is "a re-elaboration of the other's discourse" (ibid.: 84). A participant who employs such a procedure thus checks how far shared understanding has been obtained and actively takes part in the joint clarification work (ibid.: 84). Vasseur, Broeder and Roberts's (1996: 84) suggestion that such a behavior can be used very effectively by advanced speakers is clearly confirmed in example 21. As S1 takes it upon himself to provide the missing or unclear bit of information in his indicator, all S2 needs to do is to confirm S1's hypothesis. He does so by repeating this crucial piece of information in line 442 and the non-understanding is resolved instantly.

The preceding description of the clarification process already hints at the potential causes of the non-understanding. The interpretation that appears most likely in the light of the employed indicating procedure and the quick resolution is that the non-understanding was due to the trigger being an 'elliptical utterance' (Bremer 1996: 53). What S1 does in line 441 is to supply a piece of information that is not explicitly provided in lines 439 and 440. If we trace back the flow of information in the conversation – from the trigger (lines 439-440), over S2's answer (lines 431-432), to S3's initial question (lines 422-423) – it becomes obvious that S1 can infer that the trucking connections are *from dubai* and consequently he is able to formulate this as a hypothesis. Nevertheless, it seems that this inference is not a particularly easy one, because of its connection to several preceding utterances. S1 is not certain whether understanding is actually shared between himself and the other participants and therefore decides to voice his hypothetical inference and actively engages in clarifying this minor non-understanding.

Similarly to the preceding example, examples 22 and 23, which are about the same subject in meeting B and are closely linked to each other, also display the exchange of precise information as a frequent requirement of meetings and exhibit some high involvement strategies that participants employ in such a case.

Example 22 (B.6)

1	P1:	well if you go to ah (1) C-V-S there are (.) multi LAYERS of
2		shelf, (.)
3	P4:	mhm
4	P1:	okay (.) ah to: PUT (.) this kind of HI:GH (.) display (.)
5	P2:	<SOFT> (xxx) </SOFT>
6	P4:	yeah, so is it on HOOKS in the (.) in the C-V-S or (.) is it in the
7		(.) in the cartons. *Qu.*

8	P2:	it's in shelf (.) (but) (.) <1> (x) </1>	*T=Ans.*
9	P4:	<1> it's </1> LYING in the shelf <2> or (or) </2>	*I*
10	P1:	<2> it's lying </2> on the <3> shelf </3>	*R1a*
11	P2:	<3> it's lying </3> <4> on the shelf </4>	*R2b*
12	P4:	<4> AHA </4>	*RR1a*
13	P1:	and the shelf HEIGTH (.) is quite limited	*R3a*
14	P3:	<SOFT> mhm okay </SOFT>	*RR2b*

Like some preceding examples[43], example 22 is related to and seemingly brought about by a question. Contrary to the other instances, where the question itself becomes the trigger utterance, the question in this negotiation, however, elicits an answer that does not seem to suffice for achieving the degree of understanding P4 wants to achieve, when he poses the question in the first place. In example 22, it consequently is the answer to a question which triggers the non-understanding – a peculiarity which clearly seems to point towards the extraordinary need for clarity and preciseness that sets business meetings apart from casual conversations.

Structurally speaking the negotiation sequence is rather straightforward, even though it involves four different speakers. The answer, i.e. the trigger, is followed by an indicating procedure which evokes two identical responses by P1 and P2 (R1a and R2b). These responses are succeeded by a very brief reaction by P4 (RR1a), before P1 provides a third response in line 13 (R3a), which P3 acknowledges by a second reaction in line 14. At this point, the conversation slightly diverges from the topic of the negotiation and therefore the non-understanding appears to have been resolved. As will become obvious very soon afterwards in the conversation[44], however, further clarification was merely slightly postponed and the non-understanding was left 'pending' at this point.

Actively taking part in resolving the non-understanding instead of just indicating it, P4 employs an intermediate indicating procedure by re-elaborating P2's answer, a strategy very similar to the one in example 21. The way P4 formulates his indicator suggests that P2's answer is not precise and elaborate enough, i.e. the reply *it's in shelf* does not seem to fully answer the question P4 has posed in lines 6 and 7. Instead of adopting a 'wait and see' strategy, however, P4 takes matters into his own hands. He does not wait to hear out P2, but, after P2 pauses twice in line 8, utters a hypothesis himself. He re-elaborates the trigger by saying *it's LYING in the shelf*, stressing the additional verb *LYING*. Furthermore, he

---

[43] See examples 17, 18, and 19.
[44] See example 23.

indicates that his utterance is to be taken as a question – or at least a hypothesis – when he utters the word *or* afterwards.

As has been suggested in the analysis of the employed indicating procedure, the cause of the non-understanding is most likely to be found in the ellipicial nature of P2's answer. P4's question suggests that he wants precise information about how the product is stored and how it is visually presented in convenience stores (*C-V-S*) in Korea. When P2 states that the product is in the shelf, but then falters and hesitates to provide a further description, P4 provides one possible description, which is confirmed by both P1 and P2. So one the one hand, it is P4 who makes the effort of specifying the visual presentation, i.e. *LYING* as opposed to 'standing' or 'hanging', while on the other hand, P4 does not seem to allow P2 much time for providing a more elaborate answer.

Although P4 at first appears to be satisfied when P1 and P2 accept the hypothesis he provides, he nevertheless takes up the issue again only 45 seconds after the first negotiation. For one, this suggests that the non-understanding is not completely cleared up in the previous exchange. Secondly, it also again stresses the need for exchanging precise information that pertains to business talk.

Example 23 (B.7)

```
1    P4:    mhm but (.) AGAIN (.) that i understand it right (.) the products
2           are just (.) LYING in the shelf they're not HANGING on a
3           HOOK, (.) they're just LYING (.) in the in the shelf. (.)         I
4    P2:    hm                                                                R1
5    P1:    <to P2> <L1=KOREAN> (xxxx) (xx) </L1=KOREAN>
6    P2:    <to   P1>   <L1=KOREAN>    (xxxxxx)    (xx)    (xxxxxx)    (5s)
7           </L1=KOREAN>
8    P1:    <to P2> <L1=KOREAN> (xxxx) </L1=KOREAN>
9           <P2 shows S4 a picture of the products in the shop shelf>        R2
10   P4:    AHA this one you have                                             RR
```

As far as structure is concerned, example 23 exhibits a rather rudimentary negotiation sequence as there is no immediately preceding trigger utterance. The trigger is in fact to be found in example 22. Therefore, the negotiation only begins with an indicating procedure (lines 1-3). This indicator is followed only by an ambiguous *hm* as a first reaction, which is then followed by a short exchange between P1 and P2 in their first language, Korean. The second reaction, which follows in line 9, is remarkable as it is non-verbal: P2 resorts to a picture. Judging from P4's reaction, it is this picture which finally resolves the non-understanding, as it contains the information P4 has asked for.

Probably due to the distance between the trigger utterance and the indicator, the characteristics of the indicator are highly interesting in example 23, since they include a combination of indicating procedures. The major part of the indicator in lines 1 to 3 is filled again by the intermediate procedures of reformulation and reprise. P4 takes up his own words *LYING in the shelf* and elaborates his explanation by contrasting the state of 'lying in the shelf' with *not HANGING on a HOOK* and then repeats the first phrase again. But before he employs reprise and reformulation, P4 resorts to the rather explicit indicating procedure of 'metalinguistic comment', when he starts his utterance by saying *but (.) AGAIN (.) that i understand it right*. This remark draws P1 and P2's attention back to the non-understanding of example 22 and it expresses P4's wish to achieve a greater degree of clarity and understanding. Vasseur, Broeder and Roberts (1996: 88-89) note that metalinguistic indicators often represent "the final phase of a series of context-sensitive efforts to work on the understanding problem", in which participants end up going 'on record' to resolve the non-understanding, and indeed such a sequence of indicators can be observed in examples 22 and 23. The authors further maintain that the use of a metalinguistic procedure "always results in better understanding, because it clearly, precisely and cooperatively triggers working sequences" (Vasseur, Broeder & Roberts 1996: 88).

Although the potential causes of the non-understanding have already been discussed with regard to example 22, which features the trigger also of the negotiation in example 23, one additional comment has to be made at this point. Even though Bazzanella and Damiano (1999: 829) note that miscommunication can be caused by non-linguistic means, it is not the picture or the look of the shop shelfs per se that cause the non-understanding, but rather the way they are being talked about. Taking up Firth's (1996: 248) suggestion that some activities in conversation are inherently more 'fragile', i.e. less 'interactionally robust', than others, it does not seem far-fetched to propose that the the main concern of meeting B at this point, i.e. clarifying product visibility, may constitute such a 'fragile' activity. If we accept that talking about the exact visual appearance of something – in this case of the product in a particular store – is a 'fragile' activity and requires a lot of linguistic precision, it is not surprising that the participants would have needed two negotiation sequences (examples 22 and 23) to resolve the non-understanding.

In this light, it is also not diffcult to account for another striking feature of the second negotiation sequence, namely the fact that the second response (R2), i.e. the response which ultimately resolves the understanding problem, is in fact non-verbal. So in this particular case, the negotiation of meaning is finally brought to a satisfactory end, when P2 shows P4 a picture of the products in the shelf (line 9). Bazzanella and Damiano (1999: 830) describe a similar example in which an understanding problem is resolved "thanks to the clarifying use of non-linguistic means on the part of the interlocutor [...], after linguistic resources [...] have failed to produce the understanding". It would appear that, while the participants of meeting B are advanced speakers of English and normally do not resort to non-linguistic means for clarifying matters, they may be prompted to do so because of the 'fragile' nature of their task.

5.2.5 Complex sequences: multiple indicators and negotiation cycles

It has been shown that not all negotiations of meaning are confined to a single trigger-resolution sequence and a singular indicating procedure. As Gass and Varonis note, negotiation sequences may indeed "consist of multiple layers of trigger-resolution sequences" (Varonis & Gass 1985: 78) which take up considerable stretches of discourse. Since the business data that is examined in this paper often exhibits a great need for achieving understanding, it is not surprising that three of such complex and multiple negotiation sequences were found.

The first occurrence that is presented is, like other previous negotiations, triggered by a question from a participant. The example features two indicating procedures and two rather short negotiation sequences that occur immediately after each other, but are nevertheless not prompted by the same non-understanding. Structurally speaking example 24 is the least complex negotiation of meaning of the three samples that are analyzed in this section.

Example 24 (B.9)

```
98    P1:    and and and eh: (COMPANY37) which we started MAY we (.)
99           ah: couldn't sell MORE (.) to THEM (.) while we haven't started
100          to: receive returns <SOFT> which is not a good news again
101          </SOFT> (2)
102   P4:    ah: (.)
```

103	P1:	among the department store (COMPANY38) is our major (.)	
104		client, (2)	
105	P4:	ahm (.) excuse me	
106	P1:	yes (2)	
107	P4:	and <SLOW> approximately: </SLOW> (.) how many	
108		OUTLETS do they have? (1)	T=Qu.
109	P1:	which one?	I(1)
110	P4:	(COMPANY38)? (2)	R
111	P2:	(it's) two (1)	RR=Ans./T
112	P4:	<1> two? </1>	I(2)
113	P1:	<1> department </1> department store yeah MAINly in (junct-)	
114		MAIN (.) department store in downtown (1) (junction) yeah (.)	R
115	P4:	ye:ah (3)	RR

Both non-understandings are negotiated within a simple trigger-indicator-response-reaction structure, but they are connected in so far as P2's reaction (RR) in line 111 is at the same time the resolution of the first non-understanding, the answer to P4's trigger question, and the trigger of the next non-understanding.

The first indicating procedure I(1)[45], namely the one employed by P1 when he finds himself confronted with P4's question in lines 107 and 108, is situatued on the very explicit end of the continuum of indicating procedures, as it is a direct metalinguistic[46] question. By uttering the words *which one* accompanied by a rising intonation P1 clearly expresses that ta non-understanding exists with regard to P4's question. Even more so, P1 is not only rather explicit about there being a non-understanding, but he is also quite specific about the particular portion of the trigger that is responsible for its occurrence. The combination of the determiner *which* that is used "to ask someone to identify a specific person or thing out of a number of people or things" (Sinclair 1990: 200) and the numeral *one* clearly points towards the subject of the trigger question.

As far as the cause of the first non-understanding is concerned, one can therefore state with a considerable degree of certainty that it has its roots in the noun phrase of the trigger question, i.e. the pronoun *they*. Furthermore, P1's metalinguistic question indicates quite clearly that it is the referent of this deitic expression he wants to know, so that the

---

[45] If an example includes more than one indicator, these indicators will be number in the following way: I(1), I(2), I(3), etc. in order to make them more prominent in the analyzed transcript. Responses (R) and reactions to responses (RR) will always be numbered in relation to the indicator they relate to, i.e. normally the indicator that precedes them, so that their numbers will start with R1 and RR1 every time a new indicator occurs. As example 24, for instance, features two indicators but only one response and one reaction with regard to each indicator, the respective response and reaction are not numbered in this case.

[46] In the sense of Vasseur, Broeder and Roberts (1996: 88-89)

cause of the non-understanding can be subsumed under the category 'unclear/missing referent'. Since it has been noted already in the theoretical part of the paper that it is a central premise of the analysis to regard understanding as 'shared understanding' and not to blame individual participants for the occurrence of miscommunication, the following analysis is not intended to find a 'culprit' for the understanding problem, but rather to trace back the non-understanding to its orgins and to find out how the referent could have come to be unclear.

Considering P1's response in line 110, we know that the intended referent of *they* is *(COMPANY38)*. Preceding the trigger, the referent can be found in line 103, the nearest full sentence before P4's question. Therefore it seems that P4 is perfectly justified to use a pronominal expression as a subject in line 108 (T) without necessarily creating ambiguousness, because the referent of the pronoun is the subject of the preceding clause[47]. Yet, the pronoun is ambiguous for P1 and a non-understanding occurs. Through uttering the indicator *which one?*, P1 makes obvious that he understands that P4 is referring to a company, i.e. a department store in this case, but that there is more than one company that P4's question (T) – and the deictic *they* – could refer to and that he, P1, is not sure *which one* it is. This interpretation appears cogent if one considers P1's turn in lines 98 to 101, in which he talks about another company, *(COMPANY37)*. While normally P4's *they* would be interpreted as referring to the closest possible referent, i.e. *(COMPANY38)*, P1's use of the pronoun THEM – a plural form like P4's *they* – with regard to *(COMPANY37)* in line 99 could have caused ambiguity in this case.

The second non-understanding in example 24 appears to be less severe than the first one. The intermediate indicating procedure that P4 uses is a simple reprise of the word *two*, accompanied by rising intonation. P4 has in fact understood the numeral correctly, but apparently wants to re-confirm his perception in order to ensure an utmost degree of understanding. In the response (lines 113-114), whose beginning overlaps with the indicator, P1 continues P2's answer from line 111 and thereby accepts P4's repetition of *two* and also confirms it via inserting an affirmative *yeah* in line 113. To this response P4 in turn reacts with an affirmation and so the negotiation of meaning is brought to an end.

---

[47] The insertions in lines 105 and 106 neither provide an alternative referent nor are likely to distract so much from what was said in lines 103 and 104 that P1 would have had trouble recalling the subject of his own last sentence.

A certainly more complex negotiation of meaning is presented in the next extract. It starts when P1 utters an assumption that is in fact a question (lines 2-4), but is, however, not very explicitly presented as such. What follows is an accumulation of indicating procedures uttered by different participants that results in a rather complex negotiation sequence of considerable length, but is nevertheless resolved successfully in the end:

Example 25 (B.4)

1	P1:	ah <to P2> ((COMPANY2)) <LX-1=KOREAN> *(xxxxxxx)?*	
2		</LX-1=KOREAN> </to P2> (.) <to P4> <SOFT> i understand	
3		</SOFT> some other countries in the ASIA (.) we handle	
4		(COMPANY2) (1)	*T(=Qu.)*
5	P3:	<SOFT> really? </SOFT>	
6	P4:	pardon me?	*I(1)*
7	P1:	some (.) some other region in a- a- some COUNTRIES in ah:	
8		INDONESIA (.)	*R/T*
9	P4:	<L1=GERMAN> *ja?* </L1=GERMAN> <TRANSL=yes?> (.)	*I(2)*
10	P1:	s- i i i s- thought some of the our (affiliated) company handles	
11		(COMPANY2). <SOFT> no? </SOFT> (.)	*...R+I(3)*
12	P5:	indonesia?	*I(4)/T*
13	P1:	no?	*I(5)*
14	P2:	<SOFT> no </SOFT>	*R1a*
15	P4:	not <1> in </1>	*R2b*
16	P1:	<1> we </1> are the only one?	*I(6)*
17	P4:	yeah I had once a meeting with (COMPANY9) in (.) in	
18		SINGAPORE, we were <2> talking </2> about (.) VIETNAM.	
19		(.)	*R1*
20	P1:	<2> yeah </2>	*RR1*
21	P1:	mhm	*RR2*
22	P4:	because eh: they are somehow affiliated with (.) the	
23		(COMPANY28) distri<3>buto:r </3>	*R2*
24	P1:	<3> YES </3> yes <4> yes </4>	*RR3*
25	P4:	<4> in </4> vietNAM and we want- (.) we contacted THEM	
26		then fo:r (.) but it- ACTually it neve:r <5> really </5>	*...R2*
27	P1:	<5> okay </5> okay (.)	*RR4*
28	P1:	<6> (xxx) (it) </6>	*RR5*
29	P4:	<6> worked out </6> (1)	*...R2*
30	P1:	(i) understand. (4)	*RR6*

The initial non-understanding that entails this complex negotiation structure is triggered by P1's utterance in lines 2 to 4. Even though P3 seems to have understood the trigger and utters a surprise reaction in line 5, there is a non-understanding between P1 and P4, and because these two are the ones who are primarily in charge of meeting B, P4's indicating procedure in line 6 bears greater interactional weight and starts a negotiation of meaning. P4

95

deploys the explicit, but unspecific metalinguistic question *pardon me?* to indicate that he has not understood P1's utterance properly.

The fact that P4's indicator does not point towards any particular portion of the trigger as source of the non-understanding and is completely unspecific suggests that P4 is facing a general non-understanding of the whole trigger utterance. This impression is also reinforced if one looks P1's response. He does not repeat the whole trigger utterance, but only slightly reformulates its beginning, a strategy which does not suffice to clear up the non-understanding. As P3, whose proficiency in English hardly seems to differ from P4's, appears to have understood the trigger in contrast to his colleague, it seems most likely is that the non-understanding is due to flagging attention or some sort of distraction on the side of P4. This interpretation is all the more plausible if one considers that P1 utters the English trigger less than a second after he as been conversing with is colleague in Korean. During this short exchange in Korean, P4, whose first language is German, may have concentrated on something else and could therefore be taken by surprise when he is suddenly addressed again.

The response P1 provides after being confronted with P4's direct request for clarification is yet obviously not enough to resolve the non-understanding, but trigges another indicator – I(2) – on the part of P4. After having received the first half of P1's response in lines 7 and 8, P4 provides the minimal German feedback *ja?* which is paired with an interrogatory pitch movement. Although minimal feedback, as an implicit indicating procedure, is not to be interpreted as a consciously produced signal of non-understanding (Vasseur, Broeder & Roberts 1996: 75), P4's *ja?* nevertheless appears to be symptomatic of the still existent non-understanding at this point, particularly so in the light of the direct indicating procedure that precedes it in line 6.

After P4's minimal feedback, P1 continues his response in lines 10 and 11 by reformulating the remaining part of the original trigger utterance (lines 2 to 4). This reformulation is interesting in two aspects. First, it should be noticed that P1 replaces the subjective *i understand* (line 2) by the more tentative *i thought* (line 10) which expresses much more clearly that he is uttering an assumption and not a fixed belief. In addition, the shift from present tense (*understand*) to past tense (*thought*) conveys a greater distance to the statement which follows. Secondly, P1 substitutes the personal subject pronoun *we* that is used in the trigger (line 3) by the noun phrase *some of the our (affiliated) company*.

Besides reformulating the trigger, P1 lets his assumption appear in a slightly different light when he adds an interrogatory *no?* at the end. This small token at the end makes it obvious that P1's assumption, while it is not syntactically formulated as a question, is nevertheless uttered to obtain some kind of approving or disapproving feedback from (COMPANY2)'s employees, especially from P4. Furthermore, by choosing a declining *no* instead of e.g. an agreement seeking 'right', P1 already utters a hypothetical interpretation based on the others' reactions to the trigger. Therefore, P1's *no?* itself also represents an intermediate indicating procedure – I(3) – within which the participant "risk[s] a response on the basis of [his] perception of the situation" (Vasseur, Broeder & Roberts 1996: 83), namely a tentative response.

At this point P5 enters into the negotiation sequence by uttering another indicator – I(4) – in line 12. P5's reprise of the word *indonesia?* relates back to the first part of P1's response in lines 7 and 8. As an intermediate indicating procedure reprise may fulfill a number of different functions. In this instance, the reprise with rising intonation simultaneously appears to signal a minor non-understanding, as far as the perception of the reprised word is concerned, as well as surprise about the fact that P1 thinks (COMPANY2)'s products are handled in Indonesia by one of his own company's affiliates. Although a certain degree of understanding has definitely been achieved at this point, it is nevertheless clearly indicative of the still existent non-understanding that P5 does not comment on P1's assumption right away, but rather feels the need to insert an indicator.

Since P5's reprise shows that her perception of the word was correct – she is talking about the right country – P1's next contribution does not relate to her indicator I(4) any further, i.e. he does not confirm it, but he simply does not object to it. I(5) therefore is precisely the same indicating procedure P1 has already used at the end of this response in line 11. In uttering the same disbelieving *no?* P1 reacts to P5's obvious surprise and interprets it as an indication that his assumption is wrong. In doing this, he again formulates a hypothesis and produces a tentative response on the basis of his assessment of the situation. Thereby he shows a considerable degree of involvement and actively takes part in the joint clarification.

P1's high degree of engagement continues when he utters another but more elaborate hypothesis and tentative response – I(6) – in line 16, after P2 and P4 both have uttered a very short response each (R1a and R2b). It should be noted that P1 does not wait for P4 to utter a full response, but interrupts him in order to make more explicit his own intentions and the purpose of the whole negotiation sequence. By saying *we are the only one* P1 makes explicit that the negotiation of meaning has altered his initial assumption of lines 2 to 4, but simultaneously signals through rising intonation that he is not sure whether his newly formed opinion is correct. In this way, he indicates that there is still a non-understanding. He submits his hypothesis to P4's agreement and actively seeks to elicit the information he has been trying to obtain from the beginning. It seems that it is P1's active participation in the negotiation work that finally succeeds in resolving the non-understanding.

Prompted by P1's last indicator I(6) and relying on the information P1 has provided in his response (R) in lines 7 and 8 and in its continuation (...R) in lines 10 and 11, P4 eventually produces an elaborate response (R1) in lines 17 and 18 and this starts to clear up the issue. He mentions his meeting with (COMPANY9) – a company affiliated with P1 and P2's employer – but not with regard to Indonesia but with regard to Singapore and Vietnam. In offering this response, P4 shows skill in connecting different pieces of information from several utterances and in appropriately reacting to P1's last indicating procedure.

Throughout the remaining part of the negotiation, P1 repeatedly reacts to P4's responses by uttering minimal feedback (RR1, RR2, RR3, RR4). He encourages P4 to continue and signals that the non-understanding in the process of being resolved. When P4 finally brings his explanation to a close and pauses afterwards in line 29, P1 notices this transition relevance place and provides a more explicit reaction. By saying *i understand* he leaves no doubt about the fact that P4 has just provided the information he, P1, wanted to obtain. He openly signals understanding and accordingly concludes the negotiation sequence, which is acknowledged through silence by the other participants. There is a four-second gap before the conversation continues on a different topic.

The last negotiation sequence that is presented in this section is the longest and most complex negotiation of meaning found in the data. It features a number of different indicating procedures and non-understandings, all of which occur in the course of what could be described as a 'fragile' activity, namely a discussion concerning matters of copyright law, an activity which certainly would seem to require the highest degree of clarity and shared understanding. Example 26 contains the entire negotiation sequence, which lasts about one and a half minutes.

Example 26 (B.12)

1	P4:	the only (.) the only thing here i mean it's a very nice display but	
2		(.) i'm not sure what the licenser of hello kitty (.)	T
3	P5:	UH	
4	P4:	@@ will tell US (.) or	...T
5	P1:	licency?	I(1)
6	P4:	the <1> lice- </1>	R1a
7	P5:	<1> lic</1>enser	R2b
8	P4:	the licenser of hello kitty because i think that the hello kitty	
9		dispenser	...R1a/T
10	P2:	hm	
11	P4:	THERE and i'm not (.) i'm SURE that this is not approved by	...T
12	P2:	oh	
13	P4:	by what- <STRESS> (COMPANY42) </STRESS>	...T
14	P5:	<2> (COMPANY42) </2>	
15	P2:	<2> mm </2>	
16	P4:	(COMPANY42) <3> and if </3> there is like SIMPSONS (.)	
17		<4> on a </4> <STRESS> (COMPANY42) </STRESS> ah:m	...T
18	P2:	<3> mm </3> <4> <SOFT> mhm </SOFT> </4>	
19	P2:	mm	
20	P1:	<5> ah </5>	
21	P4:	<5> HEADER </5> card,	...T
22	P1:	that means (1) hello kitty should (.) a- always (1) ah: display	
23		with a (.) hello <6> kitty </6> only (.)	I(2)
24	P4:	<6> <L1=GERMAN> *nein* </L1=GERMAN> <TRANSL=no> u-	
25		</6>	R1a
26	P4:	<L1=GERMAN> *nein* </L1=GERMAN> <TRANSL=no> <7>	
27		usually </7>	R2a
28	P1:	<7> display </7> rack?	...I(2)
29	P4:	usually EVERY material <8> needs </8> to be APPROVED by	
30		the licenser.	...R2a
31	P1:	<8> aha </8>	RR1a
32	P2:	right	RR2b
33	P4:	so EVERY	R3a
34	P2:	yeah (.)	RR3b
35	P4:	every logo <9> layout </9> needs to be APPROVED.	...R3a
36	P5:	<9> <SOFT> (layout) </SOFT> </9>	R4b
37	P2:	ah:	RR4b
38	P4:	if you don't have the APPROVAL for that, and somebody from	
39		(COMPANY42) <1> goes into </1> a (COMPANY32) (.) and	
40		<2> sees that </2> their ehm dis- (.)	R5a
41	P2:	<1> ah: </1> <2> ah: </2>	RR5b+6b
42	P4:	that there is ah	...R5a
43	P1:	but (.) <3> ours </3> doesn't have a (COMPANY42) eh: the the	
44		<4> kitty </4> (.) picture	I(3)
45	P4:	<3> simpsons </3>	...R5a
46	P2:	<4> mm </4>	
47	P4:	YEAH it has the (.) kitty DISPENSER in the hand (1)	R/T

48	P1:	where (.) which one (.)	RR/I(4)
49	P5:	eh the	R1a
50	PX-3:	<SOFT> yeah the <5> clown </5> </SOFT>	R2b
51	P5:	<5> peter, </5>	R3a
52	P4:	the clown (.) <6> this one </6> is a (.) is a hello <7> kitty	
53		dispens</7>er	R4c
54	P5:	<6> (it's a) kitty </6> <7> dispenser </7>	R5a
55	P1:	AH:	RR1a
56	P2:	oh:	RR2b
57	P5:	the	R6a
58	P1:	you mean the (.) the clo:wn	RR3a/I(5)
59	P4:	i mean it's very nice but IF (COMPANY42) sees that (.) @	R1a
60	P1:	<8> oh: </8>	RR1a
61	P2:	<8> oh: </8>	RR2b
62	P5:	<8> <@> ah </@> </8> @	R2b
63	P4:	we <9>are in trou<1>ble </1> </9>	...R1a
64	P1:	<9> ah: </9>	RR3a
65	P2:	<9> ah: </9>	RR4b
66	P5:	<1> (would) </1> (n't) <2> like </2> it @@ <3> @ </3>	R3b
67	P1:	<2> okay </2>	RR5a
68	P2:	<3> mm </3>	RR6a
69	P5:	ah	R4b
70	P1:	i (.) i know what you mean	RR7a

Before the various instances of miscommunication are analyzed in detail, it appears necessary to sketch the overall structure of the sequence, because it exhibits loop character[48].

There are five different indicators, which are marked in example 26 (lines 5; 22-23, 28; 43-44; 48; 58). I(1) does not entail a longer negotiation, but is resolved rather quickly. Yet, its resolution entails a rather long contribution by P4 – interspersed with minimal feedback by P2 – which in turn comes to trigger the next indicator. The hypothesis uttered in I(2) is then opposed by P4 and brings forth another explanatory phase (lines 29-42). At some point, P1 intervenes and utters I(3), another hypothesis. This indicator only entails one response, which at the same time turns out to be another trigger and leads to the next indiating procedure I(4). This rather explicit indicator provokes a number of responses from P4, P3 and P5. These responses are briefly acknowledged by P1 and P2, before they are reacted to by the last indiator of the sequence I(5). A last main response of P4 leads to a number of interjections with which P1 and P2 seem to signal understanding, before P1

---

[48] Cf. Gass and Varonis's (1999) model of NNS miscommunication which is presented in section 3.5.2.

closes the negotiation cycle by stating explicitly that the understanding problems have been cleared up.

Since each of these indicating procedures and the understanding problems they refer to represent different cases, the whole negotiation sequence will be devided into the individual negotiations of meaning, which will then be analyzed in their own terms and in relation to each other. The first and also shortest local non-understanding of the sequence is presented in example 27.

Example 27 (B.12)

```
1   P4:   the only (.) the only thing here i mean it's a very nice display but
2         (.) i'm not sure what the licenser of hello kitty (.)              T
3   P5:   UH
4   P4:   @@ will tell US (.) or                                           ...T
5   P1:   licency?                                                          I(1)
6   P4:   the <l> lice- </l>                                                R1a
7   P5:   <l> lic</l>enser                                                  R2b
8   P4:   the licenser of hello kitty because i think that the hello kitty
9         dispenser                                                      ...R1a/T
```

Considered in isolation of the rest of the negotiation that is to follow, example 27 exhibits a rather straightforward and basic instance of non-understanding. The explicit indicating procedure, namely 'reprise of the non-understood part of the utterance' that P1 uses in I(1) is rather specific and points quite clearly to the portion of the trigger that is responsible of the non-understanding, namely the word *licenser*. Consequently, P4 and also his colleague P5, who has obviously understood P4's contribution, provide very specific responses in lines 6 and 7. Although it is mainly P4 who is in charge of the conversation at this point and who responds to the indicator first (line 6), he is supported by P5, who has also picked up the indication of the non-understanding, but just happens to utter her response (R2b) a split second after P4. The fact that both participants choose the same strategy, i.e. a repetition of the reprised word, stresses the specificity and effectiveness of P1's indicator.

Although there is no doubt about the non-understanding being triggered by the lexical item *licenser*, determining the reasons why the term turns out to be problematic is not as easy. Two interpretations appear plausible in this respect. On the one hand, it is possible to assume that the non-understanding was caused by a perceptual problem, i.e. by a mishearing of the word *licenser*. Yet, as P4's pronunciation of the term is neither conspicuous in any way nor disturbed by any noise or simultaneous talk, the conversation exhibits no observable features that suggest a perceptual problem. On the other hand, the non-understanding could also be lexical in origin, i.e. P1's indicator could point towards a problem with the meaning of the term. One reason why the causes are especially difficult to pinpoint with regard to this non-understanding is that P4 and P5's responses are not audibly reacted to by P1, i.e. we are looking at a shortened structure devoid of an RR. Therefore, one cannot be sure if the non-understanding is completely resolved at this point. Yet, it appears that, even if the understanding problem is not sorted out at this point, it is not of major gravity, because it does not cause any further negotiation of meaning in the rest of the conversation and it is not addressed again.

If one looks at the way the conversation continues in example 28, P4 appears to be very much in flow of speech. As P1 does not immediately utter a reaction to the previous clarification (line 6-7), P4 simply elaborates on the issue he has started to discuss in the first trigger (lines 1 and 2). It is noteworthy that during the ensuing stretch of the conversation (lines 8 to 19) it is not P1 who provides minimal feedback in lines 10, 12, 15 and 19, but his usually more reserved colleague P2.

Example 28 (B.12)

8	P4:	the licenser of hello kitty because i think that the hello kitty
9		dispenser ...R1*a*/T
10	P2:	hm
11	P4:	THERE and i'm not (.) i'm SURE that this is not approved by ...T
12	P2:	oh
13	P4:	by what- <STRESS> (COMPANY42) </STRESS> ...T
14	P5:	<2> (COMPANY42) </2>
15	P2:	<2> mm </2>
16	P4:	(COMPANY42) <3> and if </3> there is like SIMPSONS (.)
17		<4> on a </4> <STRESS> (COMPANY42) </STRESS> ah:m ...T
18	P2:	<3> mm </3> <4> <SOFT> mhm </SOFT> </4>
19	P2:	mm
20	P1:	<5> ah </5>
21	P4:	<5> HEADER </5> card, ...T
22	P1:	that means (1) hello kitty should (.) a- always (1) ah: display
23		with a (.) hello <6> kitty </6> only (.) I(2)
24	P4:	<6> <L1=GERMAN> nein </L1=GERMAN> <TRANSL=no> u-
25		</6> R1*a*
26	P4:	<L1=GERMAN> nein </L1=GERMAN> <TRANSL=no> <7>
27		usually </7> R2*a*
28	P1:	<7> display </7> rack? ...I(2)

While P2 utters minimal feedback, P1 adopts a 'wait and see' strategy (Voionmaa 1984 referred to in Vasseur, Broeder & Roberts 1996: 78) during this phase and leans back to observe rather than participating. On the one hand, this behavior could be labeled a 'let it pass' strategy (Firth 1996), in which case it would be symptomatic of a non-understanding. On the other hand, P4 never really pauses or invites the other speakers to participate, i.e. there is no transition relevance place between lines 8 and 21, so that P1's lack of feedback cannot completely be equated with a 'lack of uptake' (Vasseur, Broeder & Roberts 1996: 78). In this respect, P1's temporal non-participation might not be due to a non-understanding. From the analyst's position as an outside observer it is impossible to decide which of these two scenarios actually comes closer to 'the truth'.

In line 20, P1 finally breaks P4's flow of speech. By uttering the filler *ah*, P1 indicates his wish to speak and tries to gain the floor, despite the absence of a transition relevance place. As P4 completes his thought in line 21, P1 immediately takes the floor and voices I(2)[49]. What P1 utters is a reformulation and summary of P4's preceding utterances marked with T and ...T, i.e. an intermediate indicating procedure. Although his hypothesis is syntactically not structured like a question, it is nevertheless clearly spoken with interrogatory intonation, which suggests that P1 consciously produces it as a hypothesis and therefore indicates a non-understanding[50].

Judging from the nature of the indicator, the non-understanding seems to be related to the whole of P4's flow of speech between lines 8 and 21 and not just part of it. Using Bremer's (1996: 50) term, the potential cause of the non-understanding could be called a 'complex utterance' in this case. According to her, complex utterances are

> not only long and syntactically (more or less) complex, but also spoken fast and/or slurred, and accompanied by restarts, self-repair or accumulative use of particles (Bremer 1996: 50.).

These characteristics seem to describe P4's trigger utterances fairly well. In addition, the interpretation of a complex utterance as potential cause also ties in with P4's responses after line 28 (see example 29).

When P1 formulates his hypothesis I(2), P4 utters his first small exclamatory responses, R1a and R2a, even before P1 has time to complete his utterance. Looking at these responses, we see that P4 first of all feels the need to contradict P1's reformulation of his own statements. As P4 then sets out to provide an explanation as to why P1's hypothesis

---

[49] The fact that P1's next contribution to the conversation is an indicator points towards the possibility that the non-understanding might have lingered already during P1's period of silence.
[50] Cf. the remark about the difficulty of distinguishing between participants' awareness and unawareness, i.e. between non-understanding and misunderstanding, in section 3.4.

actually features a wrong assumption in line 29, he does so in a way that is much more structured than the trigger utterances:

Example 29 (B.12)

29	P4:	usually EVERY material <8> needs </8> to be APPROVED by	
30		the licenser.	...R2a
31	P1:	<8> aha </8>	RR1a
32	P2:	right	RR2b
33	P4:	so EVERY	R3a
34	P2:	yeah (.)	RR3b
35	P4:	every logo <9> layout </9> needs to be APPROVED.	...R3a
36	P5:	<9> <SOFT> (layout) </SOFT> </9>	R4b
37	P2:	ah:	RR4b
38	P4:	if you don't have the APPROVAL for that, and somebody from	
39		(COMPANY42) <1> goes into </1> a (COMPANY32) (.) and	
40		<2> sees that </2> their ehm dis- (.)	R5a
41	P2:	<1> ah: </1> <2> ah: </2>	RR5b+6b
42	P4:	that there is ah	...R5a

In providing these responses, P4 seems to account for his unstructured and slightly confusing flow of speech between lines 8 and 21 that triggered the non-understanding in example 28. P4's responses also encourage the causal interpretation of a 'complex utterance'.

What is noticeable is that P1's reactions are again very limited between lines 31 and 42. The only reaction he renders (RR1a) occurs at the very beginning of P4's explanation in line 31. After that, it is again only P2 who utters minimal feedback in lines 32, 34, 37 and 41, whereas P1 is silent and adopts a 'wait and see' strategy until his next contribution in lines 43 and 44:

Example 30 (B.12)

38	P4:	if you don't have the APPROVAL for that, and somebody from	
39		(COMPANY42) <1> goes into </1> a (COMPANY32) (.) and	
40		<2> sees that </2> their ehm dis- (.)	R5a/T
41	P2:	<1> ah: </1> <2> ah: </2>	RR5b+6b
42	P4:	that there is ah	...R5a/T
43	P1:	but (.) <3> ours </3> doesn't have a (COMPANY42) eh: the the	
44		<4> kitty </4> (.) picture	I(3)
45	P4:	<3> simpsons </3>	...R5a
46	P2:	<4> mm </4>	
47	P4:	YEAH it has the (.) kitty DISPENSER in the hand (1)	R/T
48	P1:	where (.) which one (.)	RR/I(4)

104

This utterance turns out to be another indicator – I(3) – as P1 appears to be forming another hypothesis. This hypothesis, however, is clearly opposed by P4 in line 47 (R) and therefore turns out to be a wrong hypothesis. Nevertheless, one gets the impression that P1 is rather convinced of his interpretation in lines 43 and 44, especially since he immediately challenges P4's response (R) with another indicator I(4) in line 48. As a consequence, it would seem that I(3) is not necessarily a consciously produced hypothesis and an intermediate indicating procedure pointing towards a non-understanding, but that it could very well be the result of a 'misunderstanding', i.e. a mismatch in meaning that P1 is unaware of at the time.

As has been outlined by Bremer (1996: 41) the distinction between 'non-understanding' and 'misunderstanding' is not always a categorical one. This is the case because it may be very

> difficult to assess from outside just how aware someone is about the uncertainty of his/her hypothesis. And it would exactly be this kind of awareness that decides whether a failed interpretation was a – well-concealed – lack of understanding or a real misunderstanding. (Bremer 1996: 41)

This is precisely the scenario that we are confronted with in example 30. Examining the data, I would contend that I(3) is indeed indicative of a misunderstanding – and not a non-understanding – but, being put forward from the position of an outside observer, my contention cannot be completely verified.

Besides being a fuzzy example of a 'local misunderstanding', this instance of miscommunication is very interesting concerning its potential causes and triggers. Although I have marked P4's response R5a as trigger in lines 38, 39, 40 and 42, the primary cause for the misunderstanding is the picture of a display rack that the participants are looking at. When P1 says *ours doesn't have [...] the kitty picture* he is referring to the display rack, i.e. the picture of the display rack, that his company built and that they are showing to their hosts, (COMPANY2)'s employees. This phenomenon has been observed by Bazzanella and Damiano (1999: 829), who remark that "[g]estures, behaviour, objects, situations can act as non-linguistic triggers" and can cause misunderstandings which nevertheless subsequently "undergo a linguistic handling" (ibid.: 829). In other words, "a non-linguistic misunderstanding can be detected or made explicit and negotiated on a linguistic level" (ibid.: 829) and this seems to be precisely what happens in example 30.

P4's attempt at clearing up the misunderstanding by opposing P1's assumption in line 47 is not immediately successful and triggers another indicating procedure – I(4) – on the part of P1. What P4's response yet clearly achieves is an obvious shift in P1's awareness. As P1's hypothesis is openly opposed, he cannot help but become aware of there being an instance of miscommunication. Thereby the communicative situation changes and the 'misunderstanding' – due to the new level of awareness – turns into a 'non-understanding'. It appears to be precisely this shift in awareness which puts the participants on the right track for eventually resolving the miscommunication.

The explicit indicating procedure I(4) which P1 employs in line 48 is a metalinguistic question, to be more precise a succession of two metalinguistic questions[51] referring to two different triggers. The first query *where* points to the non-linguistic trigger, i.e. the picture of the display rack, and therefore indicates that the understanding problem is to a considerable part caused by this item. P1 does not seem to share P4's understanding of why the display rack might not be approved by the licensers, i.e. which visual feature(s) might pose problems concerning copyright laws. By uttering the first minimal question, P1 not only refers to the picture but simulteaneously reacts to P4's preceding utterance (R/T) and explicitly asks *where* on the display rack there is a *kitty picture* (line 44), i.e. a *kitty DISPENSER* (line 47).

P1's second metalinguistic question, *which one*, which he utters just after a short pause, is more specific than his first *where* and clearly refers to the preceding trigger utterance. To be precise, the formulation *which one* obviously relates back to the subject of R/T, namely the pronoun *it*, and requests the specification of the referent of the pronoun. Although it is clear that, in using *it*, P4 refers to some item on the picture, i.e. on the display rack, the exact visual referent of the pronoun is never mentioned in the preceding discourse, which means that there is no linguistic referent for P4's anaphoric *it*.

Example 31 (B.12)

```
47   P4:     YEAH it has the (.) kitty DISPENSER in the hand (1)        R/T
48   P1:     where (.) which one (.)                                    RR/I(4)
49   P5:     eh the                                                     R1a
50   PX-3:   <SOFT> yeah the <5> clown </5> </SOFT>                     R2b
51   P5:     <5> peter, </5>                                            R3a
52   P4:     the clown (.) <6> this one </6> is a (.) is a hello <7> kitty
53           dispens</7>er                                              R4c
```

---

[51] Cf. Vasseur, Broeder and Roberts (1996: 88-89).

54	P5:	<6> (it's a) kitty </6> <7> dispenser </7>	*R5a*
55	P1:	AH:	*RR1a*
56	P2:	oh:	*RR2b*
57	P5:	the	*R6a*
58	P1:	you mean the (.) the clo:wn	*RR3a/I(5)*

Therefore the non-understanding in example 31 appears to be due to a combination of non-linguistic and linguistic means. Linguistically, the primary cause would seem to be a missing referent, i.e. the 'elliptical utterance' (R/T): Since P4's fails to provide a full noun phrase for the subject and only uses the pronominal reference *it*, his utterance does not contain all the information that is necessary for it to be understood and therefore would be called elliptical.

The linguistic responses that follow P1's explicit indicator I(4) exactly tie in with this interpretation. The strategy that P3, P4 and P5 all choose is a linguistic indentification of the non-linguistic referent on the display rack. It is remarkable that, at this point of the conversation, all three participants of (COMPANY2) contribute to the negotiation of meaning, which leads to an accumulation of responses between lines 49 and 54. All three of them specify that *it* is *the clown* (lines 50, 52), namely *peter* (line 51), who is holding *a hello kitty dispenser* on the picture of the display rack. These responses finally seem to steer the negotiation sequence towards its resolution, as suggested by P1's exclamation in line 55. Similar to Vasseur, Broeder and Roberts's (1996: 88) proposition and similar to the observation made with regard to example 23, it is the explicit indication of the non-understanding via metalinguistic questions that eventually proves effective in achieving better understanding.

Probably due to the length of the preceding negotiation sequence and the several understanding problems that occur within it, P1 feels the need to make sure that understanding has finally been achieved. In this respect, one should bear in mind the already mentioned need for clarity and preciseness that tends to be an important characteristic of business meetings. Furthermore, as been pointed out with regard to the whole sequence in example 28, we are looking at a 'fragile' activity concerned with legal matters which certainly do not allow for ambiguity. Therefore, it is not surprising that P1 utters a final indicating procedure – I(5) – in line 58. At this point, the negotiated instances of miscommunication appear to be almost resolved. Consequently, the remains of the non-understanding which are indicated here are only of minor gravity.

I(5) is a combination of two indicating procedures, namely of an explicit metalinguistic comment and an intermediate reprise. P1 takes up the word *clown*, i.e. the referent P3 and P4 have identified in their responses in lines 50 and 52, and combines it with the metalinguistic comprehension check *you mean*. Since P1 is able to produce such an effective and precise indicator and since he has in fact understood the others' contributions correctly, the remaining non-understanding seems to be only of a minor degree. It is probably triggered by the accumulation of responses between lines 49 and 54. Besides being spoken by three different participants, i.e. P3, P4, and P5, the responses are voiced in quick succession and include several instances of simultaneous speech, which renders their perception rather difficult.

In the final resolution, P4 does not even explicitly respond to P1's indicator, but in contrast to I(2) and I(3) he does not object to it. Through his non-contradiction, P4 accepts P1's proposition and, instead of directly commenting on it, chooses to carry on the discussion of the copyright/license issue in lines 59 and 63:

Example 32 (B.12)

58	P1:	you mean the (.) the clo:wn	*RR3a/I(5)*
59	P4:	i mean it's very nice but IF (COMPANY42) sees that (.) @	*R1a*
60	P1:	<8> oh: </8>	*RR1a*
61	P2:	<8> oh: </8>	*RR2b*
62	P5:	<8> <@> ah </@> </8> @	*R2b*
63	P4:	we <9>are in trou<1>ble </1> </9>	*...R1a*
64	P1:	<9> ah: </9>	*RR3a*
65	P2:	<9> ah: </9>	*RR4b*
66	P5:	<1> (would) </1> (n't) <2> like </2> it @ @ <3> @ </3>	*R3b*
67	P1:	<2> okay </2>	*RR5a*
68	P2:	<3> mm </3>	*RR6b*
69	P5:	ah	*R4b*
70	P1:	i (.) i know what you mean	*RR7a*

P4's response gives rise to a number of exclamatory reactions (RR1a, RR2b, RR3a, RR4b) and some acknowledging feedback (RR5a, RR6b) by P1 and P2 and is supported by P5 with a short explanatory comment (R3b), which however is drowned in overlaps. Although P1 and P2's exclamations and acknowledgements already indicate shared understanding and the resolution of the non-understanding, P1 nevertheless opts to explicitly state this understanding in line 70. By saying *i know what you mean*, he finally brings the issue to a close. The non-understandings and the temporary misunderstanding have been clarified through the repeated and adaptive use of various indicating procedures, joint negotiation and visible involvement of all participants.

5.3 Local misunderstanding and the negotiation of meaning

As opposed to 'non-understanding' discussed so far, a 'misunderstanding' is an understanding problem that no participant is aware of at the time it occurs and will be explored next. Occasionally a 'misunderstanding' may also become subject to a negotiation of meaning. Due to the potential covertness of miscommunication and due to the fact that misunderstandings are usually only brought to the surface by chance, e.g. an incoherent utterance based on a 'wrong' interpretation, it is impossible to determine how many instances of misunderstanding occur within a conversation and how many of them actually surface[52]. The following example features an instance of misunderstanding that can be called 'local', because it comes to the surface immediately after it occurs, i.e. after the utterance that triggers it. It is instantly negotiated in very much the same way as a local non-understanding, although the indicator is not consciously produced this time.

What I have marked as indicator in lines 6 and 7 in example 33 is intended by P1 as an answer to P4's question in line 5. Within Vasseur, Broeder and Roberts's (1996) continuum of indicating procedures this contribution would be labeled a 'tentative response'. What is conspicuous about this particular indicating procedure is that it only uncovers an instance of miscommunication if the resulting utterance is incohesive (Vasseur, Broeder & Roberts 1996: 83). Such incohesive utterances are then

> interpreted as symptoms of non- or misunderstanding. In this way, a tentative response may implicitly convey misunderstanding, that is to say an illusion of understanding. (Vasseur, Broeder & Roberts 1996: 83)

So even though indicating procedures are usually conceived as "procedures for indicating non-understanding" (ibid.: 73), some of them may occasionally be linked to a misunderstanding, i.e. "an illusion of understanding" (ibid.: 83), and this is precisely what happens in example 33.

Example 33 (B.11)

```
1   P1:    so action (.) o- eh DONE is a KEY ACCOUNT management
2          program we asked eh (NAME3) (.) to set up eh: some program
```

---

[52] Cf. Section 3.4.

3		(.) with imp- (.) the the important ah (.) key ACCOUNT (.) to	
4		develop some ANNUAL program (.) for ou-	
5	P4:	what is an annual program? (.)	*T=Qu.*
6	P1:	it's a YEARLY (.) based (.) <1> <SOFT> (program) </SOFT>	
7		</1>	*I*
8	P4:	<1> <L1=GERMAN> *ja ja* </L1=GERMAN> <TRANSL=yes	
9		yes> </1> i mean in regards of <2> assortment </2> in regards	
10		of placement or in regards of eh:m activities? (.)	*R1*
11	P1:	<2> (xx) </2>	
12	P4:	or in regards of PRICE off promotions or (1)	*...R1*
13	P1:	<to P2> <L1=KOREAN> *(xxxxx)* </L1=KOREAN>	
14	P2:	<to P1> <L1=KOREAN> *(xxxx)* </L1=KOREAN> (.) <to P4>	
15		ehm mainly the: ACTIVITY (.)	*RR1a*
16	P1:	promotion ac<3>tivity </3>	*RR2b*
17	P2:	<3>promotion </3> (activities) <4> yeah </4>	*RR3a*
18	P4:	<3> like </3> <4> TAS</4>TINGS or	*R2*
19	P2:	yes (.) like eh tasting but the: (.) the most im- important thing is	
20		the display. (.)	*RR4a*
21	P4:	mhm	*R3*

When P4 listens to P1's tentative response (line 6), he notices very quickly that the answer P1 provides is not at all the one he, P4, wanted to get. As soon as he recognizes this, P4 does not wait to hear out P1, but interrupts him via simulateous speech and provides a supplementary explanation (lines 8-10) to his orginal question. Since P4 starts this explanation with the metalinguistic expression *i mean*, he makes explicit that P1 has not reacted to T=Qu. the way P1 had expected him to, i.e. that a misunderstanding exists between the two speakers.

Through high involvement and considerable re-elaboration of his own question in lines 8 to 10, P4 effectively initiates a negotiation sequence. Since the understanding problem is a misunderstanding and P1 is unaware of its existence until P4 makes this explicit, P1 does not immediately react to P1's re-elaboration, but first converses with his colleague P2 in their first language Korean[53]. In line 15, it is P2 who first reacts to P1's re-elaboration and provides an answer to his question. The negotiation of meaning is then also joined by P1 (RR2b) and again continued by P2 (RR3a), before P4 utters another re-elaboration in line 18. P2's final contribution (lines 19-20) eventually seems to provide P4

---

[53] In a way, P1's short conversation with P2 in Korean is of course a reaction to P4's re-elaboration. It is, however, not addressed to P4. It is not even intelligible for P4, because it takes place in Korean. Therefore, this short exchange in Korean is considered a part of the negotiation of meaning which is conducted in English.

with the information that he intended to get in the first place and the negotiation sequence ends.

After having outlined the structural and interactional development of the negotiation phase, one can now look for the potential causes of the misunderstanding. If one examines the trigger question and P1's 'wrong' interpretation, one notices that P1's answer in fact is an explanation of the term 'annual program': *it's a YEARLY based program*. So the misunderstanding seems to stem from the fact that P1 interprets P4's trigger question as a metalinguistic question, i.e. as a signal of non-understanding, while it is actually intended as a request for information. In other words, the misunderstanding occurs because the question in line 6 looks like an indicator of a local non-understanding.

If one wants to go deeper in search of the roots of this striking concurrence of seeming non-understanding and local misunderstanding, the syntactic form of the trigger question certainly calls for further analysis. Although P1 talks about the development of *some ANNUAL program* in lines 3 and 4, P4 asks the general and rather unspecific question *what is an annual program?* in line 5. P4 employs the indefinite article *an*, instead of e.g. a deictic 'this', and therefore he does not state explicitly that he is referring to the particular annual program P1 has just mentioned. Furthermore, the interrogatory structure *what is* might also be considered imprecise, considering that P4 wants to know – as becomes clear throughout the negotiation sequence – what activities the Korean company's annual program comprises.

The analysis of this local misunderstanding clearly examplifies that "we are not always justified in saying simply that [one participant] misunderstands" (Linell 1995: 180-181). Although speakers tend to be given a "status of interpretive authority" (ibid.: 180) with regard their own utterances, they "may be mistaken in [their] choice of words" (ibid.: 180) for describing what they mean, as example 33 shows. This clearly stresses the need for adopting a non-judgmental attitude towards miscommunication, i.e. an attitude which refrains from blaming individual participants for the occurrence of miscommunication and misunderstandings, especially so when it comes to analyzing ELF interactions[54].

---

[54] Cf. Section 3.3.

5.4 Self-initiated negotiation of meaning as a means of preventing miscommunication

It has become obvious that negotiation sequences are neither always initiated through a consciously produced indicating procedure nor are they limited to non-understandings. A negotiation of meaning may, for example, be initiated through a 'wrong' hypothesis and lead to the resolution of a misunderstanding. The two examples in the current section represent another scenario, namely instances where the negotiation of meaning, i.e. the resolution via a response, is started preemptively by one participant in order to prevent the emergence of a (potentially more serious) understanding problem.

Example 34 exhibits such a negotiation sequence, although P1's trigger utterance in lines 63 and 64 is not explicitly followed by an indication procedure. At first, P4 acknowledges the trigger through minimal feedback in line 65, which, however, is still uttered during an overlap, i.e. before P1 has even concluded his sentence. After having heard the whole trigger, P4 produces another reaction, namely a surprised *REALLY?* in line 67 and it is this contribution that prompts P1 to utter a re-elaboration in line 68.

Example 34 (B.3)

60	P1:	a:s time goes by we added eh: some famous brands like (1)
61		\<STRESS\> (COMPANY4) \</STRESS\> (.)
62	P4:	\<SOFT\> mhm, \</SOFT\> (.) which you still have. (.)
63	P1:	which is eh a- at the moment the BIGGEST (1) \<4\> revenue
64		\</4\> contributor. (.) T
65	P4:	\<4\> mhm \</4\>
66	P1:	\<SOFT\> okay, \</SOFT\> (1)
67	P4:	REALLY? (.) (I)
68	P1:	y:eah this yea:r (.) i mean REVENUE not the (.) bottom line R
69	P4:	okay @@ \<5\> @@@ \</5\> \<@\> that's what i thought because
70		oth- \</@\> (.) \<6\> (xxx) \</6\> (x) (.) RR
71	P3:	\<5\> @@@ \</5\>
72	P1:	\<5\> (this ye)a:r \</5\> \<6\> this year \</6\>

P4's *REALLY?* is not precisely an indicating procedure in Vasseur, Broeder and Roberts's (1996) terms. As a reaction it may or may not point towards a failed interpretation or a misunderstanding. Nevertheless, it sequentially fulfils the function of an indicator, i.e. it elicits a response and re-elaboration by P1.

It appears that P1 considers P4's surprised reaction somehow strange or misplaced at this point and thinks it possible that P4's surprise results from a misunderstanding. As a consequence, P1 decides to ensure understanding by re-elaborating part of his own trigger utterance, when he says *REVENUE not the bottom line* in line 68. Furthermore, he introduces his explanation by the metalinguistic comment *i mean* and thereby sets it off against the preceding conversation. What is remarkable, however, is that, in uttering this response, P1 does not alter, but on the contrary re-affirms his lexical choice from line 63, where he has already used the term *revenue*. By adding the explanatory phrase *not the bottom line*, P1 chooses to make clear what he means with the term *revenue* through making explicit what he does not mean.

P4 reacts to P1's explanation with an acknowledging *okay* and laughter, which seems to encourage the assumption that P4's reaction in line 67 was indeed the result of a misunderstanding and that P4 now laughs about his own mis-interpretation. Then P4 continues by saying *that's what i thought*, which is spoken laughingly. The last portion of his reaction remains unintelligible because of simultaneous speech. The remark *that's what i thought*, however, is conspicuous, because it allows for two conflicting interpretations: if one takes the utterance literally, P4 states that understanding was shared throughout the whole sequence, which, however, does not account for his surprise in line 67 and his laughter in line 69; if one adopts a more figurative position, the remark could also mean something like 'I thought there was something wrong with my interpretation of your utterance'. In other words, P4's remark could be interpreted as both, evidence of the existence of an understanding problem and evidence of the absence of an understanding problem. Either way, at the time it is uttered, there no longer seems to be an understanding problem. In reacting to P4's 'non-indicator' (line 67), P1 has accounted for the possibility of a mis- or non-understanding and – if there ever was one – effectively prevented its continuation.

In example 35, we can observe a negotiation of meaning which is completely self-initiated, i.e. which is brought about by a comprehension check immediately ensuing the trigger within the same turn. Without any indication from the other participants, P1 reacts to his own utterance *they created some JARGON* and makes the word *JARGON* the subject of a metalinguistic comprehension check (line 5). When he asks P4 *do you know? the word JARGON?* and even proceeds to spell the term (lines 5-6), P1 self-initiates a negotiation of meaning and turns his own utterance of line 4 into a trigger.

Example 35 (B.15)

1	P1:	ah (1) actually this (.) presentation material (is) PREpared by (.)	
2		of course (NAME3) and ah (NAME5)	
3	P5:	<SOFT> mhm </SOFT>	
4	P1:	and they (3) created some (1) some ah (2) JARGON. <FAST>	T
5		do you know? </FAST> the word JARGON? (.) J-A-<@>R-	
6		</@>G-O-N? <1> jargon </1>	CC
7	P2:	<1> @ @ @ </1> @ @	
8	P4:	J?	R/I
9	P1:	J-A-R-(.) G-O-N (1) jargon	R1
10	P4:	<L1=GERMAN> ah ja (.) ja ja (.) ja ja </L1=GERMAN>	
11		<TRANSL=oh yes (.) yes yes (.) yes yes>	RR1
12	P1:	jargon (.)	R2
13	P4:	mhm	RR2

In opting for this strategy, P1 takes into account the possibility that his business partner P4 might not be familiar with the term *jargon*, although all participants are rather proficient in English.

After laughter on the part of P2, P4 reacts to P1's preceding utterance and utters a short indicator in line 8. The reprise of the letter *J?* accompanied by a rising intonation, however, clearly relates back to the spelling-portion of P1's turn and not to the word *jargon* as such. This indicator is most likely due to the fact that P4 is probably slightly surprised by P1's unexpected comprehension check and his spelling efforts. Furthermore, spelling is what Firth (1996: 248) has called a 'fragile' activity, which encourages the assumption that P4 is momentarily taken aback, not by the usage of the word *jargon* or the comprehension check, but by the sudden spelling activity. As a response to P4's indicator, P1 re-spells the word *jargon* in line 9 and after a short pause also repeats the term as a whole. This response prompts P4 to signal understanding in line 10. Although he does so in his first language German, the reaction is certainly emphatic enough to convey achieved understanding to P1. Yet, P1 decides to repeat the word *jargon* once again in line 12, to which P4 reacts with an acknowledgement token and the negotiation of meaning is brought to an end.

While some researchers might say that P1 creates a 'problem' where there is none – we will never know whether P4 would have understood the word *jargon* anyway – it is a central premise of this study not to regard the negotiation of meaning as problematic per se, but rather as a means essential to achieving, checking and maintaining understanding among ELF speakers. Negotiation sequences are not – as may be the point of view of some conventional conversation analysts – to be dimissed as unimportant 'side sequences' and deviations from the main, topic-related course of an interaction, if one is concerned with ELF discourse. Instead of regarding the negotiation of meaning and miscommunication in general as disturbing and unwanted phenomena, one should take notice of the striking interactional skills that participants very often exhibit at these occasions.

5.5 Non-understanding or strategic miscommunication?

While some researchers (e.g. Banks, Ge & Baker 1991; Weigand 1999) exclude strategic or intentional miscommunication a priori from an analysis of miscommunication, the position adopted in this paper is a different one. This is on the one hand due to the nature of the data analyzed, i.e business meetings in which participants may have opposite conversational goals, and on the other hand to the assumption that strategic miscommunication cannot always – if ever – be clearly distinguished from regular, i.e. unintentional, miscommunication[55]. In this section, three instances will be analyzed with regard to non-understanding and strategic miscommunication in order to outline the close proximity of those two phenomena in discourse.

In order to stress the fact that the appearance of a non-understanding and an instance of intentional miscommunication may be identical, the first example will be presented in two steps. If one considers example 36, it looks quite plainly like a basic negotiation of a local non-understanding:

Example 36 (A.1)

```
718   S2:                          very good because they want to
719          see HEY we are better than this (.) than this (.) OTHER
720          company. (1) <4> and ah: </4>
721   S1:   <FAST> <4> with whom are you </4> working now? </FAST>T=Qu.
722          (1)
723   S2:   again=ah: markus?                                              I
724   S1:   with WHOM? (.) <FAST> which trucking company <5> you're
725          working? </5> </FAST>                                         R
726   S2:   <5> i don't </5> i don't know. but i i'll let you know the name
727          of it.                                                        RR
```

A question (line 721) becomes a trigger, when it is followed by a short lack of uptake (line 722) and an indicating procedure (line 723). S2's explicit, yet unspecific minimal query

---

[55] For the theoretical foundation of this assumption see section 3.6

seems to point towards a general non-understanding of the trigger question. It is an invitation to S1, who is directly addressed, to repeat his question.

In his response, S1 diverges from a mere repetition and decides to 'chop up' his question into smaller syntactic bits. At first, S1 repeats the preposition and the interrogative pronoun of his initial question (*with WHOM?*), and then further clarifies the meaning of the interrogative pronoun by indicating its referent: *which trucking company*. At this point, S2 already starts to answer and therefore the non-understanding can be regarded as resolved, although S1 still adds the short phrase *you're working?* to his response. So a plausible interpretation would be that the referent of *whom* was unclear in the trigger question and once it is clarified, the non-understanding is resolved. An even more plausible interpretation, however, is to incorporate the overlap which occurs at the end of the pre-trigger turn (line 720) and the beginning of the trigger question (line 721). S2's perception of the beginning of the question, including its interrogative pronoun, is impaired by the fact that he is still talking himself. In addition, S1 utters his question quite quickly, which also suggests misperception as the cause for the non-understanding.

What seems to be a straightforward, easily negotiated and resolved non-understanding in example 36, however, suddenly appears in a new light if one considers it in relation to the context of the preceding discourse. Examining the whole sequence presented in example 37 opens up a whole new level of interpretation, namely the possibility of strategic miscommunication with regard to the supposed non-understanding between lines 721 and 724:

Example 37 (A.1)

```
694   S2:   okay. (.) i give you ALL the details marc, it's a- well i got a total
695         list. from- from dubai and we just (.) reNEWED the whole list.
696         (.) because we CHANGED ou:r (.) trucking (.) PARTNER
697         actually in dubai to a new one. and this: (.) this <8> one is very
698         good </8>
699   S3:   <8> (xxx) (are) you </8> working with?
700   S2:   oh i don't know, i forgot the name, (.)
701   S3:   <9> (COMPANY13)? </9>
702   S2:   <9> but before </9>
703         (2)
704   S2:   n=no.
705   S3:   no?
706   S2:   i don't believe so. (2) no. because WHY we changed it we had
707         some some problems (.) eh: something like (.) i don't know a
708         YEAR ago. and this trucking company, (.) when we BOOKED
```

709		something, (.) okay we ORDERED (.) i don't know (.) six seven	
710		eight trucks (.) and then they show up with only FOUR and the	
711		next day ANOTHER four that <1> eh well this </1> this is not	
712		working <2> properly </2> of course. (.)	
713	S1:	<1> hhhh </1> <2> mhm </2>	
714	S3:	but this is pretty normal in <@> dubai: </@> <SOFT> @ <3>	
715		@ @ </3> </SOFT>	
716	S2:	<3> ye:s </3> but (.) you know especially NOW because (.) we	
717		a:re (.) NOW with this new trucking company, (.) they want to	
718		perFORM them- (.) SELF (1) very good because they want to	
719		see HEY we are better than this (.) than this (.) OTHER	
720		company. (1) <4> and ah: </4>	
721	S1:	<FAST> <4> with whom are you </4> working now? </FAST>	
722		(1)	T=Qu.
723	S2:	again=ah: markus?	I
724	S1:	with WHOM? (.) <FAST> which trucking company <5> you're	
725		working? </5> </FAST>	R
726	S2:	<5> i don't </5> i don't know. but i i'll let you know the name	
727		of it.	RR

Reading through this extract, one notices that the topic of the alleged non-understanding was in fact discussed only very shortly before. The question-answer-sequence between lines 699 and 706 focusses on the same subject as the negotiation in example 36.

Therefore, it can, for once, be regarded as an instance of miscommunication that S1 poses a question to S2 (line 721) which S2 has just answered a few seconds earlier (line 700). A simple explanation for the occurrence of this miscommunication could be that S1's attention was flagging, while S2 and S3 were talking to each other and so S1 simply missed the first discussion of the topic between lines 699 and 706 and (by chance) poses the same question again. There is another possible explanation, however, which brings the issue of intentionality into play and leads us to consider the possibility of strategic miscommunication: S1 could have deliberately posed the same question to S2 again, because he was very well aware of the fact that S2 would not be able to answer it. Such a behavior would then converge precisely with House's definition of 'strategic misunderstandings' "which are deliberately used by speakers in order to gain an advantage over their interlocutor" (House 1999: 78). Yet, as the two alternative interpretations suggest, it is still open to question whether such strategic behavior and resulting miscommunication can actually be distinguished from regular, i.e. unintentional, miscommunication.

Re-analyzing the alleged non-understanding of lines 721 to 724 in the light of the question-answer-sequence in lines 699 to 706, a second instance of potential strategic miscommunication can be recognized. If one interprets S1's question in line 721 as an attempt to "gain an advantage" over S2 by forcing him to admit a second time that he does not know the name of their new trucking company in Dubai, which weakens his position in the meeting of course, it is possible to interpret S2's indicating procedure in line 723 as an attempt to mitigate the effect of S1's strategic question by delaying his own answer, an answer he is probably reluctant to provide (again), because it involves admitting his ignorance. Therefore, what, because of the use of an indicating procedure, appears to be an instance of non-understanding on a 'local' level in example 36 may as well be an instance of strategic miscommunication if it is put into the larger context of the conversation.

As example 37 shows, indicating procedures may sometimes point to instances of miscommunication where non-understanding and strategic miscommunication are both possible and legitimate interpretations. The same observation can also be made with regard to example 38:

Example 38 (A.1)

111	S1:	yeh? (.) what is your feeling where a:re is is (COMPANY1)	
112		(COMPANY1a) (.) posed together RANKING in eh: within	
113		(COMPANY5) europe?	*T*
114		(2)	*I(1)*
115	S2:	what, personally the feeling concerning that?	*I(2)*
116	S1:	yeah	*R*
117		(2)	*I(3)*
118	S2:	<1> oh: </1>	*RR/I(4)*
119	S1:	<1> sure we're not </1> eh not number one. <SOFT> this year	
120		</SOFT> (.) i would say: <SOFT> ah </SOFT> (1)	*R1*
121	S2:	actually to tell you really the true- well NOTICE of this	
122		FEELING ah personally i don't HAVE at the MOMENT	*RR*
123	S1:	hm	
124	S2:	<SOFT> (you) </SOFT> (kno:w) if you look (.) eh in working	
125		relationship which we have together with (COMPANY5) you	
126		know there is not (.) a lot of things to comPARE to see hey eh	
127		this will be <1> in </1> (imPORTANCE) or whatever (.) ...*RR*	
128	S1:	<1> yeah </1>	
129	S2:	so i cannot really say for me (.) <SOFT> eh: </SOFT> what is	
130		the difference ...*RR*	
131	S1:	mhm	
132	S2:	<FAST> i could say </FAST> PERSONALLY. that's my	*I(5)*
133		opinion. the: (1) now now in your internal picture, because you	
134		mentioned ah:m (.) in you:r email to me that some	
135		DIFFERENCE betwee:n some REGIONS? (.) maybe it's better	
136		to explain me FIRST what what what happened <1> in this </1>	
137		<2> scenario </2>	

118

At this point rather at the beginning of meeting A, the participants are talking about statistics which, as it is, have not yet been completed for the year 2003, a fact that has been talked about and therefore is already known to everybody.

Within this context, S1 then poses the question in lines 111 to 113 to S2. S2's subsequent turn (line 115) constitutes a combination of two indicating procedures, namely a direct, but unspecific minimal query (*what,*) and a fairly explicit, more specific 'reformulation as comprehension-check' (Vasseur, Broeder & Roberts 1996: 84): *personally the feeling concerning that?*. In addition, S2 does not provide this indicator immediately but only after a two-second-pause, which can be interpreted as 'lack-of-uptake' (ibid.: 78) and therefore as an implicit indicating procedure. After S1's response *yeah* in line 116, the negotiation of meaning still does not end. The response again is met with a lack-of-uptake in line 117 and when S2 and S1 then start speaking simultaneously (lines 118 and 119), S2 only provides the minimal feedback *oh:*. In line 121, S2 picks up the conversation again and explains, up until line 130, that he cannot answer S1's question because he does not have any feeling concerning the company's ranking. In lines 132 and 133, however, S2 contradicts his preceding explanation, when he states that he could give his personal opinion, which appears to be exactly what S1 wants him to do. The following *the:* (line 133) leads one to expect that S2 is now going to utter this opinion, but instead he interrupts himself and, after a short pause, simply changes the topic, a procedure similar to what Vasseur, Broeder and Roberts (1996: 77) call 'over-riding'.

Two possible interpretations present themselves. As Gass and Varonis indicate, it is possible for a speaker to "terminate the thread of the conversation" (Gass & Varonis 1991: 128) even though there is still what they call a "recognition of difficulty" (ibid.: 128), namely miscommunication. They also point out that this termination "may involve an abrupt topic shift" (ibid.: 128), which is what occurs after the pause in line 133. Therefore, it is a plausible interpretation to conclude that example 37 is a non-understanding which is not fully resolved, because S2 opts out of the negotiation sequence before understanding about the meaning of S1's question (lines 111 to 113) has been achieved and consequently – due to the still incomplete understanding – S2 does not provide an answer to S1's question.

Taking a different angle, however, example 37 can also be interpreted as 'strategic miscommunication'. From this perspective, S2's indicating procedures function to conceal his unwillingness to answer S1's – possibly tricky – question and allow him to avoid making this unwillingness explicit via an open refusal. After some further elaboration (lines 124-130) which is rather confusing in itself, S2 is able to change the topic without having answered S1's question and without appearing overtly rude or impolite. Assessing the participants' linguistic behavior from the analytical position of an outsider, both interpretations are possible within the framework of analysis.

A very similar example also occurs in meeting B, when the participants are going through the presentation material P1 has brought. They are discussing a table of last year's sales figures, when P4 asks the following question:

Example 39 (B.8)

1	P4:	but so far we had in all? (.) channels (.) INcreases right? (.)	T
2	P1:	eh:	I(1)
3	P4:	in total.	R
4		(4)	I(2)
5	P1:	so eh (1) we see some ah POTENTIALS in hypermarket and	
6		general trade. (.) okay? (.)	I(3)
7	P4:	yeah but those TWELVE per cent in C-V-S does that mean (.)	
8		<1> we </1> INCREASED (1)	R1a
9	P5:	<1> <SOFT> (twelve) </SOFT> </1>	R2b
10	P4:	twelve per cent in C-<2> V-S. </2>	...R1a
11	P1:	<2> no no </2> that's the eh	RR1a
12	P2:	general	RR2b
13	P4:	oh it's <3> general share </3>	R3a
14	P1:	<3> yeah general </3> business	RR3a
15	P4:	okay	R4a
16	P2:	hm	RR4b
17	P1:	again the major contribution- contributor. (1) in terms of (.) ah:	
18		value (.) ah: among our sales (.) OUTLETS (.) ARE (.) those	
19		two. so HYPERMARKET and general trade.	RR5a
20	P4:	mhm	R5a
21	P1:	with eh thirty-seven and (1) thirty-one per cent. (2)	...RR5a

In the sequence which succeeds P4's question (line 1) we can clearly observe an instance of miscommunication, which can again legitimately be interpreted as an instance of non-understanding as well as an instance of strategic miscommunication.

Following the non-strategic line of interpretation, we can say that P1's minimal feedback in line 2 is an implicit indicating procedure and hints at the possibility of a non-understanding, but is not enough evidence to make this clear. This possibility is reacted to by P4, when he provides the short remark *in total* to supplement his question in line 3. This attempt at clarifying his own question, however, seems to be unsuccessful because it is met with a noticeable lack-of-uptake in line 4. The fact that P1 makes a four-second pause before answering or reacting to P4's question marks an unmistakable cesura in the flow of conversation and suggests a non-understanding. When P1 finally starts to formulate an answer, he still hesitates and leaves another one-second pause at the beginning in line 5. After that P1 utters a 'tentative response', i.e. an intermediate indicating procedure. Since this response, however, does not answer P4's question, it appears to be based on a 'wrong hypothesis'.

P4 is obviously not satisfied with P1's answer (lines 5-6) and reacts to the tentative response by providing a specific example for his trigger question. He refers to a percentage in the presentation material and asks whether it stands for an increase (lines 7 and 8). In the ensuing negotiation, this issue is clarified: the percentage stands for *general share* and not for an increase. Relating back to P4's trigger question and to his own tentative response from lines 5 and 6, P1 then stresses the importance of the two channels *hypermarket and general trade* again, but he refrains from any statement concerning an increase or decrease in business.

If we remain in the non-strategic, unintentional line of interpretation, the non-understanding would seem to occur because P4's question (line 1) is uttered without an appropriate context, i.e. micro-context, in the interaction. Since the figures they are discussing have nothing to do with an increase or decrease of business, P1 is baffled with P4's trigger question, because there is no immediate context it can be related to. As a consequence, P1 does not know how to react and a non-understanding occurs. Once the general significance of the figures is clarified in lines 11 to 15, P1 simply continues to discuss the table by drawing attention to the two biggest channels (lines 17-19, 21).

There is nevertheless also an alternative interpretation which relates to the possibility of strategic behavior. Even if we assume that P4's question is uttered out of context, it seems that P1 should still be able to answer it with a simple 'yes' or 'no'. From the rest of meeting B, one can gather, however, that the year 2003 in Korea was a rather unsuccessful business year, during which sales were rather low. So if P1 were to answer P4's question directly, he would be forced to say 'no' – an answer which certainly casts an unfavorable light on the Korean company and which P1 is therefore probably reluctant to provide. In that way, P1's reply in lines 5 and 6 can also be interpreted as an attempt to avoid such an open negative answer by providing a positive formulation instead: *we see some*

POTENTIALS in hypermarket and general trade. In this case, the preceding symptoms of non-understanding in lines 2 and 4 would seem to mitigate the effect of this strategic manoeuvre. Again, also in this case, both interpretations – unintentional non-understanding and strategic miscommunication – appear legitimate.

5.6 Global misunderstanding: being in the wrong 'frame'

In this final section of analysis, one instance of miscommunication which happens on a more 'global' discourse level will be discussed. Unlike miscommunication "located at the linguistic surface" (Vasseur, Broeder & Roberts 1996: 73), which seems to be detected and indicated more frequently, "discursive-pragmatic problems" (ibid.: 73) are more difficult to identify for the participants. They are more likely to cause 'global' misunderstandings which the participants remain unaware of for a while and which only surface – if they do at all – after a considerable stretch of conversation. What we are looking at in example 40 is an instance in meeting A at which such a 'global misunderstanding' is noticed, commented on and therefore brought to the surface by S1:

Example 40 (A.2)

127	S1:	ehm we LIKE this (.) and eh it is the best way to do it, (.) ahm:
128		just make SURE (.) eh that eh: your OFFLINE stations, (.)
129	S2:	mhm (.)
130	S1:	are are doing the same, i mean (.) CLEAR you have a rate ex
131		amsterdam, and you have a rate ex frankfurt which should be
132		normally a <1> higher rate </1> (.)
133	S2:	<1> mhm </1>
134	S1:	and not a COMMON rate, (.) to amster<2>dam</2> which (.)
135	S2:	<2> mhm </2>
136	S1:	OFTEN happens with eh: eh: offline stations not only with
137		(COMPANY5) but (.) <3> (with a lot of companies,) </3>
138	S2:	<3> yeah yeah i know i know </3>
139	S1:	and also if you open your office in munich then, then=eh: for
140		(a) special QUOTATION, (.) you should offer ex amsterdam ex
141		munich (.) the same rate. (1)
142	S2:	yah. (.) <4> yah </4>
143	S1:	<4> and </4> this (.) you have to assure with the new system.
144		cuz otherwise exactly this game will <5> start. </5>
145	S2:	<5> oh. </5> markus, <6> i </6> give you a guarantee. this this
146		is (.)
147	S1:	<6> mhm </6>
148	S2:	this isn't DONE,
149	S1:	ah <FAST> wasn't <7> wasn't </7> meant as as a- THIS way

In line 149, S1 clearly notices that something has gone wrong in the way S2 has understood his preceding utterances and S1 signals this by saying *wasn't meant as as a- THIS way*. What makes him utter this explicit statement and also a quite elaborate clarification afterwards[56] obviously is S2's utterance of lines 145 and 146, giving S1 (*markus*) a *guarantee* that *this isn't DONE*.

From the point of view of pragmatics, example 40 would be a pragmatic failure similar – though not exactly – to what Thomas (1983: 99) has termed a 'pragmalinguistic failure' as the force S2 maps onto S1's utterance(s) is obviously not the one intended by S1. It seems, however, that such a pragmatic, speech act theory-based explanation is not far-reaching enough to account for the complexity that underlies this misunderstanding, a complexity that becomes particularly pronounced if one considers the development that precedes this final surfacing of the misunderstanding.

The approach that will be adopted with regard to analyzing this 'global misunderstanding' and its emergence in the discourse relies on Goffman's notions of 'frame' (Goffman 1975) and 'footing' (Goffman 1981a)[57]. What is proposed is that S1 and S2 do not 'share frames' at the time the misunderstanding in example 40 occurs and that this is the reason why the misunderstanding happens. In order to provide evidence for such an interpretation, the development of the 'misframing' that leads to S2's inappropriate reaction in lines 145 and 146 will be traced back in the discourse. In this way, I agree with Ribero and Hoyle when they note that

> [analysts] who apply the notion of framing to data share the assumption that looking at naturally occurring, connected discourse yields a fuller understanding than looking at isolated sentences or constructed texts (Ribero & Hoyle 2000: 8).

While this assumption about the importance of the 'micro-context' has also guided the preceding analyis of 'local' miscommunication and the negotiation of meaning, it gains even greater value with regard to 'global' misunderstanding and 'misframing'.

Any activity can be seen as organized into a main track and "ancillary tracks of various kinds" (Goffman 1975: 319) and 'misframings' can happen within any of these. So even though meeting A has the overall 'frame' of 'sales meeting', it is not surprising that S2 introduces – or rather, as he is not in a very powerful position, is given the opportunity to introduce – a new frame at the beginning of meeting A's second subsection (A.2):

---

[56] See extract A.2, lines 150 to 170, in the appendix.
[57] See section 3.7.1.

Example 41 (A.2)

```
5   S2:    <addressing S4> ARE there any general issues or eh (.) point of
6          vie:ws from (1) the company side. from from your side say (.)
7          concerning (COMPANY5). other things (.) like from eh: (.) i
8          don't know maybe ACCOUNTING issues eh: (1) overall
9          general issues. y- you maybe know something about? (1)
10         (COMPANY5) to to to come up from hey look THIS is maybe
11         a thing which we NEED to do better or (.) eh: <FAST> i don't
12         know </FAST> more SALES visits? or (.) just NAME it. (.)
13         you maybe have=a. (.) <1> IDEAS, thoughts </1>
```

With this turn, S2 intends to elicit some assessment of his company's – (COMPANY5)'s – performance and of its relations to the the forwarding agencies, (COMPANY1) and (COMPANY1a). To some extent, it seems that S2 expects negative feedback, which is indicated when he says *THIS is maybe a thing which we NEED to do better*. Therefore, the frame he introduces will henceforth be called 'defense frame'. As he is addressing S4 throughout the whole turn, it is S4 who responds to his invitation and mentions an incident that all participants seem to be familiar with, but which according to her account represents an exception. Her criticism is not harsh. She simply seems to comply to S2's invitation in example 41 by referring to this one problem[58].

To this, S2 responds by offering to find out more about the details of the incident – a mix-up of rates –, an offer which S4 did not ask for and which is indirectly declined in her reply (lines 50-51), which indicates that the details are not needed, because no other problem has occurred after this particular incident:

Example 42 (A.2)

```
50   S4:    (i) (xx) you took it over (of it) after that. (.) i didn't have any
51          problems actually because i had a ehm i had a
52   S1:    the problems <1> was never with (COMPANY5) side </1> (.)
53          <2> the well there was </2>
54   S4:    <1> a certain number </1> (.) <2> i had a certain </2> number
55          for your quotation which you gave me on <3> this time </3>
56   S1:    <3> yeah </3> there <4> there was- was no hiccups </4> eh:
57          with eh: the the part from (COMPANY5)
58   S4:    <4> that one was </4>
59   S2:    mhm
60   S1:    <5> it was </5> internal (COMPANY1a)
61   S4:    <5> (xx) </5>
```

---

[58] See extract A.2, lines 14 to 33, in the appendix.

At this point, S1 jumps in, making it clear that the problem *was never with (COMPANY5)*, but his utterance is drowned out by an overlap. As a consequence, S1 starts another attempt in lines 56 and 57, but again a significant part of his utterance happens while S4 is also speaking. Obviously attaching great importance to the fact that this issue be clarified, S1 tries for a third time in line 60, this time not freeing the airline, (COMPANY5), from responsibility, but explicitly blaming, so to speak, his own employer: *it was internal (COMPANY1a)*. Again, his utterance is partially disturbed by an overlap, but comes through better than the preceding ones. With these three utterances, S1 can be seen to – quite explicitly and with considerable effort – establish a 'frame' which is different from S2's 'defense frame', namely a new 'frame' which clearly does not put (COMPANY5) in the position of a defendant or culprit and which I shall henceforth refer to as 'solidarity frame'. Since S1, as the chair of the meeting, is hierarchically the most powerful participant, it seems that he has the authority to establish such a new frame and thereby perform a change of 'frame', in this chase a change towards 'solidarity' which is actually also favorable for S2.

Nevertheless, it seems that S2 does not really pick up on the introduction of the new frame, because he still continues to defend his company, (COMPANY5), quite vehemently in lines 73 to 75:

Example 43 (A.2)

```
73   S2:    we ALWAYS (.) and i tell you this honestly ALWAYS DO (.)
74          the same rate. always. (.) why? because we want to avoid (.)
75          <2> this </2> kind of conflict. (.)
76   S1:    <2> mhm </2>
77   S1:    absolutely.
```

To this vehement assurance, S1 responds with the rather strong positive acknowledgement token *absolutely*, which openly signals agreement and support and stands out from the regular minimal feedback that S1 mostly provides throughout meeting A. Therefore, S1's response can be seen as resulting from and simultaneously enforcing the new 'solidarity frame', which S1 has introduced in example 42.

Yet, as is obvious in example 44, S2 still does not cease to underline that (COMPANY5), his employer, always gives the same rates to all customers and that he would *put* his *HANDS into the fire* concerning this issue. After S2's assuring talk in lines 78 to 82, which already at this point does not seem to be necessary or called for by the other participants, S4 explains one of the possible reasons for the occurrence of such a mix-up of rates (lines 83-85, 88-90, 92-94):

Example 44 (A.2)

78	S2:	and this this is (.) really we d- mm put my HANDS into the fire
79		for it (1) this is the the scenario we only work. (.) becau:se we
80		want to make (.) no conflicts (.) and believe me <@> this is the
81		thing </@> (COMPANY5) always does. (1) and we try to
82		avoi:d (.) ALWAYS this kind of <3> things. </3>
83	S4:	<3> it's </3> not so- that's eh not (.) you never know what the
84		origins in this country are. then: (.) in the end are offering. (.)
85		<4> (and) </4> say they are coming to you, request a shipment,
86		(.)
87	S2:	<4> mhm </4>
88	S4:	or a special shipment. you give the same rate like you gave it to
89		us, (.) <5> but </5> they say mm ah: okay if i get this shipment
90		maybe i can eh: pressure them down to (.)
91	S2:	<5> mhm </5>
92	S4:	eh that i get a better rate, and then they're offering something
93		(.) LOWER? and then you have already the <6> hiccup </6> as
94		a: as a (origin) (.) so
95	S2:	<6> mhm </6>
96	S2:	yeah that's something which WE cannot help of course if <7>
97		if </7> they LOWER. <8> if if </8> THEY (.)
98	S4:	<7> sure </7> <8> sure it's </8>
99	S2:	put i don't know their commission lower or (.) thei:r whatever
100		they put lower THEMSELVES well this this is a thing (1)
101		which is a (.) well a thing which WE cannot control. (1)
102	S4:	sure. (.)

In this explanation, S4 makes it obvious that she does not hold (COMPANY5) responsible for the occurrence of such mix-ups, as she explicitly says in line 88: *you give the same rate like you gave it to us*. Then outlines further how such a *hiccup* may arise nevertheless without any fault of (COMPANY5).

It therefore seems that S4 has picked up the 'solidarity frame' introduced by S1 and also joins his efforts in enforcing it. The notions of 'frame' and 'footing', i.e. "the alignment we take up to ourselves and the others present as expressed in the way we manage the production or reception of an utterance" (Goffman 1981a: 128), are closely linked for that matter, as S1 and S4 both change their 'footing' in favor of establishing and enforcing the new 'solidarity frame'. Yet, this change in 'footing' of course also affects S2 because when as speakers we project ourselves in a current and locally active capacity, then our coparticipants in the encounter are the ones who will have their selves partly determined correspondingly (Goffman 1981a: 151).

One could say therefore that within S1's 'solidarity frame', S2 no longer inhabits his main participant role as a 'sales representative', but is assigned the new temporary role of a 'colleague'. Since S2, however, has still not picked up on the changed 'frame' and 'footing', he does not occupy this 'colleague' role and instead still feels the urge to defend his employer, (COMPANY5), in lines 96, 97, 99, 100, and 101. Thereby S2 still acts the role of the 'sales representative' of (COMPANY5) quite explicitly, when he employs an 'institutional *we*' (Drew & Heritage 1992a: 31) twice (lines 96 and 101) and even marks it with emphatic stress. Drew and Heritage (1992a: 30) note that speakers use this "self-referring *we* to invoke an institutional over a personal identity" and consequently indicate "that they are speaking as representatives, or on behalf, of an organization" (ibid.: 30).

One could say that a 'global' misunderstanding due to 'misframing' can already be observed at this point, but it is not yet openly addressed by the other participants. The *sure* S4 utters twice in line 98 and once more in line 102 again expresses solidarity with S2 and strong agreement to what he has just said. With repeating the word three times, S4 may also implicitly hint at the fact that S2 in fact need not have defended his company. But although S4 obviously projects herself as an 'understanding colleague' and attempts to reinforce the 'solidarity frame', she does not explicitly state that S2's justification was unnecessary, i.e. that S2 is acting on a wrong 'footing' in a different 'frame'.

Consequently, the sustained 'misframing' is not resolved and S2 remains in his 'defense frame', which he has introduced himself at the beginning of meeting A's second subsection in example 41 (lines 5 to 13). S2 continues to assess the situation and his own interactional role on the basis of this 'defense frame' and produces a very long turn in which he elaborately explains (COMPANY5)'s reasons for giving the same rates to everybody[59]. This is lengthy digression occurs immediately before S1's remarks and the eventual surfacing of the 'misframing' in example 40.

As it has already been mentioned before, misunderstandings on such a 'global' discourse level operate very subtly and are very difficult to detect – especially for the participants – and this is why the open misunderstanding presented in example 40 takes place the way it does. Even though S1 again reinforces the 'solidarity frame' and prepares

---

[59] See extract A.2, lines 103 to 126, in the appendix.

the ground for his next utterance(s) by providing explicit positive feedback in line 127 (*we LIKE this (.) and eh it is the best way to do it*), S2 interprets S1's obviously well-meant 'solidary' piece of advice (lines 128, 130-132, 134, 136-137, 139-141, 143-144) as a sort of mild attack or reproach. This interpretation results from the 'defense frame' within which S2 perceives and assesses S1's utterance. It is, however, not a 'defense frame' but a 'solidarity frame' within which S1 produces the utterance and within which he intends it to be understood. The result is a plain misunderstanding, which S1 then openly addresses in line 149 and subsequently tries to resolve with considerable effort.

5.7 Summary and conclusion

The analysis has presented various types of 'miscommunication' in ELF interactions and it has outlined how these different types are interactionally managed. The majority of instances of 'miscommunication' in the three hours of business data analyzed were 'local non-understandings'. These non-understandings came to the surface in the interactions because ELF speakers employed various procedures in order to indicate them more or less explicitly. Once indicated, the participants dealt with these non-understandings in negotiation sequences of varying length: While some negotiations of meaning were resolved immediately within only three turns, others featured multiple indicators and stretched over longer periods of discourse.

On the one end of the spectrum of negotiation sequences are two very short negotiations of meaning. These negotiation sequences did not feature all of the "four functional primes" of Varonis and Gass's model (1985: 73), but only consisted of trigger (T), indicator (I) and response (R). They are devoid of a reaction to the response (RR), but nevertheless functioned effectively in resolving the non-understanding. Furthermore, three instances included all four components and accordingly can be described as basic 'negotiation of meaning' structures. Two examples exhibited an enlarged negotiation structure. In these instances, the negotiation of meaning was followed by additional explanations or 'waffling'.

Although ELF participants showed involvement in all negotiations of meaning analyzed in this paper, two occasions were particularly noticeable in this respect. They were termed 'high involvement sequences'. In these sequences, the speakers contributed very actively to the joint negotiation of meaning, e.g. by formulating hypotheses as indicating procedures. Finally, three instances exhibited very complex negotiation sequences, the longest sequence lasting about one and half minutes. These extracts featured "multiple layers of trigger-resolution sequences" (Varonis & Gass 1985: 78) and various indicating procedures. They showed how ELF participants may safely and successfully manage even persistent or multiple non-understandings.

In addition, two other special cases of the negotiation of meaning could be observed. One negotiation of meaning was linked to a 'local misunderstanding'. Since a 'misunderstanding' is an instance of 'miscommunication' which neither participant is aware of at the time it occurs, it cannot be consciously indicated but only surfaces by chance. Yet, as the analysis shows, the accidental surfacing of the 'misunderstanding' may prompt a negotiation sequence very much like those sequences consciously initiated by participants. As a second special case, two negotiation sequences were self-initiated, i.e. they were started by the same participant who had uttered the trigger. In both examples, this self-initiation prevented the persistence of an understanding problem and hindered its evolvement into more serious instance of 'miscommunication'.

While many analysts exclude the possibility of strategic miscommunication prior to analysis, the present study integrated the question of intentionality into its analytical framework. With regard to three instances of 'miscommunication', the sequential development of interaction suggested that participants could have acted strategically and thereby intentionally caused understanding problems or feigned their existence. At the same time, it is impossible for the analyst to determine participants' intentions solely by looking at the data. Therefore, it is equally possible that no strategic behavior was involved and that the three extracts analyzed constitute regular, i.e. unintentional, non-understandings.

As a last type of 'miscommunication', one instance of global miscommunication was presented. A 'global misunderstanding' developed over a considerable stretch of discourse, but remained interactionally invisible to the participants for quite some time. At one point, a participant made explicit that his co-participant had misinterpreted his last utterance, i.e. that a misunderstanding had occurred. The retrospective analysis showed that this misunderstanding originated in the fact that participants had been operating in different discourse 'frames'. As a consequence, they also had differing perceptions of their roles in the current speech situation. Each participant behaved in accordance with his or her own 'frame'. But because participants did not share frames, they acted on different premises, which led to a 'global misunderstanding'.

6 CONCLUSION

The main purpose of this study was to create an initial picture of what 'miscommunication' looks like in an ELF context. Chapter 2 presented a brief overview of several theoretical approaches to 'miscommunication', namely pragmatics, conversation analysis, sociolinguistics, intercultural communication research and dialogical theory. Acknowledging what these approaches have each contributed to our understanding of language use, the chapter critically examined the different theoretical positions concerning 'miscommunication' from the position of an ELF researcher.

Chapter 3 provided the theoretical foundations for the analysis of 'miscommunication' in ELF business interactions in this paper. It sketched the ELF position, reviewed initial findings and defined the central terms used in this study. It presented the two models which were to be essential for the subsequent analysis: the procedures for indicating non-understanding and the negotiation of meaning. Furthermore, it considered the possibility of strategic miscommunication and examined the close relation between understanding and context, commenting on both the micro-contextual development of talk and macro-contextual characteristics of the situation. As a last aspect, it briefly touched upon the multicausality of 'miscommunication'.

Preceding the analysis, chapter 4 outlined some general characteristics of the recorded data. It provided general information about the two recorded business meetings and their participants. After some remarks about methodological aspects of data collection, some macro-contextual characteristics of business meetings were discussed. The structure of the meetings, the degree of formality, goals and objectives, partcipant roles and relations and the power of the chair person were examined.

The analysis of 'miscommunication' in ELF business meetings in chapter 5 primarily revealed three types of 'miscommunication': 'local non-understanding', 'strategic miscommunication' and 'global misunderstanding'. The majority of instances were 'local non-understandings', i.e. understanding problems which at least one participant is aware of at the time they occurred. They were more or less explicitly indicated by one participant and subsequently resolved in negotiation sequences of various lengths. In all these negotiations of meaning, ELF speakers were rather successful in managing understanding problems smoothly in the course of interaction.

In the short negotiation sequences, the ELF speakers indicated triggers precisely through intermediate indicating procedures, such as reformulation or reprise. In some instances, they were strikingly skilled in formulating responses which immediately cleared up non-understandings, e.g. by accounting for two possible interpretations and two potential causes of the understanding problem within the same response. Some sequences exemplified Varionis and Gass's (1985) basic four-component 'negotiation of meaning' structure. Initiated through explicit unspecific minimal queries or reformulation as comprehension check, these non-understandings were also instantly resolved.

Sometimes basic structures were enlarged through explanations which participants added to the already successful negotiation sequence. Although these additional comments did not appear to be necessary in these cases, they exemplified the ELF speakers' involvement in the interactional management of 'miscommunication' and showed their willingness to actively contribute to the negotiation of meaning. This active participation was even more pronounced in some instances where speakers formulated hypotheses and subjected them to their co-participants' agreement. Rather than simply producing a request for clarification, the speakers took initiative at these occasions. They actively shaped the negotiation sequences and steered them towards their resolution.

The long and complex negotiation sequences found in the data are neither to be underrated. In these sequences, the ELF speakers showed a flexible use of different types of indicating procedures, which they combined and adapted for their needs in the particular communicative situation. Although some of these complex negotiation loops featured several non-understandings in close proximity and lasted over a considerable stretch of discourse, they never appeared to disrupt the flow of communication. Rather on the contrary, just towards the end of the longest and most complex negotiation sequence it is noticeable that all five interactants contribute to the clarification. Through such joint negotiation work and eventual resolution, particularly complex sequences seemed to create a bond between ELF speakers.

Concerning the environments or situations, in which non-understandings were most often negotiated in the data, two environments were noticeable: questions and 'fragile' activities. Several negotiation sequences in the data were triggered by questions. Similarly, some negotiations occurred in the environment of 'fragile' activities. Both of these environments require a certain degree of precision and clarity: if a participant utters a question, s/he wants to obtain a certain piece of information; a 'fragile' activity is usually concerned with a delicate subject. It seemed to be this increased need for clarity with regard to questions and 'fragile' activities which led ELF speakers to display their understanding – or non-understanding – more explicitly in these two specific contexts. As a consequence, many negotiation sequences occurred in these two environments.

As far as the use of indicating procedures is concerned, the ELF speakers in the data most often employed intermediate and explicit procedures. Implicit procedures could only be observed within the longer negotiation sequences and never occurred in isolation, i.e. without other procedures in close proximity. Yet, it needs to be conceded that such implicit procedures are less interactionally visible than intermediate or direct procedures and, I would suggest, only scarcely lead to negotiation sequences. There were points in both meetings at which the occurrence of a non-understanding seemed possible or even likely, but at the same time there was not enough evidence in the data to confirm this impression. Due to this lack of evidence, these instances were not included into the analysis. Yet, they might be an interesting subject for further enquiry, particularly with regard to Firth's (1996) 'let it pass' principle.

Due to the multicausality of 'miscommunication', any remarks concerning the potential causes of understanding problems will never be completely decisive. Nevertheless it seems feasible to note some of the tendencies which could be recognized in the present study. Those few non-understandings possibly originating at the level of pronunciation were resolved very quickly in my data. Once indicated, these non-understandings did not require much interactional work, but were cleared up via a single response. Non-understandings related to the level of lexis or grammar were very scarce. The ELF speakers in my data were fairly proficient in English and, on the whole, they did not encounter understanding problems because of vocabulary or grammar.

The most prominent potential cause of non-understandings in my data was the occurrence of an 'elliptical utterance' (Bremer 1996: 53). Comparatively many instances of negotiation of meaning obviously resulted from the fact that the trigger turn had been 'elliptical' in one way or another. A rather frequent sub-type of these 'elliptical utterances' was what I have termed 'unclear/missing referent'. In these cases, the trigger turn contained some referential component, like a personal pronoun or a deictic expression, whose referent could not be immediately identified by the interlocutor and which therefore caused a non-understanding. An inverse situation occurred once, when a non-understanding was caused by a 'complex utterance' (Bremer 1996: 50).

Related to the potential causes of understanding problems is the second type of 'miscommunication' which appeared to be relevant in my data, namely 'strategic miscommunication'. Strategic behavior is another potential cause for the occurrence of 'miscommunication'. In some instances, the possibility of an intentionally caused understanding problem could not be completely ruled out. At the same time, it was impossible to determine participants' intentions with certainty by relying solely on evidence in the data. Therefore, in the relevant cases, the interpretation suggesting 'strategic miscommunication' stands beside the interpretation suggesting unintentional non-understanding, both interpretations being equally legitimate.

The third general type of 'miscommunication' which could be found in the recorded ELF interactions was 'global misunderstanding'. Although it only occurred once in the three hours of data, it was this type of 'miscommunication' which appeared to have the most far-reaching implications for the interaction. Since the 'global misunderstanding' was caused by sustained misframing, it spanned a considerable amount of time in the interaction. During this time, participants operated within different discourse 'frames', which had an effect on their own behavior as well as on their interpretation of the others' behavior. Since no participant was aware of this discrepancy with regard to interpretive frames for quite some time, the 'global misunderstanding' lingered persistently. Only as soon as it was recognized by one participant could it be indicated and cleared up.

As this study is qualitative in nature, its findings cannot be claimed to be relevant to all ELF interactions, but primarily to ELF business meetings. In order to arrive at insights which allow generalizations, greater amounts of data would be called for. The Vienna-Oxford Corpus of International English (VOICE) which is currently being compiled at the University of Vienna may open up new possibilities in this respect. Comprising spoken interactions among ELF speakers, this new corpus will open the door to large-scale empirical research on ELF. The different types of 'miscommunication' and the observations concerning the interactional management of 'miscommunication' among ELF speakers presented in this paper might serve as a potential starting point for any larger investigation of 'miscommuniciation' in ELF.

REFERENCES

Allwood, Jens; Abelar, Yanhia. 1984. "Lack of understanding, misunderstanding, and adult language acquisition". In Extra, Guus; Mittner, Michèle (eds.). *Studies in second language acquisition by adult immigrants.* Tilburg: Tilburg University, 27-55.

Atteslander, Peter. 1995. *Methoden der empirischen Sozialforschung.* Berlin: de Gruyter.

Auer, Peter. 1995. "Context and contextualization". In Verschueren, Jef; Östman, Jan-Ola; Blommaert, Jan (eds.). *Handbook of pragmatics 1995.* Amsterdam: Benjamins.

Banks, Stephen P.; Ge, Gao; Baker, Joyce. 1991. "Intercultural encounters and miscommunication". In Coupland, Nikolas; Giles, Howard; Wiemann, John M. (eds.). *'Miscommunication' and problematic talk.* Newbury Park: Sage, 103-120.

Bateson, Gregory. 1972. *Steps to an ecology of mind.* London: Intertext Books.

Bazzanella, Carla; Damiano, Rossana. 1999. "The interactional handling of misunderstanding in everyday conversations". *Journal of Pragmatics* 31, 817-836.

Blommaert, Jan; Verschueren, Jef (eds.). 1991. *The pragmatics of intercultural and "international communication: selected papers of the International Pragmatics Conference, Antwerp, August 17-22, 1987, and the Ghent Symposium on Intercultural Communication.* Amsterdam: Benjamins.

Blum-Kulka, Shoshana; Weizman, Elda. 1988. "The inevitability of misunderstandings: discourse ambiguities". *Text* 8, 219-241.

Bremer, Katharina. 1996. "Causes of understanding problems". In Bremer, Katharina; Roberts, Celia; Vasseur, Marie; Simonot, Margaret; Broeder, Peter (eds.). *Achieving understanding: discourse in intercultural encounters.* London: Longman, 37-64.

Bremer, Katharina; Roberts, Celia; Vasseur, Marie; Simonot, Margaret; Broeder, Peter (eds.). 1996. *Achieving understanding: discourse in intercultural encounters.* London: Longman.

Brown, Julie R.; Rogers, L. Edna. 1991. "Openness, uncertainty, and intimacy: an epistemological reformulation". In Coupland, Nikolas; Giles, Howard; Wiemann, John M. (eds.). *'Miscommunication' and problematic talk.* Newbury Park: Sage, 146-165.

Chafe, Wallace. 1987. "Cognitive constraints on information flow". In Tomlin, Russell S. (ed.). *Coherence and grounding in discourse.* Amsterdam: Benjamins, 21-51.

Coupland, Nikolas; Giles, Howard; Wiemann, John M. (eds.). 1991. *'Miscommunication' and problematic talk.* Newbury Park: Sage.

Coupland, Nikolas; Wiemann, John M.; Giles, Howard. 1991. "Talk as 'problem' and communication as 'miscommunication': an integrative analysis". In Coupland, Nikolas; Giles, Howard; Wiemann, John M. (eds.). *'Miscommunication' and problematic talk.* Newbury Park: Sage, 1-17.

Crystal, David. 1997. *English as a global language.* Cambridge: Cambridge University Press.

Cuff, E. C.; Sharrock, W. W. 1985. "Meetings". In Van Dijk, Teun A. (ed.). *Handbook of discourse analysis. Volume 3. Discourse and dialogue.* London: Academic Press, 149-159.

Dascal, Marcelo (ed.). 1985a. *Dialogue: an interdisciplinary approach*. Amsterdam: Benjamins.

Dascal, Marcelo. 1985b. "The relevance of misunderstanding". In Dascal, Marcelo (ed.). *Dialogue: an interdisciplinary approach*. Amsterdam: Benjamins, 441-459.

Dascal, Marcelo. 1999. "Introduction: some questions about misunderstanding". *Journal of Pragmatics* 31, 753-762.

Drew, Paul; Heritage, John. 1992a. "Analyzing talk at work: an introduction". In Drew, Paul; Heritage, John (eds.). *Talk at work*. Cambridge: Cambridge University Press, 3-65.

Drew, Paul; Heritage, John (eds.). 1992b. *Talk at work*. Cambridge: Cambridge University Press.

Dua, Hans R. 1990. "The phenomenology of miscommunication". In Riggins, Stephen Harold (ed.). *Beyond Goffman. Studies on communication, institution, and social interaction*. Berlin: de Gruyter, 113-139.

Duranti, Alessandro; Goodwin, Charles (eds.). 1992. *Rethinking context: language as interactive phenomenon*. Cambridge: Cambridge University Press.

Ellis, Rod. 1994. *The study of second language acquisition*. Oxford: Oxford University Press.

Erickson, Frederick; Shultz, Jeffrey. 1982. *The counsellor as gatekeeper: social interaction in interviews*. New York: Academic Press.

Extra, Guus; Mittner, Michèle (eds.). 1984. *Studies in second language acquisition by adult immigrants*. Tilburg: Tilburg University.

Firth, Alan. 1996. "The discursive accomplishment of normality: on 'lingua franca' English and conversation analysis". *Journal of Pragmatics* 26, 237-259.

Gass, Susan; Varonis, Evangeline Marlos. 1991. "Miscommunication in nonnative speaker discourse". In Coupland, Nikolas; Giles, Howard; Wiemann, John M. (eds.). *'Miscommunication' and problematic talk*. Newbury Park: Sage, 121-145.

Gnutzmann, Claus (ed.). 1999. *Teaching and learning English as a global language*. Tübingen: Stauffenburg.

Goffman, Erving. 1975. *Frame analysis*. Harmondsworth: Penguin Books.

Goffman, Erving. 1981a. "Footing". In Goffman, Erving. *Forms of talk*. Oxford: Blackwell, 124-157.

Goffman, Erving. 1981b. *Forms of talk*. Oxford: Blackwell.

Good, David A. 1999. "Communicative success vs. failure". In Verschueren, Jef; Östman, Jan-Ola; Blommaert; Bulcaen, Chris (eds.). *Handbook of pragmatics 1999*. Amsterdam: Benjamins.

Graddol, David. 1997. *The future of English?* The British Council. http://www.britishcouncil.org/english/pdf/future.pdf (16 April 2004).

Gumperz, John J. 1982. *Discourse strategies*. Cambridge: Cambridge University Press.

Gumperz, John J. 1992. "Contextualization and understanding". In Duranti, Alessandro; Goodwin, Charles (eds.). *Rethinking context: language as interactive phenomenon.* Cambridge: Cambridge University Press, 229-252.

Gumperz, John; Roberts, Celia. 1991. "Understanding in intercultural encounters". In Blommaert, Jan; Verschueren, Jef (eds.). *The pragmatics of intercultural and "international communication: selected papers of the International Pragmatics Conference, Antwerp, August 17-22, 1987, and the Ghent Symposium on Intercultural Communication.* Amsterdam: Benjamins, 51-90.

Haegeman, Patricia. 2002. "Foreigner talk in lingua franca business telephone calls". In Knapp, Karlfried; Meierkord, Christiane (eds.). *Lingua franca communication.* Frankfurt a. Main: Peter Lang, 135-162.

Holmes, Janet; Stubbe, Maria. 2003. *Power and politeness in the workplace.* Harlow: Pearson Education.

House, Juliane. 1999. "Misunderstanding in intercultural communication: interactions in English as a *lingua franca* and the myth of mutual intelligibility". In Gnutzmann, Claus (ed.). *Teaching and learning English as a global language.* Tübingen: Stauffenburg, 73-89.

Humphreys-Jones, Claire. 1986. "An investigation of the types and structure of misunderstandings". Unpublished Ph.D. Dissertation. Newcastle-upon-Tyne: University of Newcastle-upon-Tyne.

International Phonetic Association. 1996. "The international phonetic alphabet". www2.arts.gla.ac.uk/IPA/fullchart.html (3 June 2004).

Jenkins, Jennifer. 2000. *The Phonology of English as an International Language.* Oxford: Oxford University Press.

Jenkins, Jennifer. 2002. "A sociolinguistically based, empirically researched pronunciation syllabus for English as an international language". *Applied Linguistics* 23, 83-103.

Kachru, Braj B. (ed.). 1992a. "Teaching World Englishes". In Kachru, Braj B. (ed.) *The other tongue: English across cultures.* (2nd edition). Urbana: University of Illinois Press, 355-365.

Kachru, Braj B. (ed.). 1992b. *The other tongue: English across cultures.* (2nd edition). Urbana: University of Illinois Press.

Knapp, Karlfried; Meierkord, Christiane (eds.). 2002. *Lingua franca communication.* Frankfurt a. Main: Peter Lang.

Koole, Tim; Ten Thije, Jan D. 1994. *The construction of intercultural discourse: team discussions of educational advisers.* Amsterdam: Rodopi.

Kordon, Kathrin. 2003. *Phatic communion in English as a lingua franca.* Unpublished MA thesis, Universität Wien.

Labov, William. 1978. *Sociolinguistic patterns.* Oxford: Blackwell.

Linell, Per. 1995. "Troubles with mutualities: towards a dialogical theory of misunderstanding and miscommunication". In Markova, Ivana; Graumann, Carl F.; Foppa, Klaus (eds.). *Mutualities in dialogue.* Cambridge: Cambridge University Press, 176-213.

McGregor, Graham. 1985. "Utterance interpretation and the role of the analyst". *Language and Speech* 28, 1-28.

Meeuwis, Michael. 1994. "Leniency and testiness in intercultural communication: remarks on ideology and context in interactional sociolinguistics". *Pragmatics* 4, 391-408.

Meeuwis, Michael; Sarangi, Srikant. 1994. "Perspectives on intercultural communication: a critical reading". *Pragmatics* 4, 309-313.

Meierkord, Christiane. 1996. *Englisch als Medium der interkulturellen Kommunikation. Untersuchungen zum* non-native/non-native-speaker-*Diskurs*. Frankfurt / Main: Lang.

Meierkord, Christiane. 2002. "'Language stripped bare' or 'linguistic masala'? Culture in lingua franca conversation". In Knapp, Karlfried; Meierkord, Christiane (eds.). *Lingua franca communication*. Frankfurt a. Main: Peter Lang, 109-133.

Meierkord, Christiane; Knapp, Karlfried. 2002. "Approaching lingua franca communication". In Knapp, Karlfried; Meierkord, Christiane (eds.). *Lingua franca communication*. Frankfurt a. Main: Peter Lang, 9-28.

MICASE. 1999. "MICASE Transcription and spelling conventions. B. Spelling conventions". http://www.lsa.umich.edu/eli/micase/transcription.html (10 July 2004).

Milroy, Lesley. 1984. "Comprehension and context: successful communication and communication breakdown". In Trudgill, Peter (ed.). *Applied sociolinguistics*. London: Academic Press, 7-31.

Milroy, Lesley. 1987. *Observing and analysing natural language*. Oxford: Blackwell.

Ochs, Elinor. 1991. "Misunderstanding children". In Coupland, Nikolas; Giles, Howard; Wiemann, John M. (eds.). *'Miscommunication' and problematic talk*. Newbury Park: Sage, 44-60.

Pan, Yuling; Wong Scollon, Suzanne; Scollon, Ron. 2002. *Professional communication in international settings*. Malden: Blackwell.

Ribeiro, Branca Telles; Hoyle, Susan M. 2000. "Frame analysis". In Verschueren, Jef; Östman, Jan-Ola; Blommaert, Jan; Bulcaen, Chris (eds.). *Handbook of pragmatics 2000*. Amsterdam: Benjamins.

Riggins, Stephen Harold (ed.). 1990. *Beyond Goffman. Studies on communication, institution, and social interaction*. Berlin: de Gruyter.

Roberts, Celia. 1996. "A social perspective on understanding: some issues of theory and method". In Bremer, Katharina; Roberts, Celia; Vasseur, Marie; Simonot, Margaret; Broeder, Peter (eds.). *Achieving understanding: discourse in intercultural encounters*. London: Longman, 9-36.

Sarangi, Srikant. 1994. "Intercultural or not? Beyond celebration of cultural differences in miscommunication analysis". *Pragmatics* 4, 409-427.

Sarangi, Srikant. 1995. "Culture". In Verschueren, Jef; Östman, Jan-Ola; Blommaert, Jan (eds.). *Handbook of pragmatics 1995*. Amsterdam: Benjamins.

Schegloff, Emanel A. 2000. "When 'others' initiate repair". *Applied Linguistics* 21, 205-243.

Scollon, Ron; Wong Scollon, Suzanne. 1995. *Intercultural communication. A discourse approach*. Oxford: Blackwell.

Seidlhofer, Barbara. 2001. "Closing a conceptual gap: the case for a description of English as a lingua franca". *International Journal of Applied Linguistics* 11, 133-158.

Seidlhofer, Barbara. 2002a. A concept of international English and related issues: from 'real English' to 'realistic English'? Strasbourg: Council of Europe. http://www.coe.int/T/E/Cultural_Co-operation/education/Languages/Language_P olicy/Policy_development_activities/Studies/SeidlhoferEn.pdf (29 August 2003).

Seidhofer, Barbara. 2002b. "The shape of things to come? Some basic questions about English as a lingua franca". In Knapp, Karlfried; Meierkord, Christiane (eds.). *Lingua franca communication*. Frankfurt a. Main: Peter Lang, 269-302.

Sinclair, John (ed.). 1990. *Collins Cobuild English grammar*. London: Collins.

Spencer-Oatey, Helen (ed.). 2000. *Culturally speaking. Managing rapport through talk across cultures*. London: Continuum.

Stubbs, Michael. 1983. *Discourse analysis*. Oxford: Blackwell.

Tannen, Deborah. 1986. *That's not what I meant! How conversational style makes or breaks your relations with others*. New York: Morrow.

The Princeton Language Institute (eds.). 1999. *Roget's 21st century thesaurus in dictionary form*. 2nd edition. New York: Dell.

Thomas, Jenny. 1983. "Cross-cultural pragmatic failure". *Applied Linguistics* 4, 91-112.

Tomlin, Russell S. (ed.). 1987. *Coherence and grounding in discourse*. Amsterdam: Benjamins.

Trudgill, Peter (ed.). 1984. *Applied sociolinguistics*. London: Academic Press.

Tzanne, Angeliki. 1999. *Talking at cross-purposes: the dynamics of miscommunication*. Amsterdam: Benjamins.

Van Dijk, Teun A. (ed.). 1985. *Handbook of discourse analysis. Volume 3. Discourse and dialogue*. London: Academic Press.

Varonis, Evangeline Marlos; Gass, Susan M. 1985. "Non-native/non-native conversations: a model for negotiation of meaning". *Applied Linguistics* 6, 71-90.

Vasseur, Marie-Thérèse; Broeder, Peter; Roberts, Celia. 1996. "Managing understanding from a minority perspective". In Bremer, Katharina; Roberts, Celia; Vasseur, Marie; Simonot, Margaret; Broeder, Peter (eds.). *Achieving understanding: discourse in intercultural encounters*. London: Longman, 65-108.

Verschueren, Jef; Östman, Jan-Ola; Blommaert, Jan (eds.). 1995. *Handbook of pragmatics 1995*. Amsterdam: Benjamins.

Verschueren, Jef; Östman, Jan-Ola; Blommaert; Bulcaen, Chris (eds.). 1999. *Handbook of pragmatics 1999*. Amsterdam: Benjamins.

Verschueren, Jef; Östman, Jan-Ola; Blommaert, Jan; Bulcaen, Chris (eds.). 2000. *Handbook of pragmatics 2000*. Amsterdam: Benjamins.

Vion, Robert. 1986. "Les diverses phases d'une interaction". Paper presented at ESF meeting on Understanding, London, March 1986.

VOICE Project. 2003. "VOICE Transcription and mark-up conventions. Version 3.0, June 2003".

Voionmaa, Kaarlo. 1984. "Lexikal overföring och rationaletet". Papers presented to the 4th Scandinavian Conference on Bilingualism, Uppsala.

Vollstedt, Marina. 2002. "English as a language for internal company communications". In Knapp, Karlfried; Meierkord, Christiane (eds.). *Lingua franca communication.* Frankfurt a. Main: Peter Lang, 87-107.

Wardhaugh, Ronald. 1998. *An introduction to sociolinguistics.* (3rd edition). Oxford: Blackwell.

Weigand, Edda. 1999. "Misunderstanding: the standard case". *Journal of Pragmatics* 31, 763-785.

Weizman, Elda. 1999. "Building true understanding via apparent miscommunication: a case study". *Journal of Pragmatics* 31, 837-846.

Widdowson, Henry G. 1994. "The ownership of English". *TESOL Quarterly* 28, 377-389.

Widdowson, Henry G. 1997. "EIL, ESL, EFL: global issues and local interests". *World Englishes* 16, 135-146.

Widdowson, Henry G. 1998. "Context, community, and authentic language". *TESOL Quarterly* 32, 705-716.

Widdowson, Henry G. 2003. *Defining issues in English language teaching.* Oxford: Oxford University Press.

Wong, Jean. 2000. "Delayed next turn repair initiation in native/non-native speaker English conversation". *Applied Linguistics* 21, 244-267.

APPENDIX

Data A: Meeting A

Type:	business meeting at international forwarding agency
Place:	Luxembourg
Time:	January 2004
Overall length:	more than three hours
Length of data analyzed:	one hour
Number of speakers:	four S1, S2, S3: present during Extract A.1
	S1, S2, S4: present during Extract A.2

	L1	gender	age	pseudonym	status
S1	German (Ger.)	male	35+	markus	chair (COMPANY1a)
S2	Dutch	male	30+	joseph	visitor (COMPANY5)
S3	German (Ger.)	male	30+	marc	host (COMPANY1a)
S4	German (Ger.)	female	35+	mia	host (COMPANY1a)

Extract A.1

(9:11 – 40:05; *length 30:54*)

```
1   S2:  shall we start?
2   S1:  yes, we start eh eh directly with marc <1> e:h </1> eh
3   SX-3:<1> <SOFT> yeah </SOFT> </1>
4   S2:  okay
5   S1:  as he's eh: expect another visitor, he also will not join for lunch,
6        (.)
7   S2:  <2> okay </2>
8   S1:  <2> yeah? </2> so: ah (2)
9   S2:  get something
10  S1:  <SOFT> makes (.) makes more sense </SOFT> (1)
11  S2:  <SOFT> ah @ </SOFT> (2)
12       <S2 rummaging about a little (5)>
13  S1:  <addressing S3> <SOFT> (it's just a) (x) i would say (.) (i think)
14       (.) </SOFT> YEAH <SOFT> (no) problem ah </SOFT> (3)
```

15	S2:	yeah first of all of course (1) again many thanks for this (.) NICE
16		and brilliant year of last (.) year of course the two thousand and
17		THREE, want to thank you (.) ALL of you of course of the
18		turnover which you eh (.) performed already, (.) ah:m i wanted to
19		take some statistics which i did actually LAST year
20	S1:	mm
21	S2:	the: the problem is we didn't finish yet the WHOLE year, <1> so
22		i'm WAITING on the </1> last part? (.)
23	S1:	<1> <SOFT> @ @ @ @ @ @</SOFT> </1>
24	S1:	yeah
25	S2:	i can give you some details but <S2 starts leaving through his
26		papers (50)> ple:ase don't have a look at the rest (3) eh:m (2)
27		just to get you an idea
28		(11)
29	S2:	<SOFT> uh </SOFT> (it's a) mess with papers
30		(4)
31	S1:	looks like my desk
32	S2:	hh <1> @ @ @ @ @ </1>
33	S1:	<1> @ @ @ @ @ @ </1>
34		(7)
35	S2:	<SOFT> uh </SOFT> (2) (maybe i) took it separate (5) <SOFT>
36		i give you: </SOFT> (1) you can see, as the LAST (5) let me see
37		i (.) made this (.) in very early in the morning
38	S1:	but that's a good one <1> let me have look to it. let let me have
39		look to it. ok </1>
40	S2:	<1> @ @ @ @ @ @ @ @ @ @ </1>
41	S1:	(COMPANY1) above (COMPANY2) and (COMPANY3) that's
42		already <2> good </2>
43	S2:	<2> @ @ @ </2> <3> okay </3>
44	S1:	<3> so. </3> my friend @ <4> @ </4> @ @
45	S2:	<4> @ </4>
46	S1:	<5> (COMPANY2) </5> a hundred and three tons, o- one
47		hundred tons from us
48	S2:	<5> okay what-</5>
49		<door to conference room opens and S10 – not part of the
50		conversation/meeting – looks in>
51	S10:	<LN = French> xxxxxx? </LN = French>
52	S1:	uh?
53	S2:	okay but how come-
54	S3:	<to S10> <LN = French> eh: ce pour le: (1) lunch</LN =
55		French> <TRANSL=that is for lunch>
56	S10:	<LN = French> xxxxxxxxx? </LN = French>
57	S3:	<to S10> <LN = French> oui (c'est aussi ici) </LN = French>
58		<TRANSL=yes (that also here)>
59	S1:	<to S10> <LN = French> ce lunch? </LN = French>
60	S10:	<LN = French> xxxxxx </LN = French>
61	S1:	<to S10> <LN = French> oui oui (cause) y </LN = French>
62	S3:	<to S10> <LN = French> (cause) y </LN = French>

63		<S10 leaves room again and closes door>
64		(1)
65	S2:	ah what i just want to let you know is ah you know that you:
66		ACTUALLY the LAST month was not very good in mine
67		opinion because well maybe we struggle you know with
68		capacities and eh all kinds of things like that, we had the same
69		problems. (.) but just to let you know ah or for example this was
70		the NOVEMBER month <1> that </1> eh you were (on) number
71		one
72	S1:	<1> mhm </1>
73	S2:	but this all has to do of course also with the beaujolais, (.) so the
74		turnover automatically (.) is INTONAGE is pretty HIGH,
75		automatically gives you: oh very high yield also (.) which is an
76		average of <2> three point four three </2>
77	S10:	<S10 just opened the door again> <LN = French> <2> xxx </2>
78		xxxxx? </LN = French>
79	S3:	<3> <to S10> <LN = French> c'est fermé? </LN = French>
80		<TRANSL=it is closed?> </3>
81	S1:	<3> <to S2> sorry </3>
82	S10:	<LN = French> (xxxxxxx) </LN = French>
83	S1:	mm
84		(9) <S1 gets up and signs some papers S10 hands him>
85	SX-10:	(xxxxx) <1> (x) </1>
86	S1:	<1> (x) </1>
87		(4) <S1 sits down at the conference desk again>
88	S2:	and what you're seeing here is actually all the beauJOLAIS
89		people
90	S3:	yeah
91	S1:	yeah @ @ @
92	S2:	i'm always open in this eh: (.)
93	S1:	but you <1> know </1> this is (COMPANY4) (.) not us
94	S2:	<1> no- </1>
95	S2:	yes i know but- well we count you in of course
96	S1:	sure
97	S2:	as a total picture (.) so that's why. but what i do, eh: WHEN we
98		got the december month (.) FINISHED (.) i will send to an
99		overall statistical ah perfor<1>mance</1>
100	S1:	<1> mm </1>
101	S2:	and i believe it's always good to see for you, (.) to have well
102		maybe a motivation again for (hey) LOOK we can do better this
103		<2> or </2>
104	SX-3:	<2> <SOFT> mm </SOFT> </2>
105	S2:	whateve:r (.) this is too much to (COMPANY5) (or fo:r)
106		whatever you can analyze yourSELF (.) and then ah: i believe
107		it's a good picture to this year <1> <SOFT> to (.) this year
108		</SOFT> </1>
109	S1:	<1> yeah absolutely </1> we're happy about that
110	S2:	<SOFT> oh, </SOFT> (.) okay?

111	S1:	yeh? (.) what is your feeling where a:re is is (COMPANY1)
112		(COMPANY1a) (.) posed together RANKING in eh: within
113		(COMPANY5) europe?
114		(2)
115	S2:	what, personally the feeling concerning that?
116	S1:	yeah
117		(2)
118	S2:	<1> oh: </1>
119	S1:	<1> sure we're not </1> eh not number one. <SOFT> this year
120		</SOFT> (.) i would say: <SOFT> ah </SOFT> (1)
121	S2:	actually to tell you really the true- well NOTICE of this
122		FEELING ah personally i don't HAVE at the MOMENT
123	S1:	hm
124	S2:	<SOFT> (you) </SOFT> (kno:w) if you look (.) eh in working
125		relationship which we have together with (COMPANY5) you
126		know there is not (.) a lot of things to comPARE to see hey eh
127		this will be <1> in </1> (imPORTANCE) or whatever (.)
128	S1:	<1> yeah </1>
129	S2:	so i cannot really say for me (.) <SOFT> eh: </SOFT> what is
130		the difference
131	S1:	mhm
132	S2:	<FAST> i could say </FAST> PERSONALLY. that's my
133		opinion. the: (1) now now in your internal picture, because you
134		mentioned ah:m (.) in you:r email to me that some
135		DIFFERENCE betwee:n some REGIONS? (.) maybe it's better
136		to explain me FIRST what what what happened <1> in this </1>
137		<2> scenario </2>
138	S1:	<1> hhh </1> <2> ahm </2> we will do this in in in the second
139		eh round when we talk with mia just eh for this point eh:
140		important is we are heading towards a a splitting of department,
141		(.)
142	S2:	<1> mhm </1>
143	S1:	<1> ah: </1> the far east and middle east department will be split
144		into two departments and this should have done on eh already to
145		the first of january, (.)
146	S2:	mhm
147	S1:	is now postponed to the first of april. (.)
148	S2:	mhm
149	S1:	<SOFT> so </SOFT> there will be a middle east department,
150		middle east south asia, (.) <2> which is </2> INDIA (.)
151	S2:	<2> mhm </2>
152	S1:	at the end of the day, (.) which eh (NAME1) (LAST NAME1)
153		will run, (.)
154	S2:	mhm
155	S1:	yeah, and marc and (NAME2) (.) will be his sales staff for this
156		area. (.)
157	S2:	mhm

158	S1:	and there will be a far east department (.) headed by myself, (1)
159		and that will be (had) now, (.) <1> all </1> the transitions
160		already done, (.)
161	S2:	<1> mhm </1>
162	S1:	for example as you know marc handled (.) middle east plus
163		bangkok taipei and eh SINGAPORE, (.) bangkok taipei and
164		singapore are now transferred to clemens (.) to (1) sylvain,
165	S2:	<2> mhm </2>
166	S1:	<2> <L1=GERMAN> ja? </L1=GERMAN> <TRANSL=yes?>
167		</2> and that's also (what is) the splitting on the CHINA DESK,
168		(.) (NAME3) is taking care only for main land china, (.)
169	S2:	mhm
170	S1:	yeah? and clemens only for shanghai. (.)
171	S2:	aha
172	S1:	hongkong <1> (bangkok) </1> taipei.
173	S3:	<1> <coughs 2x> </1>
174	S1:	clemens what- toDAY will <FAST> present us as well main land
175		china as (NAME3) has a d- day of holidays today </FAST>
176	S2:	mhm
177	S1:	yeah? but (.) MARC is now (1) in charge for the middle east
178		together with (NAME1) who's also on holidays, ah: no, he's on
179		business trip he'll come later this this <1> afternoon, </1>
180	S3:	<1> he will come </1> today
181	S1:	yeah? so=ah: i'm stepping more and more out, (.) <2> of </2>
182		the middle east,
183	S2:	<2> <SOFT> hm </SOFT> </2>
184	S2:	mhm
185	S1:	so=ah: if you have something for dubai? (1) he's your partner.
186	S2:	(is) the: right person <3> eh: </3>
187	S1:	<3> <FAST> okay. </FAST> </3>
188	S2:	hey eh just to explain you more about (COMPANY5), it's a (1)
189		LAST year (.) it was a (.) well let's say a struggle year (.) ah our
190		performance was okay, if you look to the total performance and
191		i'm talking in eh LOAD FACTORS is more ah (.) ah: well an
192		average between the ninety and the ninety-two. (.) TONS load
193		factor, and this is cumulalative back to january, so it's still a
194		pretty high performance, even THOUGH you can see especially
195		in the last year (.) tha:t well YIELDwise it's a TREMENDOUS
196		(.) cutdown if you compare o:r you know- well YOU GUYS
197		know especially also with eh: (.) eh the rates are going down
198		TREMENDOUSLY and eh: well this this was a TOUGH (.)
199		PART of the year, so: (.) especially if you know maybe the
200		hongkong people, (.) they're very keen to keep levels up (.) to
201		the scenario which is actually not (.) market-conform anymore
202		(.) so in that way we are struggling a lot things (.) you know eh:
203		well to get those aGGRESSIVE rates into the market (2) you can
204		notice also wi:th with you guys because last half year eh from
205		the other year the two thousand and three, eh:m (.) well i

206		LOWERED your rate in that concern, (.) to get you more car-
207		mar- mar- market-conform rate, to MAYBE attract some more
208		business, (1) eh:m in that se:nse in the beginning i noticed (.)
209		your turnover (.) some dubai (even) but there was more=ah: (.)
210		more i believe OVERFLOW dubai? if i say it correct? (.) from
211		<1> your- from your sight? </1>
212	S3:	<1> eh: dubai: </1> it's dubai it's always difficult <2> eh:m
213		</2> (.)
214	S2:	<2> no? </2>
215	S3:	cuz ah: especially end of the year we operate in a lot of of ah:
216		own charter flights but i think i've explained you that already
217		during some phone conversations
218	S2:	mhm
219	S3:	and ah that's (.) BASICally what i can give away, is overflow
220		cargo from all these charter flights. we had up to: up to six
221		charter flights a WEEK. (.)
222	S2:	mhm
223	S3:	so=ah:m (.) it- it makes it difficult to give=eh: some cargo away:
224		if eh you <1> have to fill the: <SOFT> (xxx) </SOFT> </1>
225	S2:	<1> oh. (.) but those those </1> RATES? yeah? were they:
226		COMPETITIVE enough or say STRONG enough for you to
227		use?
228	S3:	not any more <SOFT> @ </SOFT>
229	S2:	not <2> any more </2> okay
230	S3:	<2> @ @ @ @ @ </2>
231	S1:	@ @
232	S3:	@ @ <3> @ @ </3>
233	S2:	<3> we are </3> now in a different (.) well <4> time zone again
234		</4>
235	S3:	<4> again it's a </4> again it's a different thing cuz you know in
236		eh: (.) especially: eh beginning of the year, (1) eh:m well the
237		capacity is still there,
238	S2:	mhm
239	S3:	and eh: (1) the cargo is gone. cuz the production is is eh is going
240		tremendously down during eh: <1> christmas new year's eve
241		(xx) </1>
242	S2:	<1> and how's how's the situation (now) </1> the production is
243		not <2> oh: </2> optimal at the moment is because of the year
244		beginning?
245	S3:	<2> well </2>
246	S3:	let's say i still have the production.
247	S2:	mhm
248	S3:	but eh: to be very honest the CURRENT rates we're buying
249		dubai is fourty-five cents
250	S2:	mhm (.)
251	S1:	on actual weight, (.)
252	S3:	on actual weight.
253	S1:	@ @ @ @ (.)

254	S2:	now now we sitting around here again you know and (1) to come
255		up- and i'm always open in this you know (.) that eh: try to get
256		maybe this this level up again or down again and concerning the
257		rate? what what what would be NECESSARY to come up? (1)
258		OR that we do it the other way around, i will give you some
259		indication but eh: (1) i give you a nice offer say let's say for the
260		first half year (.) eh: as a KICKOFF (.) fo:r this six months you
261		know especially i really don't know what's gonna happen (.)
262		eh:m
263	S3:	<SOFT> who knows </SOFT>
264	S2:	NOBODY does
265	S3:	<SOFT> @ @ </SOFT>
266	S2:	but also now for US, this YEAR is gonna be a (.) well we need
267		to be very successful this year as you maybe know that we are
268		OPENING our doors again (.) in expansion. eh: especially in
269		EUROPE (.) so for US it's an additional capacity we need to
270		fulFILL (1) as i told you last YEAR ah that we're gonna (.)
271		OPEN the german offers, (.)
272	S1:	<SOFT> mhm </SOFT>
273	S2:	eh: hh about GERMANY eh (COMPANY5) is so particular (.)
274		eh: maybe the strange word is (.) i:s (1) ah: how can i say it in a
275		nice decent english word they are so ah (2) you know
276		particularly CAMOUFLAGING (.) themselves to say WHICH
277		destination it's gonna be, (.) camouflage is maybe not the correct
278		word but (.) <claps hands together> they are really not opening
279		yet? but i can say it it's gonna be MUNICH (1) eh: this this is the
280		destination which we're gonna: OPEN. (.) eh:m we TRY to had
281		this (.) IN as from (.) I believe so (.) from JUNE or either july.
282		(2) they PROMISED us to have it earlier but this all has to do, eh
283		because of the turnover a new plane, which actually is already in,
284		but they're now already (.) building up this, into the: well the
285		cargo conversion which we need to have to <1> FLY </1> it of
286		course (.)
287	S1:	<1> <SOFT> mhm </SOFT> </1>
288	S2:	and this is eh: well they promised us aGAIN but- WE are
289		particular. i'm DUTCH you know we all say <2> first see and
290		then </2> (1)
291	S1:	<2> <SOFT> @ @ @ </SOFT> </2>
292	S2:	ah: we see it's a really active year (on)line and then eh belie:v-
293		we belie:ve it's coming around july (.) june (.) around then (.)
294		deadline. well aGAIN if we have this additional capacity (.) then
295		I believe it's also for YOU quite interesting maybe what we tal:-
296		oh: well last year we discussed a little ALSO concerning this,
297		that EITHER well you could choose that part. EITHER you
298		could choose the amsterdam site
299	S1:	<coughs 1x>
300	S2:	well in that sense (.) WE have enough capacity (.) to offer. (1)
301		BUT (.) I believe (.) if you look to the MARKET (.) the:n well

302		it's too much capacity (1) in that term we need to agree
303		SOMETHING and maybe something a- very attractive. (.) so in
304		that sense i want to MAKE you an OFFER? (1) eh: i only want
305		to: get some hints from you from okay what will be an
306		INTERESTING (.) level? (.) from (1) eh an idea <1> maybe
307		</1> from okay this this is a thing that we maybe have (.)
308	S1:	<1> mhm </1>
309	S2:	REGULAR loads, (.) say, let's say on a WEEKLY basis (1) and
310		maybe maybe this is <2> a point of view </2>
311	S1:	<2> my: the:- </2> there would my question towards eh marc. (.)
312		have you EVER explained to (.) to joseph, (.) the WAY (.) the
313		business works. (es-) espec<1>ially (COMPANY1) business
314		</1>
315	S3:	<1> yeah. i think we </1> HAVE discussed (it-) about it but but
316		it's always difficult to judge. you can- you know from from one
317		day on on the OTHER (.) there might be a booking popping up
318		for one thousand cubic meters.
319	S2:	mhm
320	S3:	that's eh: (1) always a little bit depending especially beginning
321		of the month they have problems eh: to: obTAIN the: necessary
322		invoices from (COMPANY7) (xxx). usually: (.) let's say
323		between the first and the fifth of each month, (.) we have very
324		low production of cargo. (.) eh:m (1)
325	S1:	sta- start a little bit different. (.) we have (.) JUST down the hill
326		(COMPANY6). (.) as distribution center for (COMPANY7). (.)
327		<1> so </1> all (COMPANY7) cargo is coming (in)to HERE, (.)
328	S2:	<1> mhm </1>
329	S1:	into the (COMPANY8) part. hhh in the meantime. eh:m they're
330		sitting on the cargo.
331	S2:	mhm
332	S1:	but then they get the INVOICES from (COMPANY7), and then
333		the cargo is ready to move. (.) from THAT (.) day on (.)
334		normally within TWO days the cargo has to be in DUBAI, (1)
335		<background noise from plane (8)> (workers) three four days
336		sometimes <FAST> <SOFT> (you never can be) (x). </SOFT>
337		</FAST>
338	S2:	<SOFT> mhm </SOFT>
339	S1:	but you NEVER KNOW when it's popping up, <1> you never
340		know: </1> (1)
341	S3:	<1> <coughs 3x> </1>
342	S1:	<SOFT> <FAST> (just wait for the) </FAST> plane, </SOFT>
343		ah:m how MUCH it is? (.)
344	S2:	<2> mhm </2>
345	S1:	<2> it can </2> be: ONE HUNDRED cubic meters (.) it can be
346		eh: like this week one thousand four hundred cubic meters. (.)
347	S2:	<3> mhm </3>
348	S1:	<3> yesterday </3> afternoon <FAST> one thousand four
349		hundred cubic meters </FAST> a:re READY to go.

350	S2:	mhm
351	S1:	SO. (.) ehm eh we start. (.) eh we call for full charters,
352	S2:	<SOFT> mhm </SOFT>
353	S1:	yeah? which is (some) (.) VOLUME amount as you know, yeah?
354		and eh: (1) then we look what what possibilities do we have. (.)
355	S2:	mhm
356	S1:	yeah? (.) so we have TRIED at the beginning with eh several
357		carriers also with (COMPANY9), (.) to have (.)
358		ALLOCATIONS for pallets on this flight so eight on that flight
359		<1> eh: but it- it- it is not working </1> out it's absolutely not
360		working out
361	S2:	<1> (it's ni- it's quite eh:) (xx) </1>
362	S1:	in ADDITION comes what what marc has mentioned then as
363		WELL, hh the DIScrepancy between the beginning of the month
364		towards the end of the <2> month </2>
365	S2:	<2> mhm </2>
366		(2)
367	S1:	<3> that's eh the tricky part </3>
368	S2:	<3> okay but then eh </3> <4> i eh: i understand eh: </4>
369	S3:	<4> (xx) would always- it would always </4> be on (ad hoc) (.)
370		it would ALWAYS be <SOFT> on ad hoc </SOFT>
371	S2:	mhm
372	S3:	we cannot fix something regu<5>lar</5>
373	S2:	<5> oh. </5> (.) oh- okay. but then maybe you know what we
374		did like last year, (.) we give you a phone call, in that kind of
375		sense <6> and </6> say <7> hey </7> marc, (.)
376	SX-3:	<6> <SOFT> yeah </SOFT> </6>
377	SX-1:	<7> mhm </7>
378	S2:	maybe you have something, maybe you don't? (.) BUT (.) i
379		THINK we need to agree something <FAST> you know in-
380		</FAST> on the RATES in advantage. (1) <FAST> what what
381		would be the hint from your side what would be </FAST> eh (.)
382		what would be NECESSARY, would it (.) be necessary to have
383		only PALLET rates? KILO rates? o:r whatever? eh: (1)
384	S3:	<SOFT> well </SOFT> (2) what markus said already the
385		CURRENT (.) buying scenario is that we are buying fourty-five
386		cents, (.)
387	S2:	oh. (.)
388	S3:	and we have eh we get charged on actual weight.
389	S2:	mhm (1)
390	S3:	so meaning, eh doesn't matter if the U-L-D the Q seven has two
391		thousand or three thousand kilos, we got charged for the actual
392		weight per <1> kilo </1>
393	S2:	<1> mhm </1>
394	S1:	hh
395	SX-3:	and per manifest let's say. (.) <2> i'd say </2>
396	S2:	<2> ah </2>
397	S1:	the cargo will be ONLY (.) come in (.) <3> built up units </3>

398	S3:	<3> U-P units </3>
399	S1:	U-P units
400	S2:	okay
401	S1:	eh: <FAST> (COMPANY6) is is we deliver U-(L-)M to U-L-Ds,
402		they build up Q sevens Q sixes </FAST> WHATEVER, (.) and
403		we deliver (.) ONLY built up <1> cargos</1>
404	S3:	<1> (xxx) </1> <2> (do you know) (xx) </2>
405	S2:	<2> okay. (.) okay, </2> what what i gonna do MARC i give you
406		an OFFER, (.) i make this on EMAIL (.) <3> eh: </3>
407	S3:	<3> <SOFT> please </SOFT> </3>
408	S2:	tomorrow is <4> WEDNES</4>day yeah? (.)
409	S1:	<4> <SOFT> mhm </SOFT> </4>
410	S2:	so: i will make you an OFFER we:ll together with he
411		conversations which i'm gonna have here today, (.) <5> and
412		</5> make MORE offers of course <6> and in that sense </6>
413		i'm- i make you an offer and WELL i KNOW this (1)
414	S1:	<5> <SOFT> mhm </SOFT> </5>
415	S3:	<6> are you:? </6>
416	S2:	GUIDELINE which you just mentioned (.) this is more or less
417		the well (.) the level of rates which is at the moment (1) <7>
418		even (if) </7>
419	S3:	<7> are you </7> serving some some more destinations ah: in
420		the middle east?
421	S2:	again?
422	S3:	do you have some more destinations in the middle east? or it's
423		purely dubai?
424	S2:	YES. i PROMISE(D) you actually i've- sorry
425	S3:	still not <1> get it @ @ @ @ </1>
426	S2:	<1> i've (.) i for</1>got <2> @ (.) @ </2>
427	S3:	<2> <SOFT> @ @ @ </SOFT> </2>
428	S2:	i FORGOT eh you are recording this <3> (now) </3>
429	S1:	<LOUD> <3> @ </3> @ <4> @ @ @ @> </4> </LOUD>
430	S3:	<4> @ @ @ @ </4>
431	S2:	<4> @ @ </4> i forgot last year actually to mention it, yes. we-
432		we have a lot of ah: destinations within (.) the middle east (1)
433		<5> eh: </5>
434	S3:	<5> send me </5> (.) send me JUST a LIST (.)
435	S2:	yes.
436	S3:	with destinations you can offer, what kind of services, (1) <6>
437		you </6> have, (1) <7> a:nd </7>
438	S2:	<6> yes </6>
439	S2:	<7> it's all </7> to to let you know now immediately it's all of
440		course it's a TRUCKING (.) connection eh:
441	S1:	<SOFT> <FAST> from du<1>bai</1> </FAST> </SOFT>
442	S2:	<1> FROM </1> (.) our dubai station. (2)
443	S1:	<SOFT> okay. </SOFT>
444	S2:	but it it's a very GOOD. to to give you a lot of example we we
445		had (.) last time we have a lot of dama:l shipments even riad o:r

446		just name all the destinations we: we get those also. (1) and=ah: i
447		believe the service which we can offer THERE is (.) oh it's quite
448		good. (.) and ah: well an- anyway i make you an a total <1> (.)
449		summanary of destinations </1>
450	S3:	<1> <SOFT> i need </SOFT> what i need is a list of </1>
451		destinations, what <2> kind of servi:ce (and eh) (.) then the (xx)
452		the transit (.) yeah that would be </2>
453	S2:	<2> even even with HOURS, a:nd the trucking company, (.)
454		PHONE numbers, (.) WHATEVER. </2>
455	S3:	(exactly) (.) that's <3> what </3>
456	S2:	<3> and i('ll) </3> make you a whole summarary of this
457	SX-1:	yeah
458	S3:	and then i: i can come back to you to see okay ah ah where we
459		are in need and=ah: what (.)
460	S2:	uh.
461	S3:	what conditions we will need (2)
462	S1:	coming back to dubai. (.) ah:m another question's you're
463		interested is also to make CHARTER flights.
464	S2:	mhm. (1)
465	S1:	is this an <1> option? </1>
466	S2:	<1> we? </1> (.) yes.
467	S1:	for you.
468	S2:	especially:=eh (.) now to tell you also something (.) AS we're
469		gonna have again a new PLANE, now we have in totally four. (.)
470		but the fifth one is (sure) (here) to come also. (.) ah: we are
471		working out a CORRIDOR system. (.) so in OTHER words it
472		means that we quickly (x) aggressively h- ha:ve BIG LOTS (.)
473		park lots or total planes whatever, (.) IMMEDIATLEY eh: can
474		offer this into the market (.) <1> so: </1> for example if you
475		ha:ve i don't know (.)
476	S1:	<1> mhm, </1>
477	S2:	DOHA, we have many good requests to doha for example (.) like
478		(.) eighty tons ninety tons whatever <2> then we can </2>
479		corridor
480	S3:	<2> (xx) (thirty) (xx) </2>
481	S2:	this this <3> kind </3> of possibility (.)
482	S1:	<3> mhm </3>
483	S2:	to those costumers. and this ESPECIALLY (.) eh: starting from
484		this year, (.) we gonna: well MORE aggressively opening (.)
485		this kind of concept (.)
486	S1:	mhm (.)
487	S2:	i will let you know something about this also? (.) eh:m you know
488		the strange thing within (COMPANY5), it's a f- it's a POLICY.
489		(.) they say tha:t for EACH (1) destination which you want to
490		FLY as a (COMPANY5), (.) ONE of us needs to be (.) send over
491		to this destination? (1) eh: arrange everything like the handli:ng,
492		COVering all the (.) the necessary action <1> which is </1>
493		necessary to operate this plane (.)

494	S1:	<1> <L1=GERMAN> *ja* </L1=GERMAN> <TRANSL=yes>
495		</1>
496	S2:	but the POINT is (1) we ha:ve SUCH a big list (.) that we are
497		now actually CUTTING (.) destinations like THIS because we
498		are not ONLY looking to the MIDDLE east? (.) because we say
499		eh: AMSTERDAM. (.) you fly maybe: you know eh maybe
500		ITALY? i don't know this (is) maybe a (.) a GOOD corridor
501		destination? (.) or say: SWITZERLAND, whatever, you know
502		the: ROUGHLY in a (.) i- i- in a RANGE for the particular (.) i
503		don' know (.) fifteen to two thousand miles or something,
504		something like that, we make CORRIDOR destinations ALL the
505		way up to: HONGKONG (.) (and they) route you(r) flight,
506	S1:	mm
507	S2:	and (COMPANY5) say this is their policy (.) (well) you need to
508		have (1) one (COMPANY5) people send over FIRST to arrange
509		all those things, and THIS is what we are doing now already (1)
510		so: a lot of people from hongKONG, they're really flying
511		themselves CRAZY
512	S1:	<SOFT> @@ </SOFT>
513	S2:	<SOFT> @@@ </SOFT> to all kinds of <1> (.) destinations
514		</1>
515	S1:	<1> hey, (.) you need </1> somebody for this? @ <2> @@@@
516		</2>
517	S2:	<2> @@ </2> no (but-) it's WEIRD you know they say (1) they
518		only need to: have a (check) you know? <FAST> y- you could
519		pick up the phone i i can pick up the phone </FAST> with italy
520		and say HEY (.) you want to: have a contract together with (.)
521		with us and we make a: a HANDLING contract whatever it's it's
522		so quite easy. no, THEY say: (.) you need to be LIVE (.) active
523		(1) in this (.) eh particular destination. (1) and beLIEVE me we
524		had something i: i don't know we had (.) thirty-eight destinations
525		or something? which we picked up, i:n this who:le route? (.) and
526		THEN we heard this policy? it's oh: i'll (call) you eh <1> w:ff
527		</1>
528	SX-1:	<SOFT> <1> @@ </1> @@ </SOFT>
529	S2:	we took out a LOT of (.) of those destinations. (1) but this is
530		particular the chine:se they they they they('re) really VERY (.)
531		put everything in: in in <2> BOOKS, </2> manuals (.)
532	SX-3:	<2> <SOFT> mhm </SOFT> </2>
533	S1:	(wait)?
534	SX-3	<SOFT> @@ <3> (xx:) </3> </SOFT>
535	S2:	<3> but it's a </3> it's a good thing you: you COORDINATE in
536		this matter. but ah. (.) okay, but that's (.) i('ll) let you know also,
537		(.) <4> and </4> then ah: (2)
538	S3:	<4> <SOFT> please </SOFT> </4>
539	S3:	well <1> in c- just in </1> in case we are in need of let's say a
540		full flight, (.)
541	S2:	<1> my (xx) </1>

152

542	S3:	ah: just to trust it to you (and) say OKAY (.) then and
543		<L1=GERMAN> *dann* </L1=GERMAN> <TRANSL=then> we
544		would have sufficient cargo to operate a full flight with you (1)
545		ah: these are the conditions we can ah: APPLY o:r (.) whatever
546		then ah: we can see case by case
547	S2:	oh. Oh. (.) okay,
548		(6)
549	S1:	as indication for eh dubai full charter (2) out of msterdam (.)
550		<1> seven </1> four seven
551	S2:	<1> mhm </1>
552	S2:	mhm (.) what, the co<2>st?</2>
553	S1:	<2> (we p)</2>ay: eh: (.) for time being eh y- (.) what do you
554		think is the PRICE?
555		(4)
556	S2:	it's a tough question but eh: i belie:ve (6) let's say: (2) two
557		hundre:d (2) thirty? (.) thousand (2)
558	S1:	o<3>kay,</3>
559	S3:	<3>amster</3>dam dubai?
560	S2:	yeah,
561	S1:	sixty thousand. <4> (a lot) </4>
562	S2:	<4>SIX</4>TY? (.) okay. Then eh: yeah. (.)
563	S1:	<LOUD> that <5> you </5> know which area we're <6> talking
564		about. (.) yeah? </6> </LOUD>
565	S2:	<5> well </5>
566	S3:	<6> <SOFT> @ @ @ </SOFT> </6>
567	S2:	no- <7> (but) </7>
568	S3:	<7> i </7> thought you were talking about a round-trip price
569		<8> eh: </8> amsterdam <9> dubai: hongkong </9> eh:
570		amsterdam @ @ @
571	S2:	<8> @ @ @ </8>
572	S1:	<9> two hundred thirty thousand pfff </9>
573	S2:	no actually we- WE are quite (.) you know=ah
574	S3:	(x) (the pixies) (.) @ @ @ @ (1)
575	S2:	in PRICES concerning this CHARTERing (.) we never did
576		actually in- a separate charter for this. (1) but then (.) aGAIN it's
577		it's something new for also <1> but </1>
578	S3:	<1> yeah </1>
579	S2:	i'm (.) well SURPRISED but actually also NOT surPRISED, (.)
580		because if you look to those sixty THOUsand well it's mo:re (.)
581		<2>eh: more con</2>form the PRICE (.)
582	S1:	<2> <SOFT> <FAST> i mean </FAST> </SOFT> just think
583		about </2>
584	S2:	if you to: look to the kilo rate (2) <3> in total. </3>
585	S1:	<3> and look and </3> look back eh: just to the amsterdam
586		airport, (.) which far east carriers all are based there, and have
587		empty flights going back, in the <4> (xx) </4> (it's- we) take
588		one day out o:f of the operations
589	S3:	<4> (x) </4>

153

590	S1:	(.) <5> fly </5> to middle east for this ONE
591	S2:	<5> <SOFT> mhm </SOFT> </5>
592	S2:	<SOFT> mhm </SOFT>
593	S1:	and fill the next day's flight
594	S2:	oh.
595	S1:	<SOFT> yeah? </SOFT>
596	S2:	and if you: look in that kind of price you kno:w (.) is is is this
597		based on (.) each day? <SOFT> (you see?) </SOFT> (1) hh <1>
598		(does it matter?) </1>
599	S1:	<1> (it is) </1> based on EACH day. <2> mo:re </2> or less,
600		whenever:, okay. we have to see it (then) when when we have
601		enough cargo (you'd-) like this one thousand four hundred cubic
602		meters, (.)
603	S2:	<2> mhm </2>
604	S1:	we (ASK) several carriers, (.)
605	S2:	<SOFT> mhm </SOFT> (.)
606	S1:	and we get (1) SEVERAL carriers. (COMPANY10 – truncated!,
607		only first syllable) (.) <1> eh: </1>
608	S2:	<1> <SOFT> mhm </SOFT> </1>
609	S1:	it's not only ONE carrier. (.) it's carriers in luxemburg, it's
610		carriers in amsterdam, (.)
611	S2:	mhm
612	S1:	<L1=GERMAN> ja? </L1=GERMAN> <TRANSL=yes> and
613		it's carriers in frankfurt. (.) <2> they </2> say ah: we have the
614		availability or not, or we can, or we cannot. (.)
615	S2:	<2> <SOFT> mhm </SOFT> </2>
616	S2:	<3> <SOFT> oh </SOFT> </3>
617	S1:	<3> yeah? </3> for this and this price. (.) but the market is <4>
618		eh </4>
619	S3:	<4> even </4> even we get requests from the carriers coming to
620		us saying hey do you want to operate a flight?
621	S1:	yeah.
622	S2:	mhm
623	S3:	so it's eh: (.) it's eh: easy
624	S2:	mhm
625	S1:	best example is eh: (COMPANY11) and and (COMPANY12).
626		whenever they have a free: quoTATION, yeah, they just give us
627		a call=eh: and saying i have in two days a flight available, do
628		you want? yes no. (.)
629	S2:	mhm (.)
630	S1:	yeah?
631	S2:	(but) this- in this (.) SCENARIO i want to have (COMPANY5)
632		also you know that (.) OUR people: they need to (be:) (.) well
633		CALLING you, (1) that you get CRAZY of us eh:
634	S3:	<1> <SOFT> @ @ @ @ </SOFT> </1>
635	S1:	<1> <SOFT> @ @ @ @ </SOFT> </1>
636	S2:	<SOFT> @ </SOFT> marc? (.) <2> no no but in that </2> sense
637		they they they need to have you know eh: a CALL. (.)

638	SX-3:	<2> <SOFT> @ @ @ @ </SOFT> </2>
639	S2:	eSPECIALLY once once a week twice a week an:d just to: see
640		okay well (.) is there any load available whateve:r (.) and
641		then=ah well (.) we can build up anything (.) concerning a-
642		(better) deal o:r just NAME it (.) in that sense, (1) but again i'm
643		i'm not surprised about you:r (1) your price. (1) you know
644		SOMEtimes what WE do (.) i:s to let you know our monday:
645		flight is quite WEAK (1) eh:m (.) in in holland (1) eh:m (.) our
646		monday flight (.) sometimes (.) we: try to (.) eh: DELAY it in
647		terms if it's possible commercialwise, (.) why? because there's a
648		TREMENDOUS market with (.) eh: plants, flowers, to dubai. (.)
649		in THAT sense (.) eh: we build up (.) even the FLOWER option,
650		not the AGENTS but (.) the SHIPPERS. (.) and with those
651		SHIPPERS (.) which we KNOW the agents (1) they
652		TOGETHER (.) try to succeed to fill the flight (.) and actually
653		that's a sort of (.) (part) (x) (.) CHARTERING actually also the
654		flight (.) just to know (well) lately it works out pretty good. (.)
655		but then ah: well it's the TIMING because CUTOFF for flowers
656		on a monday is (.) is not a good day hh <1> suppose </1> it was
657		a TUESday (.)
658	SX:	<1> (x) </1>
659	S2:	it's a BRILLIANT day. (.)
660	S1:	<SOFT> (yeah) (yes) </SOFT>
661	S2:	this this is also a SCENARIO (.) to let you know also (.) ah: WE
662		are (.) working out to have a flight on this tu:esday. (.) becau:se a
663		MONDAY well i believe everywhere in europe, maybe certain
664		routes not? but (.) i:t's it's it's a weak (.) weak day of course eh:
665		to operate (1) this kind of flight if you want to fulFILL <1> to
666		get </1> it FULL
667	S1:	<1> yeah </1>
668	S1:	<SOFT> (x) <2> (xxxx) </2> </SOFT>
669	S2:	<2> so: we are really </2> looking DESPERATELY to have this
670		(.) flight on MONDAY (.) go into the tuesday. (.) but this is very
671		tough especially with [swippal], with slots and whatever it's (.)
672		it's a tough decision
673	S1:	calling <3> eh: </3>
674	S2:	<3> a TOUGH thing to </3> get ARRANGED. (.)
675	S1:	what do you think if you could arrange it w- how long would it
676		take? (2) to put on tuesdays. (1) cuz LATER for the
677		HONGKONG discussion we will talk about the MONDAY
678		flight hh (.) hh so it would be important to have the monday
679		flight
680	S2:	mhm (.) okay,
681	S1:	<LOUD> @ @ @ @ @ so be CAREFUL what you're SAYING
682		now <4> @ @ @ @ </4> </LOUD>
683	S2:	<4> yah yah okay </4> okay @ (.)
684	S1:	@
685	S2:	always be careful what i'm saying <5> (but eh) </5>

686	S1:	<5> @@ </5> @@ (1)
687	S2:	okay well RECAP? ahm (.) i will give you (1) a: (.) GOOD (1)
688		hopefully a very <6> good OFFER, </6> and eh: of course i give
689		you the: eh: (.)
690	SX-3:	<6> <SOFT> @@@@ </SOFT> </6>
691	S2:	(in)land or say the: eh the [smut] <7> eh: </7>
692	S3:	<7> the distribution </7> to the middle east (and) (.) that's
693		basically what i need
694	S2:	okay. (.) i give you ALL the details marc, it's a- well i got a total
695		list. from- from dubai and we just (.) reNEWED the whole list.
696		(.) because we CHANGED ou:r (.) trucking (.) PARTNER
697		actually in dubai to a new one. and this: (.) this <8> one is very
698		good </8>
699	S3:	<8> (xxx) (are) you </8> working with?
700	S2:	oh i don't know, i forgot the name, (.)
701	S3:	<9> (COMPANY13)? </9>
702	S2:	<9> but before </9>
703		(2)
704	S2:	n=no.
705	S3:	no?
706	S2:	i don't believe so. (2) no. because WHY we changed it we had
707		some some problems (.) eh: something like (.) i don't know a
708		YEAR ago. and this trucking company, (.) when we BOOKED
709		something, (.) okay we ORDERED (.) i don't know (.) six seven
710		eight trucks (.) and then they show up with only FOUR and the
711		next day ANOTHER four that <1> eh well this </1> this is not
712		working <2> properly </2> of course. (.)
713	S1:	<1> hhhh </1> <2> mhm </2>
714	S3:	but this is pretty normal in <@> dubai: </@> <SOFT> @ <3>
715		@@ </3> </SOFT>
716	S2:	<3> ye:s </3> but (.) you know especially NOW because (.) we
717		a:re (.) NOW with this new trucking company, (.) they want to
718		perFORM them- (.) SELF (1) very good because they want to
719		see HEY we are better than this (.) than this (.) OTHER
720		company. (1) <4> and ah: </4>
721	S1:	<FAST> <4> with whom are you </4> working now? </FAST>
722		(1)
723	S2:	again=ah: markus?
724	S1:	with WHOM? (.) <FAST> which trucking company <5> you're
725		working? </5> </FAST>
726	S2:	<5> i don't </5> i don't know. but i i'll let you know the name
727		of it. (1) we just had (.) i believe it was in december, we
728		cha:nged this WHOLE schedule (.) we ADDED some
729		destinations
730	S1:	mhm
731	S2:	eh: better price:s
732	S3:	so <1> you have </1> as WELL:
733	S2:	<1> yeah </1>

734	S3:	<SOFT> let me (say). </SOFT> you you can offer as well a: a
735		one-way trucking from dubai to riad and jiddah (2)
736	S2:	yes. i believe so: yes. (.) but i- i need to check. because (.) i have
737		NOW a total (.) summarary: of <2> ALL </2> the destinations,
738		inclu:ding what is necessary (.)
739	S3:	<2> mhm </2>
740	S2:	you know eh suppose it is NOT bonded, or (.) it IS bonded,
741		whatever. i can tell you immediately. (.) <3> it's it's just </3>
742	S3:	<FAST> <3> yeah because i need to </3> know the <4>
743		conditions </4> because especially saudi arabia it's pretty
744		difficult </FAST> <5> hh cuz i </5> KNOW in in let's say in
745		riad and jiddah they have no FREE zone available.
746	S1:	<4> mhm, </4>
747	S2:	<5> even even </5>
748	S2:	oh.
749	S3:	that means usually (.) the: custom clearance needs to be done at
750		the border already, (.) or already in dubai,
751	S2:	mhm
752	S3:	ah: which is making it pretty difficult for the: for the consignees
753		to obtain the cargo. (.) a:nd it's as well high costs involved (.)
754	S2:	<1> eh </1>
755	S3:	<1> and </1> the only free zone in saudi arabia is in DAMAL.
756		(.)
757	S2:	EVEN (.) even i can tell you (now). necessary documentatio:n,
758		and what- all- all kinds of details?
759	S3:	hm (.)
760	S2:	it's it I will explain to you. it's a just a (.) i make a copy of what
761		we <2> have here </2>
762	S3:	<2> (no but) </2> once i have THAT i can have a look
763		THROUGH and then ah:
764	S2:	oh. (2)
765	S3:	mi:ght <3> come </3> might become more (xx)
766	S2:	<3> it's (x) </3>
767	S2:	cuz last last time we: had a: very big shipment to: i believe it was
768		DAMAL (.) and there was something ALSO with with
769		BONDed. (.) but actually what we did, (.) we we trucked it
770		DIRECTLY actually to the consignee.
771	SX:	<SOFT> yeah </SOFT>
772	S2:	but the PROBLEM was he had no bonded warehouse (xx) but
773		THEN (.) we had some PEOPLE (.) also BY this company (.)
774		and THEY arranged (.) at the BORDER (1) that already could
775		CLEAR it, (.) and THEN they could continue the whole thing.
776	S3:	yeah but this is always a: a cost factor. (.)
777	S2:	yeah okay but- <1> well </1>
778	S3:	<1> cuz </1> if you if you can clear in the free zone ah: you're
779		(.) m- maybe a lot of companies are duty exempt(ors) so they
780		HAVE to clear in the free zone
781	S2:	mhm

782	S3:	eh: if they DO: clear their cargo at the BORDER they might to
783		have (.) eh to pay duties eh: whatsoever <2> eh: </2> which is
784		quite expensive in saudi arabia.
785	S2:	<2> oh. </2>
786	S2:	oh.
787	S3:	so i nee- DEFINITELY (1) with this offer i will need ALL
788		conditions (.) ALL the <3> possibilities you're offering there
789		</3>
790	S2:	<3> you will you will get it </3> (.) definitely. <4> you will get
791		</4> ALL (1)
792	S3:	<4> that's eh: </4>
793	S2:	NECESSARY information <5> which you wanted about this,
794		</5> you <6> you will get (it) </6>
795	S3:	<5> @ @ @ @ </5> <6> in case i </6> have additional questions
796		i will let you know ANYWAY <7> @ @ @ @ </7> <8> @ @
797		</8>
798	S2:	<7> @ @ @ @ </7>
799	SX-1:	<8> <SOFT> okay </SOFT> </8>
800	S2:	NO, we're ta- well we we definitely NOTICED this because (1)
801		on PURPOSE (.) we kept it (.) a little: QUIET let's say it like
802		that, (.) because we wanted to SORT out FIRST (all) kinds of
803		problems (.) STRUGGLE problems from we:ll let's- supPOSE
804		you: you book something and (.) afterwards we need to explain
805		to you YEAH. because it's this. eh: bla bla bla eh but (.) on
806		PURPOSE we did this (.) and THEN our GUY: eh say in
807		DUBAI (.) eh: well he sorted out A:LL those kind of details. (.)
808		and he made a big summarary out of it. (.) so we now know
809		exACTly (2) to each destination which we could offer (1) eh:
810		which is (.) eh FIRST of all it's (.) the STANDARD trucks we
811		could offer. BESIDES that (.) we can offer also within that
812		region (.) MORE destination but it (is) on AD HOC. (.) it me:ans
813		that (.) we can make the request? (1) but it's not in this list. we
814		can OF COURSE make the request? (.) but we need to ask first
815		to ou:r (.) person in dubai who's in charge of that, (.) and try to
816		find OUT (.) from oka:y eh possibilities eh could it be done, eh
817		whatever
818	S3:	<SOFT> okay </SOFT> (.)
819	S2:	because well you know RIAD i: riad (.) from out of dubai it
820		takes three days eh special documentations and all kinds of- (.)
821		well this this <@> kind of things </@> (.) <1> you get with
822		ALL kinds </1> of destinations <2> like that </2>
823	S3:	<1> i know @ @ @ </1>
824	S3:	<2> @ @ </2> okay, (.) no that's fine with me,
825	S2:	mhm (1)
826	S3:	and i'm waiting your <3> (xx) </3>
827	S2:	<3> okay </3> (.) you maybe have some more questions eh:
828		marc. (1)

829	S3:	no basically my major questions are answered. i:'m just waiting
830		your proposal. (.) <4> and then </4> ah: we can continue (1)
831	S2:	<4> okay </4>
832	S2:	okay (.) for NEXT year (1) you guys (.) you gonna come to
833		amsterdam eh?

Extract A.2

(51:57 – 59:02; *length 7:05*)

1	S1:	hh okay let's let's first go to the general issues, (.) yeah? and
2		then i give a <1> call upstairs ah: </1>
3	S2:	<1> yes (.) maybe </1> i can ask you the question. from- (.)
4	S4:	sure
5	S2:	<addressing S4> ARE there any general issues or eh (.) point of
6		vie:ws from (1) the company side. from from your side say (.)
7		concerning (COMPANY5). other things (.) like from eh: (.) i
8		don't know maybe ACCOUNTING issues eh: (1) overall
9		general issues. y- you maybe know something about? (1)
10		(COMPANY5) to to to come up from hey look THIS is maybe
11		a thing which we NEED to do better or (.) eh: <FAST> i don't
12		know </FAST> more SALES visits? or (.) just NAME it. (.)
13		you maybe have=a. (.) <1> IDEAS, thoughts </1>
14	S4:	<1> (i) (x) (say) (x) like </1> that so far: when i was working
15		befor- WITH you. because i had also a certain time that i had
16		the backup of (NAME2)'s when she was taking care about the
17		hongkong trophey hh (.) i had eh the:se BIG ni:ce eh shipment
18		MAINLY (y-) reminded it's wa- from PORTUGAL. (.) was
19		this very, (.)
20	S2:	<SOFT> (don't) you <2> know? </2> </SOFT>
21	S4:	<2> (it')s: </2> it was a DENSE cargo but was (.) not very nice
22		to build up and so on
23	S2:	hh all <3> this </3> <4> this is the thing </4> <5> i remember
24		</5>
25	S4:	<3> and </3>
26	S1:	<4> mm (and) i (thought) </4>
27	S4:	<5> it was in </5> (.) AUGUST.
28	S1:	august. <6> (yeah) </6>
29	S4:	<6> august </6> (1) end of august. i was eh dealing with
30		(NAME4). (.) about that. (1)
31	S2:	hh and this <7> this i remember </7>
32	S4:	<7> and so FAR it was </7> working very well i didn't (.)
33		didn't had any problems
34	S1:	it was this eh: eleven (lower) (dockage) or s- something <8>
35		like this (.) (shipment) eh </8> nightmare <9> shipment. </9>
36	S4:	<8> <L1=GERMAN> ja. (.) ja ja. ja ja. </L1=GERMAN>
37		<TRANSL=yes (.) yes yes. yes yes.> correct. </8> <9>
38		because </9> we could not (xx) up on (main deck as) it was
39		<1> to </1> <2> (x) </2>

159

40	S1:	<1> hm </1>
41	S2:	<2> oh. </2> (.) you know at THAT time i t- i t- i traveled
42		ALSO a LOT. (.) and=ah I was not really in the OFFICE at
43		THAT time and i HEARD something BETWEE:N (.) ah
44		conCERNING this eh from portugal whatever but (.) what I
45		underSTOOD there was a (.) a MIXTURE (.) of a MIX-UP o:f
46		(.) of RATES which they give to YOU i belie:ve and say to:
47		somebody else. but i don't KNOW (.) who the other (.) was, i
48		really don't know. (.) but i can FIND OUT more details if you
49		prefer to hear it. (.) STILL (1) in that kind of particular case (1)
50	S4:	(i) (xx) you took it over (of it) after that. (.) i didn't have any
51		problems actually because i had a ehm i had a
52	S1:	the problems <1> was never with (COMPANY5) side </1> (.)
53		<2> the well there was </2>
54	S4:	<1> a certain number </1> (.) <2> i had a certain </2> number
55		for your quotation which you gave me on <3> this time </3>
56	S1:	<3> yeah </3> there <4> there was- was no hiccups </4> eh:
57		with eh: the the part from (COMPANY5)
58	S4:	<4> that one was </4>
59	S2:	mhm
60	S1:	<5> it was </5> internal (COMPANY1a)
61	S4:	<5> (xx) </5>
62	S4:	<6> okay </6>
63	S2:	<6> BUT </6> but ov- overALL (.) NONE of US got it (.)
64		what i believe (.) we didn't either also got it eh i believe YOUR
65		side, (we) didn't get it, so in that sense eh: @ (1) <FAST> it's
66		(not in particular) </FAST> t- to tell you SOMETHING.
67	S1:	<SOFT> yeah </SOFT>
68	S2:	SUPPOSE we we get INQUIRIES (.) eh: sometimes that
69		happens. (.) we get the same inquiries which you ha:ve (.) a:nd
70		we get them from out of <1> germany </1> belgium france
71		whatever, just name it (.)
72	S1:	<1> <SOFT> (ge-) </SOFT> </1>
73	S2:	we ALWAYS (.) and i tell you this honestly ALWAYS DO (.)
74		the same rate. always. (.) why? because we want to avoid (.)
75		<2> this </2> kind of conflict. (.)
76	S1:	<2> mhm </2>
77	S1:	absolutely.
78	S2:	and this this is (.) really we d- mm put my HANDS into the fire
79		for it (1) this is the the scenario we only work. (.) becau:se we
80		want to make (.) no conflicts (.) and believe me <@> this is the
81		thing </@> (COMPANY5) always does. (1) and we try to
82		avoi:d (.) ALWAYS this kind of <3> things. </3>
83	S4:	<3> it's </3> not so- that's eh not (.) you never know what the
84		origins in this country are. then: (.) in the end are offering. (.)
85		<4> (and) </4> say they are coming to you, request a shipment,
86		(.)
87	S2:	<4> mhm </4>

88	S4:	or a special shipment. you give the same rate like you gave it to
89		us, (.) <5> but </5> they say mm ah: okay if i get this shipment
90		maybe i can eh: pressure them down to (.)
91	S2:	<5> mhm </5>
92	S4:	eh that i get a better rate, and then they're offering something
93		(.) LOWER? and then you have already the <6> hiccup </6> as
94		a: as a (origin) (.) so
95	S2:	<6> mhm </6>
96	S2:	yeah that's something which WE cannot help of course if <7>
97		if </7> they LOWER. <8> if if </8> THEY (.)
98	S4:	<7> sure </7> <8> sure it's </8>
99	S2:	put i don't know their commission lower or (.) thei:r whatever
100		they put lower THEMSELVES well this this is a thing (1)
101		which is a (.) well a thing which WE cannot control. (1)
102	S4:	sure. (.)
103	S2:	but you know WHY why we do this particular with
104		(COMPANY5), and i say again we we we REALLY don't do
105		this. why? (w-) we have LEARNED. you know if you look to
106		(.) a PARTICULAR business in HOLLAND you have (.) the
107		FLOWER and the plants business hh well believe me (.) this is
108		a (.) a business (.) which is (.) we have a very big (1) BASKET
109		(.) of cargo? (.) and all those (.) flower (.) AGENTS (.) around
110		us (.) they're JUMPING on this. (.)
111	S4:	<1> mhm</1>
112	S2:	<1> and </1> if you say from hey (.) uh i like you BETTER (.)
113		o:r or this lady is eh (.) is more beautiful: than that lady,
114		whatever, (.) you give her a better PRICE? (.) it doesn't work
115		out because they- (.) around, (.) they'll come back to you, say
116		hey joseph? (.) ah: i don't believe it you gave HER (.) or you
117		gave HIM (.) a better PRICE because of this. (.) so in THAT
118		respect (.) we learned from ourselves and said okay well eh: @
119		this is (.) too much. because (.) at the END of all. (.) you'll be a
120		REFEREE. it's (.) it's it's it's incredible. (.) and in in THAT
121		way we (1) give everybody the same chance (1) if (.) well a- a-
122		again WE still need to get the shipment <2> also </2> but (.)
123	S4:	<2> sure </2>
124	S2:	we give them the same rates
125	S1:	hh
126	S2:	to make SURE we don't (hit) this CONFLICT in (.)
127	S1:	ehm we LIKE this (.) and eh it is the best way to do it, (.) ahm:
128		just make SURE (.) eh that eh: your OFFLINE stations, (.)
129	S2:	mhm (.)
130	S1:	are are doing the same, i mean (.) CLEAR you have a rate ex
131		amsterdam, and you have a rate ex frankfurt which should be
132		normally a <1> higher rate </1> (.)
133	S2:	<1> mhm </1>
134	S1:	and not a COMMON rate, (.) to amster<2>dam</2> which (.)
135	S2:	<2> mhm </2>

136	S1:	OFTEN happens with eh: eh: offline stations not only with
137		(COMPANY5) but (.) <3> (with a lot of companies,) </3>
138	S2:	<3> yeah yeah i know i know </3>
139	S1:	and also if you open your office in munich then, then=eh: for
140		(a) special QUOTATION, (.) you should offer ex amsterdam ex
141		munich (.) the same rate. (1)
142	S2:	yah. (.) <4> yah </4>
143	S1:	<4> and </4> this (.) you have to assure with the new system.
144		cuz otherwise exactly this game will <5> start. </5>
145	S2:	<5> oh. </5> markus, <6> i </6> give you a guarantee. this this
146		is (.)
147	S1:	<6> mhm </6>
148	S2:	this isn't DONE,
149	S1:	ah <FAST> wasn't <7> wasn't </7> meant as as a- THIS way
150		but we KNOW </FAST> that this (.)
151	S2:	<7> the- </7>
152	S1:	OFTEN happens. especially in your offices and you have to
153		promote this flight
154	S2:	mhm
155	S1:	and you forget about the truckings, eh: you HAVE it with: with
156		a lot of carriers. hh
157	S2:	<8> oh. </8>
158	S1:	<8> (COMPANY14), </8> (COMPANY15), and and and a:ll
159		w-
160	S2:	mhm
161	S1:	whatever you name it. (.) yeah? and THERE especially then the
162		hiccups start(ed).
163	S2:	mhm
164	S1:	and THEN it starts really this this this GAMES, (.) and we all
165		know in europe the worst case we HAVE at (COMPANY16),
166		hh eh you pick up the phone, you call frankfu:rt, eh: you have a
167		rate A, <FAST> you call brussels, you have a rate B, you call
168		amsterdam, you have a rate C, and then you start to call the
169		round aGAIN, and you tell everybody, and at the end of the day
170		you decrease <1> (the) (xx) </1> </FAST>
171	S2:	<1> i know but </1> this this <2> this is the thing </2>
172	S1:	<FAST> <2> it's not wealthy </2> for the AIRLINES, and it's
173		not wealthy fo:r the BROKERS, like WE are, </FAST> (.) it's
174		not wealthy for the whole market. i mean (all) (xx) can ONLY
175		be (.) which is (.) eh for OUR lengths to the far east eh nearly
176		impossible for two thousand four, but hh we should ALL try to
177		keep as high as possible

Data B: Meeting B

Type: business meeting at food company
Place: Linz (Austria)
Time: February 2004
Overall length: more than three hours
Length of data analyzed: two hours and nine minutes
Number of speakers: five   P1, P2, P3, P4, P5: present during all extracts

	L1	gender	age	pseudonym	status
P1	Korean	male	40+	-	visitor (COMPANY6)
P2	Korean	male	40+	mister wu	visitor (COMPANY6)
P3	German (Aut.)	male	25+	max	host (COMPANY2)
P4	German (Aut.)	male	35+	robert maier	chair (COMPANY2)
P5	German (Aut.)	female	30+	nina	host (COMPANY2)

Extract B.1

(6:01 – 8:31; *length 2:30*)

```
1   P4:  mhm (1) SO (do you) first of all PLEASE let me introduce
2        MYSELF?
3   P1:  okay?
4   P4:  ahm (.) i'm in the company fo:r (.) the- the seventh YEAR now,
5        (.)
6   P1:  okay
7   P2:  <SOFT> (xx) <3> (x) </3> </SOFT>
8   P4:  <3> ah:m </3> (.) i USED to be: (1) responsible fo:r south-east
9        asia,
10  P2:  <SOFT> ah: </SOFT>
11  P4:  ah (.) meaning you know thailand in- indonesia singapore
12       malaysia philippines (.) and AUSTRALIA, (1) and also in in
13       EUROPE some countries like NORTHERN europe and
14       SOUTHERN europe (1) a:nd since ah <STRESS> (NAME1)
15       </STRESS> is taking more and more ah (.) management
16       responsibilities in reg- in regard of (.) MARKETING <4> and
17       </4> and ah: (1)
```

18	P1:	<4> mhm </4>
19	P4:	a:nd management within the HOUSE, ahm (.) he gave over the
20		responsibility also for (.) the northern part of asia
21	P1:	mhm
22	P4:	except for japan,
23	P1:	<SOFT> m<1>hm </1> </SOFT>
24	P4:	<1> ah: </1> (.) to myself,
25	P1:	<SOFT> mhm </SOFT>
26	P4:	and (.) beginning of this ye:ar ah (1) ah we hired also max,
27	P1:	<2> mhm </2>
28	PX-2:	<2> mhm </2>
29	P4:	who will
30	PX-m:	mm (.)
31	P4:	basically it will be (.) TOGETHER that we: that we ah (2) are
32		here for you for your
33	P1:	mhm (.)
34	P4:	ah for your market, (.)
35	P1:	mhm
36	P4:	so whenever (.) in the <1> FUTURE </1> you will ah basically
37		communicate to the (.)
38	PX-1:	<1> mhm </1>
39	P4:	TWO of us, (.)
40	P1:	m<2>hm </2>
41	P2:	<2>m</2>hm
42	P4:	ah:m (1) the only thing is that ahm (.) since we have never MET
43		and <3> (NAME1) </3> is not here,
44	P1:	<3> mhm </3>
45	P1:	mhm
46	P4:	there was a past history and the knowledge
47	P1:	m<5>hm</5>
48	P2:	<5>m</5>hm
49	P4:	ahm is basically
50	P2:	<6> nina </6>
51	P1:	<6> you get </6> through:
52	P4:	in <7> NINA'S <7/>
53	P1:	<7> nina </7>
54	P2:	<SOFT> <7> @ @ </7> @ @ </SOFT>
55	P4:	in nina's hands because she (.) probably knows more about the
56		<8> history and wha</8> what (.)
57	PX-1:	<8> yes (.) (exactly) </8>
58	P4:	what used to be (.) and ah frankly speaking i also: am not (.)
59		TOO familiar yet <9> or </9> too much involved yet <1> ah
60		</1> (.)
61	P1:	<9> mhm </9> <1> mhm </1>
62	P4:	ah:m (.) into (.) KOREA,
63	P1:	mhm (.)
64	P4:	that's why (1) maybe we will have also time to FIRST of all (.)
65		speak about your company,

164

66	P1:	mhm
67	P4:	in order for me to get a (.)
68	P1:	mhm
69	P4:	get a picture to know y- i mean (.) we have to come to korea
70		anyway:
71	P1:	mhm
72	P4:	to to to (1) to get deeper (.) in- involved in the market but i
73		appreciate your: your VISIT as a kind of first ah:m
74	P1:	<SOFT> (sure) </SOFT> (.)
75	P4:	ah:m let's call it (2) RE-START <2> since </2> last year was
76		not the: the: (.)
77	P1:	<2> <SOFT> mhm </SOFT> </2>
78	P4:	the best ye:ar, eh as i saw in the files maybe we can also talk
79		about that,
80	P1:	<SOFT> (sure) </SOFT> (.)
81	P4:	ahm (1) <L1=GERMAN> ja </L1=GERMAN>
82		<TRANSL=yes> and then we will present you also the news for
83		this year,
84	P1:	<SOFT> mhm </SOFT>
85	P2:	<SOFT> mhm </SOFT>

Extract B.2

(10:09 – 10:20; *length 0:11*)

1	P4:	so <6> you don't </6>
2	P1:	<6> we have to </6> join them tonight (.) about ten o'<7>clock?
3		</7>
4	P4:	<7> boah </7> (.) so you don't have any JET LAG or so?
5	P2:	<SOFT> @@ </SOFT>
6	P1:	uh?
7	P4:	jet lag?
8	P1:	because we arrived eh PARIS (.)
9	P2:	i am eh: <8> in europe for </8>
10	P1:	<8> yah yah </8> eh: WEDNESDAY. (.)
11	P4:	oKAY, WOW

Extract B.3

(12:40 – 14:40; *length 2:00*)

1	P4:	ahm and (.) since WHEN are you distributing (COMPANY2)?
2		(.) in korea?
3	P1:	ah: (2) i think it's good (2) (good) three years? <SOFT> (xxxxx)
4		</SOFT>
5		<P5 enters with coffee>
6	P2:	<to S1> <SOFT> (xx) ninety-nine </SOFT>

165

7	PX-m:	<SOFT> @ @ </SOFT>
8	P2:	<to P1> <SOFT> ninety-seven? ninety-eight? </SOFT>
9	P1:	<to P2> <SOFT> (xxx) <1> (xx) </1> </SOFT>
10	P2:	<to P1> <SOFT> <1> nine</1>ty-nine? </SOFT> (2)
11	P1:	<to P4> it's either:
12	P4:	NINETY-NINE? <2> or </2>
13	P1:	<2> ninety-</2> <3>eight </3> or ninety-<4>nine yeah </4>
14	P2:	<SOFT> <3> ninety </3> <4> ninety-nine </4> </SOFT>
15		(2) <P5 hands out coffee>
16	P5:	okay
17		(5) <P5 hands out coffee>
18	P5:	<5> ninety-</5>nine? (.)
19	P1:	<5> (and) </5>
20	P1:	yeah. (.) and 1- last
21	P3:	<to P2> <SOFT> (like milk?) </SOFT>
22	P1:	give you some (.)
23	P3:	<to P5> <SOFT> <L1=GERMAN> *(ist die milch eh genug?)*
24		</L1=GERMAN> <TRANS=is there enough milk?>
25	P5:	<SOFT> mhm </SOFT>
26	P1:	background
27	P5:	<to P3> <SOFT> <L1=GERMAN> *(x)* <6> *(xxx)* </6> *(xxxx)*
28		</L1=GERMAN> </SOFT>
29	P4:	<to P1> <6> mhm </6>
30	P1:	of myself and mister wu as well as our company
31	P4:	MHM
32	P1:	(just) as- (.) as you (.) mentioned we have to (1) know each other
33		a little bit better, before we eh
34	P5:	<SOFT> @ @ <LX-1=GERMAN> *(xxxx)* </LX-1=GERMAN>
35		</SOFT>
36	P4:	<to S5> <SOFT> <L1=GERMAN> *(2s)?* </L1=GERMAN>
37		</SOFT> (.)
38	P1:	ahm
39	P4:	<to P1> sorry (.) </to S1> <SOFT> (xxxxx) </SOFT> (.)
40	P1:	ah i joined this company (1) nineteen ninety-<1>six </1>
41	PX-2:	<SOFT> <1> thank </1> you </SOFT> <P5 has been pouring
42		out coffee>
43	P4:	OKAY, (.)
44	P1:	but at the time i was (.) responsible LOGISTICS. (.)
45	P4:	mhm (1)
46	P1:	ah: a- and i took over this eh: (.) management (1) early two
47		thousand (.) JANUARY two thousand TWO
48	P4:	mhm,
49	P1:	okay? (.) ah:m (.) and the COMPANY started (1) consumer good
50		business (1) ah:=eh nineteen ninety-FIVE. (.)
51	P4:	mhm, (.)
52	P1:	ah: with (2) one or two eh: international brands such as eh (1) ah
53		(.) <STRESS> (COMPANY3) </STRESS> (writing)
54		(instruments) (.) you <2> know (COMPANY3)? </2> (.)

55	P4:	<2> mhm, </2>
56	P1:	an:d we- we- we have some PET FOOD (.) from: STATES (1)
57		those are- (.) those were the two ah: items we start with. <3>
58		then </3> WE added (.)
59	P4:	<3> mhm </3>
60	P1:	a:s time goes by we added eh: some famous brands like (1)
61		<STRESS> (COMPANY4) </STRESS> (.)
62	P4:	<SOFT> mhm, </SOFT> (.) which you still have. (.)
63	P1:	which is eh a- at the moment the BIGGEST (1) <4> revenue
64		</4> contributor. (.)
65	P4:	<4> mhm </4>
66	P1:	<SOFT> okay, </SOFT> (1)
67	P4:	REALLY? (.)
68	P1:	y:eah this yea:r (.) i mean REVENUE not the (.) bottom line
69	P4:	okay @ @ <5> @ @ @ </5> <@> that's what i thought because
70		oth- </@> (.) <6> (xxx) </6> (x) (.)
71	P3:	<5> @ @ @ </5>
72	P1:	<5> (this ye)a:r </5> <6> this year </6>

Extract B.4

(31:02 – 31:52; length 0:50)

1	P1:	ah <to P2> ((COMPANY2)) <LX-1=KOREAN> (xxxxxxx)?
2		</LX-1=KOREAN> </to S2> (.) <to P4> <SOFT> i understand
3		</SOFT> some other countries in the ASIA (.) we handle
4		(COMPANY2) (1)
5	P3:	<SOFT> really? </SOFT>
6	P4:	pardon me?
7	P1:	some (.) some other region in a- a- some COUNTRIES in ah:
8		INDONESIA (.)
9	P4:	<L1=GERMAN> ja? </L1=GERMAN> <TRANSL=yes?> (.)
10	P1:	s- i i i s- thought some of the our (affiliated) company handles
11		(COMPANY2). <SOFT> no? </SOFT> (.)
12	P5:	indonesia?
13	P1:	no?
14	P2:	<SOFT> no </SOFT>
15	P4:	not <1> in </1>
16	P1:	<1> we </1> are the only one?
17	P4:	yeah I had once a meeting with (COMPANY9) in (.) in
18		SINGAPORE, we were <2> talking </2> about (.) VIETNAM.
19		(.)
20	P1:	<2> yeah </2>
21	P1:	mhm
22	P4:	because eh: they are somehow affiliated with (.) the
23		(COMPANY28) distri<3>buto:r </3>
24	P1:	<3> YES </3> yes <4> yes </4>
25	P4:	<4> in </4> vietNAM and we want- (.) we contacted THEM
26		then fo:r (.) but it- ACTually it neve:r <5> really </5>

27	P1:	<5> okay </5> okay (.)
28	P1:	<6> (xxx) (it) </6>
29	P4:	<6> worked out </6> (1)
30	P1:	(i) understand. (4)

Extract B.5

(32:19 – 33:39; *length 1:20*)

1	P1:	and we brought some ah: (3) presentation material, (.) <1> for
2		</1> you,
3	P4:	<1> <SOFT> mhm </SOFT> </1>
4		<P1 hands material to P4 who hands one to P3 and keeps the
5		second one> (2)
6	P5:	(it's okay)
7	PX-2:	@ @ @
8	P4:	we'll we <2> look together </2>
9	P5:	<2> we always </2> share
10	P2:	<SOFT> @ @ @ </SOFT> (2)
11	P1:	and if you ALLOWED me about (.) let's say (2) an HOUR we
12		can go through, because
13	P4:	m<3>hm </3>
14	P1:	<3> it </3> gives you ah as as the CONTENT shows you
15	P4:	yeah (.)
16	P1:	the MARKET overview: eh: what was the KOREAN ecommu-
17		economy look(ed) like (1) in two thousand and three and eh it's
18		OUTLOOK for THIS year (2)
19	P4:	mhm (.)
20	P1:	then eh we can go over to=eh: (.) year two thousand three
21		business review,
22	P4:	<4> mhm </4>
23	P5:	<4> mhm </4>
24	P1:	(1) what was our TARGET and what was our ACHIEVEMENT
25		(.) and what was (.) the PROBLEMS, (.) <5> and </5> what
26		actions we: (1) eh took.
27	P4:	<5> mhm </5>
28	P4:	OKAY,
29	P1:	and the LAST (.) last one is the business plan fo- plan for this
30		year
31	P4:	<SOFT> mhm </SOFT>
32	P1:	our objectives and strategies (.)
33	P4:	mhm
34	P1:	a:n- eh and w- we do have some A and P eh summary
35	P4:	okay, (1)
36	P1:	is it okay that i (.) GO with this <6> presentation? <SOFT> okay
37		okay </SOFT> </6>
38	P4:	<6> PLEASE (.) PLEASE <L1=GERMAN> *ja,*
39		</L1=GERMAN> <TRANSL=yes> </6> (5)

Extract B.6

(66:29 – 66:57; *length 0:28*)

1	P1:	well if you go to ah (1) C-V-S there are (.) multi LAYERS of
2		shelf, (.)
3	P4:	mhm
4	P1:	okay (.) ah to: PUT (.) this kind of HI:GH (.) display (.)
5	P2:	<SOFT> (xxx) </SOFT>
6	P4:	yeah, so is it on HOOKS in the (.) in the C-V-S or (.) is it in the
7		(.) in the cartons.
8	P2:	it's in shelf (.) (but) (.) <1> (x) </1>
9	P4:	<1> it's </1> LYING in the shelf <2> or (or) </2>
10	P1:	<2> it's lying </2> on the <3> shelf </3>
11	P2:	<3> it's lying </3> <4> on the shelf </4>
12	P4:	<4> AHA </4>
13	P1:	and the shelf HEIGTH (.) is quite limited
14	P3:	<SOFT> mhm okay </SOFT>

Extract B.7

(67:42 – 68:09; *length 0:27*)

1	P4:	mhm but (.) AGAIN (.) that i understand it right (.) the products
2		are just (.) LYING in the shelf they're not HANGING on a
3		HOOK, (.) they're just LYING (.) in the in the shelf. (.)
4	P2:	hm
5	P1:	<to P2> <L1=KOREAN> *(xxxx) (xx)* </L1=KOREAN>
6	P2:	<to P1> <L1=KOREAN> *(xxxxx) (xx) (xxxxx)* (5s)
7		</L1=KOREAN>
8	P1:	<to P2> <L1=KOREAN> *(xxxxx)* </L1=KOREAN>
9		<P2 shows S4 a picture of the products in the shop shelf>
10	P4:	AHA this one you have
11	P2:	this one we made eh: (.) made eh:m (.) se- eh september? (.) o:r
12		october. (.)

Extract B.8

(73:37 – 74:37; *length 1:00*)

1	P4:	but so far we had in all? (.) channels (.) INcreases right? (.)
2	P1:	eh:
3	P4:	in total.
4		(4)
5	P1:	so eh (1) we see some ah POTENTIALS in hypermarket and
6		general trade. (.) okay? (.)
7	P4:	yeah but those TWELVE per cent in C-V-S does that mean (.)
8		<1> we </1> INCREASED (1)

169

9	P5:	<1> <SOFT> (twelve) </SOFT> </1>
10	P4:	twelve per cent in C-<2> V-S. </2>
11	P1:	<2> no no </2> that's the eh
12	P2:	general
13	P4:	oh it's <3> general share </3>
14	P1:	<3> yeah general </3> business
15	P4:	okay
16	P2:	hm
17	P1:	again the major contribution- contributor. (1) in terms of (.) ah:
18		value (.) ah: among our sales (.) OUTLETS (.) ARE (.) those
19		two. so HYPERMARKET and general trade.
20	P4:	mhm
21	P1:	with eh thirty-seven and (1) thirty-one per cent. (2)
22	P4:	<SLOW> general trade? ah (1) you sell DIRECTLY to or whole
23		salers o:r </SLOW>
24	P2:	whole sellers
25	P4:	<4> to ah </4>
26	P1:	<4> whole sellers </4>
27	P2:	to the whole seller (.)
28	P4:	mhm (3)

Extract B.9

(75:24 – 79:21; *length 3:57*)

1	P1:	there's eh some ah
2	P2:	<to P5> yeah <1> (xx) </1>
3	P1:	<1> frequent </1> turn over (.) for the (product) manager fo:r (.)
4		eh: (COMPANY2), (1) we did in ah: less than ONE year time
5		(1) from (NAME7) to (NAME6) then NOW
6	P5:	<SOFT> (NAME5) </SOFT>
7	P1:	<STRESS> (NAME5) </STRESS> (.) (LAST NAME5), (1) ah:
8		so THAT was- that was ALSO <2> cause ehm </2> (.)
9	P2:	<2> <SOFT> (xxxxx) </SOFT> </2>
10	P1:	NOT smooth ah: ah internal (.) ah operation as well a- as well as
11		understanding of market.
12	P4:	right
13	P2:	to be <3> (true) </3>
14	P1:	<3> to be </3> FRANKLY with you.
15	P4:	<L1=GERMAN> *ja ja* </L1=GERMAN> <TRANSL=yes yes>
16		that's- (.) that's CLEAR if you change the (.) product managers
17		(.) frequently then (.)
18	P2:	<SOFT> yes </SOFT> (.)
19	P4:	'cuz everybody needs TIME to get INTO the business <4> and
20		once he's in</4>to another CHANGE so
21	P2	<4> that's yeah </4>
22	P2:	mhm
23	P1:	ah:
24	P4:	but THIS one is now (1) (NAME3)

25	P2:	j-
26	P4:	(LAST NAME8) <similar to (LAST NAME3)> (.)
27	P2:	(LAST NAME3)
28	P4:	(LAST NAME3)
29	P2:	<5> yeah </5>
30	P1:	<5> (NAME3) </5> (LAST NAME3)'s divi- division <6>
31		manager </6>
32	P2:	<6> division </6>
33	P4:	<L1=GERMAN> *ach so ok* </L1=GERMAN> <TRANSL=i see
34		okay>
35	P1:	and (NAME5) (LAST NAME5) is the eh: the product manager
36	P4:	<SOFT> okay </SOFT> and <L1=GERMAN> *sie*
37		</L1=GERMAN> <TRANSL=she> (.) she's here to stay. (1)
38	P5:	@@
39	P4:	@@ (1) <SOFT> <L1=GERMAN> *(oder auch nicht)*
40		</L1=GERMAN> <TRANSL=well maybe not> </SOFT>
41	P5:	<1> or </1>
42	P3:	<1> @@ </1> @@ <2> @@ </2>
43	P4:	<L1=GERMAN> <2> *oh* <3> *je* </3> </2> </L1=GERMAN>
44		<TRANSL=oh dear>
45	P5:	<3> is she </3> not?
46	P4:	oh oh (.)
47	P5:	oh oh (.)
48	P4:	oh oh
49	P1:	WE (1) appreciate these TWO (NAME3) (LAST NAME3) and
50		(NAME5) (LAST NAME5) is REALLY (.) ah: ah important ah:
51		(1) staff from ours
52	P4:	mhm (.)
53	P1:	ah and w- they are really (1) ah: DYNAMIC (.) and challenge (.)
54		ah for their ah SUCCESS because (.) those teams are also (.) ah:
55		handles ah (COMPANY4) and (COMPANY4) is really (.)
56		successful brand ah we have (1) <SOFT> okay? </SOFT>
57	P4:	mhm (5)
58	P2:	(and also) (NAME3) (LAST NAME3) knows the eh <STRESS>
59		(COMPANY2) </STRESS> very well because eh (.) eh: he has
60		been in (.) ENGLAND fo:r (.) from (.)
61	P1:	he was RAISED in eh england
62	P2:	in eng<4>land so: </4>
63	P1:	<4> (with) ah: </4> <5> also </5>
64	P4:	<5> it's a </5> big FRIEND there right?
65	P2:	yes <@> right <@> <6> @ </6>
66	P1:	<6> he </6> knows ah:
67	P4:	@@ <7> @@ </7>
68	P1:	<7> (COMPANY2) </7>
69	P2:	<SOFT> <7> @@ </7> <8> @@ </8> </SOFT>
70	P5:	<SOFT> <8> (from his) </8> <9> (childhood) </9> </SOFT>
71	P1:	<9> from his </9>
72	P5:	@@ <1> @@ </1>

171

73	P1:	<1> childhood </1> <SOFT> okay? </SOFT>
74	P5:	childhood dreams
75	P4:	right
76	P2:	so <2> she's very (sure) </2> @@@ to: to (promote) eh the
77		(COMPANY2) business
78	P5:	<2> <SOFT> (xxxx) </SOFT> </2>
79	P4:	mhm (.) okay? (1)
80	P1:	the next one is eh (1) our (.) year two thousand three SALES (.)
81		BY ah major account, (2) ah: the <STRESS> C-V-S </STRESS>
82		(1) we have (.) three major, (.) (COMPANY31) (.) and eh (.)
83		<STRESS> (COMPANY30) </STRESS> which is owned by
84		(COMPANY36) (1) and (COMPANY37) (.)
85	P4:	mhm (.) so (COMPANY29) is NOT there? (.)
89	P1:	(COMPANY29) no.
90	P4:	okay, (2)
91	P1:	uh: (1) <STRESS> (COMPANY30) </STRESS> as you see we
92		did very (.) ACTIVELY: from (.) FEBRUARY (.) til=eh
93		MARCH, (.) then we start to have some (1) ah: continuous
94		RETURNS, (2) same as <STRESS> (COMPANY31),
95		</STRESS> (2) (and) (COMPANY37) (.)
96	P4:	<to P5> <SOFT> <L1=GERMAN> *(4s) (2) (xxx) (1) (2s)*
97		</L1=GERMAN> </SOFT> (.)
98	P1:	and and and eh: (COMPANY37) which we started MAY we (.)
99		ah: couldn't sell MORE (.) to THEM (.) while we haven't started
100		to: receive returns <SOFT> which is not a good news again
101		</SOFT> (2)
102	P4:	ah: (.)
103	P1:	among the department store (COMPANY38) is our major (.)
104		client, (2)
105	P4:	ahm (.) excuse me
106	P1:	yes (2)
107	P4:	and <SLOW> approximately: </SLOW> (.) how many
108		OUTLETS do they have? (1)
109	P1:	which one?
110	P4:	(COMPANY38)? (2)
111	P2:	(it's) two (1)
112	P4:	<1> two? </1>
113	P1:	<1> department </1> department store yeah MAINly in (junct-)
114		MAIN (.) department store in downtown (1) (junction) yeah (.)
115	P4:	ye:ah (3)

Extract B.10

(87:37 – 88:09; length 0:29)

1	P1:	and we eh: developed (1) (to) (.) to (a) fit eh size rack. eh
2		which=eh (.) i eh: showed the
3	P4:	mhm

4	P1:	pictures on page twenty-eight (1) and also we called it wire rack,
5		(2) so that was a bi- eh: that was our eh A and P eh (1)
6	P2:	<SOFT> seventeen </SOFT>
7	P1:	page seventeen?
8	P2:	<SOFT> mhm </SOFT>
9	P1:	oh yeah pa- sorry page seventeen
10	P5:	mhm (.)
11	P1:	we produced about three hundred <[vðær]> (1)
12	P4:	of those? (2)
13	P2:	<SOFT> yeah </SOFT>

Extract B.11

(90:04 – 90:51; *length 0:47*)

1	P1:	so action (.) o- eh DONE is a KEY ACCOUNT management
2		program we asked eh (NAME3) (.) to set up eh: some program
3		(.) with imp- (.) the the important ah (.) key ACCOUNT (.) to
4		develop some ANNUAL program (.) for ou-
5	P4:	what is an annual program? (.)
6	P1:	it's a YEARLY (.) based (.) <1> <SOFT> (program) </SOFT>
7		</1>
8	P4:	<1> <L1=GERMAN> *ja ja* </L1=GERMAN> <TRANSL=yes
9		yes> </1> i mean in regards of <2> assortment </2> in regards
10		of placement or in regards of eh:m activities? (.)
11	P1:	<2> (xx) </2>
12	P4:	or in regards of PRICE off promotions or (1)
13	P1:	<to P2> <L1=KOREAN> *(xxxxx)* </L1=KOREAN>
14	P2:	<to P1> <L1=KOREAN> *(xxxx)* </L1=KOREAN> (.) <to P4>
15		ehm mainly the: ACTIVITY (.)
16	P1:	promotion ac<3>tivity </3>
17	P2:	<3>promotion </3> (activities) <4> yeah </4>
18	P4:	<3> like </3> <4> TAS</4>TINGS or
19	P2:	yes (.) like eh tasting but the: (.) the most im- important thing is
20		the display. (.)
21	P4:	mhm

Extract B.12

(96:39 – 98:04; *length 1:25*)

1	P4:	the only (.) the only thing here i mean it's a very nice display but
2		(.) i'm not sure what the licenser of hello kitty (.)
3	P5:	UH
4	P4:	@ @ will tell US (.) or
5	P1:	licency?
6	P4:	the <1> lice- </1>
7	P5:	<1> lic</1>enser

8	P4:	the licenser of hello kitty because i think that the hello kitty
9		dispenser
10	P2:	hm
11	P4:	THERE and i'm not (.) i'm SURE that this is not approved by
12	P2:	oh
13	P4:	by what- <STRESS> (COMPANY42) </STRESS>
14	P5:	<2> (COMPANY42) </2>
15	P2:	<2> mm </2>
16	P4:	(COMPANY42) <3> and if </3> there is like SIMPSONS (.)
17		<4> on a </4> <STRESS> (COMPANY42) </STRESS> ah:m
18	P2:	<3> mm </3> <4> <SOFT> mhm </SOFT> </4>
19	P2:	mm
20	P1:	<5> ah </5>
21	P4:	<5> HEADER </5> card,
22	P1:	that means (1) hello kitty should (.) a- always (1) ah: display
23		with a (.) hello <6> kitty </6> only (.)
24	P4:	<6> <L1=GERMAN> *nein* </L1=GERMAN> <TRANSL=no> u-
25		</6>
26	P4:	<L1=GERMAN> *nein* </L1=GERMAN> <TRANSL=no> <7>
27		usually </7>
28	P1:	<7> display </7> rack?
29	P4:	usually EVERY material <8> needs </8> to be APPROVED by
30		the licenser.
31	P1:	<8> aha </8>
32	P2:	right
33	P4:	so EVERY
34	P2:	yeah (.)
35	P4:	every logo <9> layout </9> needs to be APPROVED.
36	P5:	<9> <SOFT> (layout) </SOFT> </9>
37	P2:	ah:
38	P4:	if you don't have the APPROVAL for that, and somebody from
39		(COMPANY42) <1> goes into </1> a (COMPANY32) (.) and
40		<2> sees that </2> their ehm dis- (.)
41	P2:	<1> ah: </1> <2> ah: </2>
42	P4:	that there is ah
43	P1:	but (.) <3> ours </3> doesn't have a (COMPANY42) eh: the the
44		<4> kitty </4> (.) picture
45	P4:	<3> simpsons </3>
46	P2:	<4> mm </4>
47	P4:	YEAH it has the (.) kitty DISPENSER in the hand (1)
48	P1:	where (.) which one (.)
49	P5:	eh the
50	PX-3:	<SOFT> yeah the <5> clown </5> </SOFT>
51	P5:	<5> peter, </5>
52	P4:	the clown (.) <6> this one </6> is a (.) is a hello <7> kitty
53		dispens</7>er
54	P5:	<6> (it's a) kitty </6> <7> dispenser </7>
55	P1:	AH:

56	P2:	oh:
57	P5:	the
58	P1:	you mean the (.) the clo:wn
59	P4:	i mean it's very nice but IF (COMPANY42) sees that (.) @
60	P1:	<8> oh: </8>
61	P2:	<8> oh: </8>
62	P5:	<8> <@> ah </@> </8> @
63	P4:	we <9>are in trou<1>ble </1> </9>
64	P1:	<9> ah: </9>
65	P2:	<9> ah: </9>
66	P5:	<1> (would) </1> (n't) <2> like </2> it @ @ <3> @ </3>
67	P1:	<2> okay </2>
68	P2:	<3> mm </3>
69	P5:	ah
70	P1:	i (.) i know what you mean

Extract B.13

(103:32 – 103:45; *length 0:13*)

1	P5:	<1> (xxx) </1>
2	P1:	<1> it's like a INsurance </1> you know?
3	P4:	pardon me <clears his throat>
4	P1:	it's like an INsurance you buy (.)
5	P4:	<@> right </@>
6	P1:	the CHANCE you (.)
7	P4:	RIGHT
8	P1:	get in the <2> acci </2>dent is really really low
9	P4:	<2> right </2>

Extract B.14

(107:06 – 107:32; *length 0:26*)

1	P4:	<L1=GERMAN> *na ja* </L1=GERMAN> <TRANSL=well> if
2		(.) if i m- may ehm (.) make a comment there,
3	P2:	mhm (1)
4	P4:	the (.) <['ɪmpʊls]> channel (.) ehm
5	P1:	<['ɪmpʌls]> chann<1> el? </1>
6	P4:	<1> the </1> <['ɪmpʊls]> channel or the C-V-S eh channel
7		(.) is very much ah (.) LICENSE driven. (.) meaning (1) if it's (.)
8		in the <['ɪmpʊls]> channel (1) the LICENSE is very important (.)

Extract B.15

(117:15 – 117:46; *length 0:31*)

1	P1:	ah (1) actually this (.) presentation material (is) PREpared by (.)
2		of course (NAME3) and ah (NAME5)
3	P5:	<SOFT> mhm </SOFT>
4	P1:	and they (3) created some (1) some ah (2) JARGON. <FAST>
5		do you know? </FAST> the word JARGON? (.) J-A-<@>R-
6		</@>G-O-N? <1> jargon </1>
7	P2:	<1> @ @ @ </1> @ @
8	P4:	J?
9	P1:	J-A-R-(.) G-O-N (1) jargon
10	P4:	<L1=GERMAN> ah ja (.) ja ja (.) ja ja </L1=GERMAN>
11		<TRANSL=oh yes (.) yes yes (.) yes yes>
12	P1:	jargon (.)
13	P4:	mhm

Extract B.16

(121:15 – 123:18; *length 2:03*)

1	P1:	again ah we (.) expect that we would (.) GET (.) your
2		contribution of ten per cent of our (1) (actual) we purchase
3		which will: which we (.) we will ah provide you shortly (.) for
4		our purchase plan (2)
5	P1:	<to P2> <L1=KOREAN> *(3s)* </L1=KOREAN> (1)
6	P2:	<to P1> <L1=KOREAN> *(4s)* </L1=KOREAN> (.)
7	P1:	ah it will be (2) early (.) early march. okay? (.)
8	P4:	what?
9	P1:	the the FIGURE for the purchase (.) figure (bec-) <1> because
10		</1> (1)
11	P4:	<1> <L1=GERMAN> *ach so* </L1=GERMAN> <TRANSL=oh i
12		see> </1>
13	P2:	ah:
14	P1:	we- we'll be back (.) we'll be back eh: (1) (the) twenty-eighth (2)
15	P2:	<SOFT> (end of) <2> (xx) </2> </SOFT>
16	P1:	<SOFT> <2> ah not </2> twenty-eighth </SOFT> (.) <3>
17		twenty-SEVENTH </3>
18	P2:	<3> (twenty-seventh) </3> mhm (.)
19	P1:	i'll be <4> back </4> in in the office (.)
20	P4:	<4> <SOFT> mhm </SOFT> </4>
21	P4:	mhm
22	P1:	so i need (.) couple of more days to eh to (review) in detail (.)
23		then we'll give you ah: our PURCHASE plan (.) for year two
24		thousand four
25	P4:	right <5> because </5>
26	P1:	<5> (yeah:) </5> WITHOUT that (.) <6> (xx) </6>
27	P4:	<6> you cannot </6> really calculate <7> what </7>
28		promotions you <8> can (have) </8>
29	PX-2:	<7> (xxx) </7>

30	P1:	<8> of course you </8> SHOULD (.) you should have that
31		number to to: (.) plan your your your part. (.)
32	P4:	right
33	P1:	<SOFT> okay, </SOFT> (4)
34	P1:	<SOFT> okay? </SOFT> <turning the page> (.)
35	P4:	and i hope we have a (2) seventy per cent INcrease then this year
36	P3:	<SOFT> @ @ @ </SOFT>
37	P2:	<SOFT> @ @ @ @ </SOFT>
38	P4:	after a seventy per cent DEcrease
39	P2:	@ @ @ @ (2)
40	P1:	our marketing objectives (2) are made of three: (2) points eh
41		increase distribution coverage level (1) and also enhance (that)
42		consumer TRIAL and repeat. (2) and also successfully launch
43		new product items like the (1) eh hello kitty and (.) the others
44		maybe eh: you will show us (.) eh: right after my presentation,
45		(.) your plan, (.)
46	P4:	mhm,

VOICE Transcription and mark-up conventions (Version 3.0, June 2003)

slightly adapted

Transcription	Explanation
SPEAKER ID	
S1 (S2, S3, etc.): at the beginning of each turn	speaker IDs, assigned in the order they first speak
SX:	unknown speaker, gender not identified
SX-f:, SX-m:	unknown speaker, with gender identified
SX-1: (2, 3, etc.)	probable but not definite identity of speaker
SS:	two or more (indistinguishable) speakers in unison
PAUSES	
(.)	(period) for brief pause (up to a good ½ sec)
(1), (3)	longer pause, timed to the nearest second; e.g. (1) = 1 second, (3) = 3 seconds
BREATH	
hh, hhh	noticeable breathing in/out: hh = relatively short; hh = relatively long
INTONATION	
?	clause(s) spoken with rising intonation
.	clause(s) spoken with falling intonation
,	clause(s) spoken with level tone
EMPHATIC STRESS	
TEXT	syllables spoken with emphatic stress are written in capital letters
LENGTHENING	
te:xt	lengthened sounds are marked with a colon
SELF-INTERRUPTION	
te-	speaker's self-interruption is marked with a hyphen
REPETITION	
text text text	repeated words and phrases (self-interrupted words included) are fully transcribed, e.g.: i i i think it's it's ri- right.
CONTEXTUAL EVENTS	
<contextual event> <contextual event (3)>	contextual events (non-speech), indicated only when they are relevant for the interaction or for understanding the transcription; e.g. <telephone

	rings>; <S3 enters the room>, <S1 points at S2>, etc.; the length of the event (in seconds) is added in parentheses if relevant, e.g. <S1 reading quietly (3)>
LAUGHTER	
@ @ @	all laughter is transcribed with the @ symbol, expressing approximate syllable number (hahaha = @ @ @)
<@> text </@>	utterances spoken laughingly ("/" denotes end)
OTHER SPEAKING MODES	
<READING> text </READING> <ON PHONE> text </ON PHONE> <QUOTATIVE> text </QUOTATIVE> <FAST> text </FAST> <SLOW> text </SLOW> <LOUD> text </LOUD> <SOFT> text </SOFT> ...	utterances which are read, telephone exchanges, direct speech or imitating someone's speech etc. (this is an open list, additions possible!)
FOREIGN WORDS	
<L1=GERMAN> *text* </L1=GERMAN> <L1=X> *xxx* </L1=X>	utterances in the participants' L1 are written in *italics* and in Roman alphabet and the L1 is specified; unknown L1 is marked <L1=X>
<LN> *text* </LN>	other non-English utterances are also written in *italics* and in Roman alphabet; (LN = non-English, non-L1 of speaker)
<TRANSL=text>	translations into English should be provided if possible, immediately after the end-tag </L1=LANGUAGE>
<L1=VIETNAMESE> *xxx* </L1=VIETNAMESE> <LN> *xxx* </LN> <LN> *(5s)* </LN>	unintelligible utterances, either in participants' L1 or in LN are written with *x*'s, approximating syllable number; if more than 4-5 syllables: specify length in seconds (also in *italics*)
UNINTELLIGIBLE SPEECH	
(xxx)	unintelligible words are marked by x in parentheses, approximating syllable number
UNCERTAIN SPEECH	
(text)	uncertain transcription is written in parentheses
PRONUNCIATION VARIATION	

text <[dekst]> (x) <[dekst]> (text) <[dekst]>	phonemic/phonetic symbols are used only when a pronunciation is used that affects the interaction; what you hear goes in pointed and square brackets, also when unintelligible or uncertain
OTHER VARIATIONS	
<SIC> text </SIC>	any other variation which clearly affects the interaction (e.g. an unexpected wording that causes communication problems)
OVERLAPS	
S1: <1> text </1> text <2> text </2> S2: <1> text </1> <2> text </2>	whatever happens simultaneously in the recording (also contextual events (see above) and backchanneling (e.g. yeah, mhm) is transcribed in gray and numbers are used to indicate the overlaps: everything that is simultaneous gets the same number. Start with <1>, then next overlaps are <2>, then it will often be best to use <1> again for the next overlap. With many overlaps in close proximity it may be clearer to go up to <3> or more – up to a maximum of <9>; then start again with <1>. All overlaps are approximate and words may be split up if appropriate. As always, start a new line for every new speaker; utterances immediately following the overlap continue in the same line, for others start a new line (see examples below, esp. Example 3 and comments following it)
CONTINUATION	
S1: text text text te= S2 =xt text	immediate other-continuation is marked by = (no space between "text" and "=")
NAMES	
pseudonym	when names occur of people involved in the interaction, they are changed to pseudonyms in the transcript, except in some clearly public speech events. Pseudonyms can also be used for non-present people if this seems appropriate.
(NAME)	when names of people or institutions/companies occur that need to be anonymized, replace the name with (NAME) – for more than one name-replacement use (NAME1), (NAME2), etc. and match identical ones
COMBINING TAGS	
<TAG1> <TAG2> text </TAG2></TAG1>	when more than one tag is used to mark an utterance, order them 'ab ba' (see Example 4 below)

VDM publishing house ltd.

Scientific Publishing House
offers
free of charge publication
of current academic research papers, Bachelor´s Theses, Master's Theses, Dissertations or Scientific Monographs

If you have written a thesis which satisfies high content as well as formal demands, and you are interested in a remunerated publication of your work, please send an e-mail with some initial information about yourself and your work to *info@vdm-publishing-house.com*.

Our editorial office will get in touch with you shortly.

VDM Publishing House Ltd.
Meldrum Court 17.
Beau Bassin
Mauritius
www.vdm-publishing-house.com

Printed in Great Britain
by Amazon